**WORKBOOK**

# Focus on GRAMMAR 5

**FOURTH EDITION**

Rachel Spack Koch

ALWAYS LEARNING

PEARSON

**FOCUS ON GRAMMAR 5: An Integrated Skills Approach, Fourth Edition Workbook**

Pearson Education, Inc., 10 Bank Street, White Plains, NY 10606

**Staff credits:** The people who made up the *Focus on Grammar 5, Fourth Edition Workbook* team, representing editorial, production, design, and manufacturing, are: Aerin Csigay, Christine Edmonds, Nancy Flaggman, Ann France, Stacey Hunter, Lise Minovitz, and Robert Ruvo.

Cover images: Shutterstock.com
Text composition: ElectraGraphics, Inc.
Text font: New Aster

Text credits: **p. 6** Based on *The Virtual Doctor*, from Smartmoney.com, March 26, 2010. **p. 12** Table from the Population Reference Bureau, http://www.prb.org. Used with permission. **p. 28** Adapted from "File 11a: The largest Urban Agglomerations Ranked by Population Size at each point in time 1950–2025" in World Urbanization Prospects, The 2007 Revision, United Nations, http://esa.un.org./unup/. Used by permission. **p. 53** Menu from the Mitsitam Native Foods Café, National Museum of the American Indian, Washington, D.C. Used with permission. **p. 68** Based on the article *Is English Changing?*, from the website of the Linguistic Society of America, www.lsadc.org. **p. 96** Based on an article from *The Wall Street Journal*, July 29, 1994, by Eric Morgenthaler. **p. 122** Based on *The Discovery of Radium, Address by Madame M. Curie at Vassar College, May 14, 1921*, Ellen S. Richards Monographs No. 2 (Poughkeepsie: Vassar College, 1921). **pp. 125, 180** Based on material from *Amazing Facts*, by Richard B. Manchester. New York: Bristol Park Books, 1991. **p. 138** Based on an article in *The Washington Post*, October 27, 2004, by Anthony Faiola; an article in *The Mainichi Daily News*, March 6, 2003, by Makoto Kawanabe and Mainichi Shimbun; and an article on EverestNews.com, March 1, 2004. **p. 143** From "How to Procrastinate Like Leonardo da Vinci" by William A. Pannapacker in *The Chronicle Review*, Vol. 55, Issue 24, February 20, 2009. Used by permission of the author. **p. 150** From "Is Human Activity a Substantial Cause of Global Climate Change?" on http://climatechange.procon.org. Used by permission of ProCon.org. **p. 170** Based on material found at Shakira.com. **p. 190** Based on material from *Extraordinary Origins of Everyday Things*, by Charles Panati, Perennial Library, Harper & Row, 1987, revised 1989.

Photo credits: **Page 22** Shutterstock.com; **p. 73** Shutterstock.com; **p. 76** Shutterstock.com; **p. 125** David R. Frazier Photolibrary, Inc./Alamy; **p. 131** Shutterstock.com; **p. 143** iStockphoto.com; **p. 158** Shutterstock.com

Illustrations: **ElectraGraphics:** pp. 25, 30, 34, 36, 41, 53, 55, 62, 63, 80, 85, 90, 95, 99, 108, 115, 122, 159, 164, 182, 191; **Steve Schulman:** pp. 131–132

ISBN 10: 0-13-216985-1
ISBN 13: 978-0-13-216985-1

Printed in the United States of America

6 7 8 9 10—V001—18 17 16

# Contents

# CONTENTS

# ABOUT THE AUTHOR

**Rachel Spack Koch** has been developing ESL materials and has taught ESL for many years, principally at the University of Miami, and also at Harvard University, Bellevue Community College, and Miami-Dade College. In addition to the *Focus on Grammar 5 Workbook*, she has contributed to other widely used ESL workbooks. A participant in and developer of interactive student activities on the Internet since the early 1990s, she also writes online English teaching materials and content for ESL software.

## PART I

PRESENT, PAST, AND FUTURE

UNIT

# 1 Present Time

## EXERCISE 1: Present-Time Verbs

*Look at Carol's comments on a book discussion forum. Complete her comments. Circle the correct verb forms.*

(Have you read)/ Do you read any good books lately? This question often <u>begins / is beginning</u> a
1.                                                                                                          2.

conversation. These days, when you <u>are seeing / see</u> people in airports and on buses and planes, they
3.

<u>are not necessarily reading / don't necessarily read</u> printed pages. They may be reading e-books. An
4.

e-book (an electronic book) is also called a *digital* book. It is an electronic version of a printed book.

You <u>read / are reading</u> it on a personal computer, or on a special hand-held device.
5.

E-books <u>have become / become</u> extremely popular in the last several years. People <u>like / are liking</u>
6.                                                                                                                    7.

e-books because they <u>are / are being</u> quickly available. You can download an e-book in 90 seconds,
8.

and you <u>don't need / aren't needing</u> to wait to get it from a bookstore or a library. In addition, you
9.

can carry hundreds of books with you at one time. They are all stored in your device and they

<u>don't weigh / aren't weighing</u> anything. You <u>always have / are always having</u> a book with you to read
10.                                                                    11.

while you <u>are traveling / have been traveling</u> or waiting in a doctor's office.
12.

But print books are still very popular. A lot of people <u>are preferring / prefer</u> print books because
13.

the books <u>are feeling / feel</u> good in your hands, and they <u>smell / are smelling</u> good. Print books
14.                                                                          15.

are traditional, and people <u>enjoy / are enjoying</u> seeing them on bookshelves. I myself
16.

<u>have been contemplating / contemplate</u> the idea of getting an e-book reader for a while now, but I
17.

<u>decide / have decided</u> not to get one. That's because I <u>love / am loving</u> the feel, the smell, and
18.                                                              19.

the look of real books.

## EXERCISE 2: Simple Present and Present Progressive Verbs

*Look at the ad on a job website. Complete the ad with the correct forms of the verbs: simple present or present progressive. Use the verbs from the box.*

### Help-Desk Representative

| | |
|---|---|
| answer | look for |
| communicate | pay |
| ~~contemplate~~ | solve |
| have | train |
| like | try |

Are you tired of long rides to work? Does your family have to do without your attention? Maybe at this moment you _____ *are contemplating* _____ changing your job. You can change your life.
**1.**
Work from home!

Our dynamic, growing, small software company _____ a self-motivated
**2.**
and responsible person for the position of help-desk representative. The person in this position

_____ questions from computer users and _____
**3.** **4.**

their computer and software problems, all from home! Your profile:

- You _____ at least two years of experience with Internet technology.
  **5.**
- You _____ with people easily and clearly by phone.
  **6.**
- You _____ people and are patient with them.
  **7.**

What we offer you:

- We _____ you on our software.
  **8.**
- We _____ a good starting salary and offer health insurance.
  **9.**
- We _____ to expand our company, and there is opportunity for you
  **10.**
  to grow with us.

Our customer support desk is open 24/7, and you may arrange your working hours for your own

convenience. Say good-bye forever to long commutes, and say hello to telecommuting!

## EXERCISE 3: Non-Action Verbs

*Read the letter to the editor. Underline the non-action verbs.*

Dear Editor:

We <u>need</u> higher taxes in this town. Probably nobody believes me, but this is true. Nobody wants to pay more money, but everybody desires more services and a better quality of life. I know that these things are true:

1. We don't have enough police officers. More police officers mean safer streets and safer neighborhoods.

2. We love our children, and we want a good education for them. However, it doesn't appear that we are going to get the smaller classes, pre-kindergarten classes, and proper student advising that our young people deserve until we find more money.

3. We drive on some roads that are in bad condition and are badly lit. We need to fix the roads and put up more and better lighting.

We owe it to ourselves and our children to maintain and improve our community. When our citizens understand the value of their tax contributions, they will not mind paying a little more now toward a better future.

Jonathan Jeffries, a citizen

## EXERCISE 4: Action and Non-Action Verbs

*An interviewer is taking a survey about popular, modern technological devices. Complete the conversations between the interviewer and the interviewees. Use the simple present or present progressive forms of the verbs.*

**Conversation 1**

INTERVIEWER: Hello, Ma'am! We _____*are taking*_____ a survey this morning. Could you please
                    **1. (take)**

tell us this: What is the most important modern device in your everyday life?

WOMAN: I really _____ my cell phone. I _____
               **2. (need)**                    **3. (talk)**

to my friends and family whenever and wherever I want. I am always in touch

with my colleagues and stay on top of everything in my office. Of course, I

_____ it only for conversations. I _____ a
   **4. (not / use)**                            **5. (text)**

lot too. And I _____ photos instantly. That's fun. Oh, . . . listen.
       **6. (send)**

*(continued on next page)*

It _____ now. That's my assistant's ring tone. I think something

       **7. (ring)**

important _____ in the office right now. Excuse me, please.

           **8. (happen)**

**Conversation 2**

INTERVIEWER: Hello, Sir! Could you please tell us this: What is the most important modern device in

your everyday life?

MAN: No problem. It's my GPS, my global positioning system. I _____ it.

                                            **9. (love)**

INTERVIEWER: Why is it so important to you?

MAN: Well, I _____ a lot in my work. I _____ all

           **10. (travel)**                         **11. (drive)**

over the state. I never _____ lost. It _____

                 **12. (get)**               **13. (tell)**

me exactly what road to take. It _____ which lane of the highway

                                  **14. (know)**

I am on and it _____ me to the correct lane. If I take a wrong

                 **15. (direct)**

turn, or _____ my route, it recalculates for me. And when I

              **16. (change)**

_____ a restaurant or a hotel, it _____ one for

         **17. (want)**                         **18. (find)**

me. Look. Right now I _____ it for a good breakfast restaurant,

                 **19. (ask)**

and it _____ me 24 suggestions. Awesome!

      **20. (give)**

**Conversation 3**

INTERVIEWER: Hello, Sir! Could you please tell us this: What is the most important modern device in

your everyday life?

MAN #2: Oh, that's easy. My iPad. I do everything with it: I _____ music

                                             **21. (download)**

and books. I _____ my email. I _____

               **22. (get)**                  **23. (write)**

notes to myself and I _____ my own voice messages. And it

                 **24. (record)**

_____ less than half a pound.

      **25. (weigh)**

INTERVIEWER: Is there anything that it _____?

                          **26. (not / do)**

MAN #2: Yes. It _____ pictures and it _____ a phone.

          **27. (not / take)**                        **28. (not / be)**

*Complete the sentences. Circle the correct adjective or adverb. Draw an arrow to the verb it describes.*

1. My accountant's calculations don't seem very (exact) / **exactly**. I am going to find a new accountant.

2. The jeweler measured the diamond very closely and then found the perfect setting for it; the diamond fit the new setting **exact / exactly.**

3. The diamond looks **beautiful / beautifully** in its new setting.

4. Hmm . . . this problem seems very **hard / hardly**. I don't think that I can solve it.

5. The student answered the difficult math problem **correct / correctly** in just a few minutes.

6. This soup tastes **delicious / deliciously**! What did you put in it?

7. The baby tasted the cereal **quick / quickly** and then spit it all out.

8. Uh-oh—this noise doesn't sound **good / well**. I'm going to pull over and take a look at the engine.

9. You look very **sad / sadly** today. Is something the matter?

10. Domingo sings very **well / good**. He hopes to become an opera singer.

11. When we invited Barbara to join us after the concert, she replied, "Sorry, I'm going home now. I'm feeling really **tired / tiredly**."

12. It's taking a long time for the show to begin. The children are **impatient / impatiently**.

13. The teacher answered the question **patient / patiently**. As a result, Gina gained more confidence and began to feel **good / well** about herself.

14. The meaning of this sentence does not seem **clear / clearly**. If you use commas, it means one thing; if you don't use commas, it means something else. Please punctuate **clear / clearly**.

*Read the Hiccup (a social networking site) entry from Kim. Complete it with the correct forms of the verbs. Use the simple present, the present progressive, the present perfect, or the present perfect progressive.*

Right now I _____*am waiting*_____ for my doctor. I _____ for
              **1. (wait)**                                       **2. (wait)**

him for 15 minutes. Oh, here he is now.

First we greet each other. Then he asks, "What _____ you today?" I
              **3. (bother)**

tell him about my sore throat and my cough. He asks, "How long _____
              **4. (be / you)**

sick? How long _____ this cough?" I tell him. He asks about my
          **5. (have / you)**

blood pressure and temperature. I _____ what they are because I
              **6. (know)**

_____ them already and have recorded the numbers. Finally, he says,
      **7. (take)**

"Open your mouth wide,"—and at this point, I _____ clearly that this
                            **8. (realize)**

doctor's visit is different from all the other doctor's visits I have ever had. I twist myself like

a pretzel into an odd position and open my mouth in front of the webcam. At this moment, I

_____ at the real doctor's office and he _____
      **9. (be / not)**                                   **10. (look / not)**

into my real mouth. I _____ here at my computer as my doctor
              **11. (sit)**

_____ at his computer, 40 miles away, at the other end of this webcam
      **12. (sit)**

connection. We are not in the same room. This is the new world of virtual medicine.

Many doctors and their patients _____ the world of virtual medicine
              **13. (enter)**

in recent years. This is how it works: Doctors set up online offices with secure websites. Here

patients _____ information about their symptoms, history, and
      **14. (input)**

medications, as well as blood pressure and temperature readings they've taken themselves.

They _____ questions. They _____ all of
      **15. (ask)**                                   **16. (do)**

this and they _____ their beds or sofas or desks. In many cases, they
          **17. (leave / not)**

_____ to visit with the doctor; the doctor just reads the data and responds.
      **18. (need / not)**

But today, I _____ an appointment for an actual visit with my doctor. A
          **19. (have)**

webcam—like the one we _____ today—is a very important tool.
              **20. (use)**

The doctor tells me, "You have an infection in your throat. Right now I _____
                                                                                    **21. (send)**
a prescription by computer to your pharmacy. Take the medicine, get plenty of rest, and schedule a

virtual follow-up visit in two weeks."

I _____ virtual medicine because it is convenient and it
        **22. (like)**
_____ a lot of time. My doctor _____ it too, for the
        **23. (save)**                                    **24. (like)**
same reasons.

## EXERCISE 7: Editing

*Read the email from Marco. There are twenty-one mistakes in verb forms. The first mistake*
*is already corrected. Find and correct twenty more.*

From: MarcoM21@upe.edu
To: Ricardo09876@itmail.com
Subject: My new life

Hey, Ricardo,

    *am writing*
   I ~~write~~ to you in English today so we can both get more practice. Sorry that I don't write sooner,

but I have been really busy. Classes in my intensive English program in Chicago are going on for

about six weeks. The instructors has given homework every day, and I have been study every night in

order to stay on top of the assignments. In fact, I study right now because I have a big test tomorrow.

Besides that, we have an assignment to write a two-page essay. It's due tomorrow, but I have not

been writing it yet. You may remember that I tend to put difficult things off until the last minute—I

am a procrastinator.

   I am complaining about all the homework, but the truth is that my English is improving rapidly.

   Besides in my classes, I have learn a lot of English in the past six weeks by talking with people

around me in the city. In my apartment building, most people are speaking English, and when I am

needing something, I speak to the manager in English. For example, the plumbing in my apartment

often doesn't work, and I'm explaining the problem to the manager several times already. Now, I am

knowing the plumber pretty well because the same plumber is coming every week!

*(continued on next page)*

On the negative side, the weather has being terrible this month. It's raining almost every day. In addition, I don't like the food here. I am missing real home cooking. Of course, I don't do without meals. I just don't enjoy them. In fact, I'm get thinner. I lose about five kilos so far. And I feel lonely. I'm talking to many people every day, but I don't make any new friends yet. What's new with you? What happens at home? Send me an email soon.

Your friend, Marco

## EXERCISE 8: Personal Writing

*On a separate piece of paper, describe which items of technology are most useful to you. Write two or three paragraphs about them. Use some of the phrases from the box.*

| | |
|---|---|
| I have . . . | Every day / year, I . . . |
| I like . . . | For the past two years, . . . |
| I really need . . . | Right now, . . . |
| I use . . . | Since I have had it, . . . |
| I want . . . | When I turn it on, . . . |
| It does . . . | |

# 2 Past Time

## EXERCISE 1: Past-Time Verbs

*Read the wedding announcement in* The Times. *Complete the announcement. Circle the correct verbs.*

## Stone–Barber Wedding

Lillian B. Stone and Julius Barber were married on Saturday night at the Downtown Center Hotel. The ceremony was performed by Ms. Stone's nephew. About one hundred people (attended) / were attending the event, including
**1.**
the two children and three grandchildren of Ms. Stone, and the son and grandson of Mr. Barber.

The couple met late in life, after both have lost / had lost their spouses. Ms. Stone is
**2.**
not a stereotypical senior citizen. She drives a small sports car. She runs a mile every day, takes yoga classes, and plays competitive bridge. After her first husband has died / died in 2005, she felt
**3.**
lonely. She missed / was missing her husband.
**4.**
She and her husband would often go / were
**5.**
often going to concerts together, so she continued to attend concerts with her friends. In 2007, one of her friends wanted to introduce her to a man who also enjoyed concerts. She hesitated before she accepted the invitation. But she was ultimately glad that she did accept. The man turned out to be Julius Barber.

Julius fell / was falling in love immediately.
**6.**
He said, "I wasn't looking for another wife. I already had had / would have a very happy
**7.**

marriage, but I didn't think I would be / had been
**8.**
lucky enough to have one again. I was just glad to have the prospect of friendship." But things changed for him as soon as he met Lillian. "It was like a bolt out of the blue," he said. "I knew right away that I was going to see / used to see
**9.**
her again."

After that, they saw each other every day. After they had been dating / have been dating
**10.**
for about a month, one Saturday night at dinner, he asked her to "tie the knot." At first, she thought that everything was going too quickly, but by the time dessert arrived, she had accepted
**11.**
/ had been accepting his proposal happily.

Mr. Barber is not a stereotypical senior citizen, either. He works full time as a researcher at the Food and Agriculture Organization of the United Nations. He has several hobbies, including playing the piano and cooking international dishes. He used to be / would be
**12.**
an active biker until he broke / had broken his
**13.**
hip three years ago.

The couple has recently bought / would
**14.**
recently bought a new condominium, where they will live after their honeymoon in Paris.

## EXERCISE 2: Ordering Actions in the Past

*Read the passage. In each set of sentences, write 1 in front of the action that began first or happened first and 2 in front of the action that happened second. If the actions happened at the same time, write S on both lines.*

### A Famous Unarranged Marriage

English royalty had married people from other royal families for more than 400 years. These marriages were usually arranged for political or family reasons.

1. In 1981, though, that custom changed when Prince Charles married Princess Diana, a young

   Englishwoman who was not from a royal family.

   ___2___ Prince Charles married Princess Diana.

   ___1___ English royalty married people from other royal families.

2. Diana was teaching children in kindergarten when she started seeing the Prince.

   _____ Diana was teaching children in kindergarten.

   _____ She started seeing the Prince.

3. After they started seeing each other, a romance blossomed.

   _____ They started seeing each other.

   _____ A romance blossomed.

4. They married after they had been engaged for about six months.

   _____ They married.

   _____ They were engaged.

5. Millions of people all over the world watched them on TV as they tied the knot.

   _____ Millions of people all over the world watched them on TV.

   _____ They tied the knot.

6. After they married, they had two sons.

   _____ They married.

   _____ They had two sons.

7. At the beginning, everything seemed perfect. Diana would take care of her children while

   Charles would take care of his royal duties.

   _____ Diana took care of her children.

   _____ Charles took care of his royal duties.

**8.** Diana was a good mother, and she also did charity work.

_____ Diana was a good mother.

_____ She did charity work.

**9.** As time went on, though, the marriage was not working well.

_____ Time went on.

_____ The marriage wasn't working well.

**10.** Although they used to be very happy together, things changed.

_____ They were happy together.

_____ Things changed.

**11.** They were pondering divorce when they decided to separate.

_____ They pondered divorce.

_____ They decided to separate.

**12.** Charles and Diana ultimately divorced in 1996 after they had been married for 15 years.

_____ They divorced in 1996.

_____ They were married for 15 years.

**13.** Soon afterwards, Diana died in a car crash while she was vacationing in France.

_____ Diana died in a car crash.

_____ She was vacationing in France.

**14.** When she died, people all over the world mourned her early death.

_____ She died.

_____ People all over the world mourned her early death.

**15.** People remembered the beautiful couple who had led, they thought, a beautiful life, even

though it didn't turn out well.

_____ It didn't turn out well.

_____ People thought that the couple led a beautiful life.

*Read the table and passage about world population. Complete the passage. Circle the correct verb forms.*

| YEAR | POPULATION |
|---|---|
| 50,000 B.C.E. | 2 |
| 8000 B.C.E. | 5,000,000 |
| C.E. 1 | 300,000,000 |
| 1200 | 450,000,000 |
| 1650 | 500,000,000 |
| 1750 | 795,000,000 |
| 1850 | 1,265,000,000 |
| 1900 | 1,656,000,000 |
| 1950 | 2,516,000,000 |
| 1995 | 5,760,000,000 |
| 2002 | 6,215,000,000 |

How many people (have ever lived) / had ever lived on Earth? It is impossible to know that, but
**1.**
demographers (experts in population studies) have pondered this figure and came up with an

estimation. They based their estimates on the idea that humans first have lived / lived on Earth in
**2.**
the year 50,000 B.C.E. The demographers also guessed the average size of the human population at

different periods. At the beginning of the agricultural period, about 8000 B.C.E., about 5 million people

have been living / were living in the entire world. That is about the population of the city of Baghdad
**3.**
today, or of the whole country of Denmark.

Over the years, populations in different regions were / would increase or decline in response to
**4.**
famines, the condition of cattle herds, wars between people, and changing weather and climate.

There was a high birth rate, but also a very high death rate. People's life spans used to be / are very
**5.**
short; statistically, life expectancy at birth probably averaged only about 10 years throughout most

of human history. Today, in contrast, it is about 57 years, worldwide, and as high as 80 in some

countries.

The population of the entire world <u>would be / was</u> about 300 million in C.E. 1—about the size of
6.
the United States today—according to one estimate. By 1650, the entire world population <u>had risen /</u>
7.
<u>was rising</u> to about 500 million, or about 8 percent of what it is today. The population <u>had been</u>

<u>growing / has grown</u> more slowly for several hundred years before that due to the tremendous toll of
8.
the plague, or Black Death. By 1800, however, the world population had passed the 1 billion mark,

and it <u>had continued / continued</u> to grow after that. Populations <u>were benefiting / used to benefit</u>
9.                                                                              10.
from better hygiene and public sanitation, more widely available food supplies, improved nutrition,

and, more recently, vastly improved medicine.

In the 1990s, demographers predicted that early in the 21st century, the population of the

world <u>reaches / would reach</u> 6 billion. They were right: In 2002, the population of the world actually
11.
<u>has reached / reached</u> 6 billion, which was about 5.8 percent of all the people who were ever born.
12.
Statisticians estimate that about 106 billion people <u>have lived / have been living</u> on Earth since the
13.
beginning of the human race.

## EXERCISE 4: Past-Time Verbs

*Read the excerpt from a young woman's memoir. Circle the correct verb forms.*

My parents and I came to live in the United States when I was five years old. We (had thought)/

<u>have thought</u> that everybody in America was very rich. Imagine our surprise when we <u>learned / have</u>
1.                                                                                              2.
<u>learned</u> that it was very difficult for many people, my father included, to make a living in our new

country.

My father <u>was / has been</u> a dentist in Europe before we <u>have come / came</u> 31 years ago.
3.                                                           4.
Here he couldn't work as a dentist right away because he <u>hasn't passed / hadn't passed</u> the state
5.
examinations yet. While he <u>had studied / was studying</u> for the dentist examinations, he <u>worked / had</u>
6.                                                                              7.
<u>worked</u> in a dental laboratory in order to support our family. Within a year, he <u>was passing / passed</u>
8.
the examinations and <u>established / used to establish</u> himself in a practice with a local dentist. Things
9.
turned out well for my father. He had a long and successful career as a dentist. By the time he <u>retired /</u>

<u>was retiring</u> last year, he <u>was practicing / had been practicing</u> dentistry here for over 25 years. During
10.                              11.

*(continued on next page)*

his career, he earned the respect of his peers and the devotion of his patients, as well as the love of the poor immigrants whom he <u>would treat / has been treating</u> free of charge.
**12.**

My mother too <u>has been / had been</u> happy here. She <u>got / has gotten</u> a degree in finance five
**13.**                          **14.**
years ago, and she now owns and operates her own profitable copy center. She <u>has been taking / had</u>
**15.**
<u>been taking</u> courses for a long time before she actually <u>got / had gotten</u> her degree. She <u>would take /</u>
**16.**                          **17.**
<u>has taken</u> only one or two courses each semester because she was busy looking after my father, my brother, and me. Now she is an independent woman who runs her own business.

I myself <u>have had / had had</u> a very good life so far. Three years ago, I <u>got / have gotten</u> my law
**18.**                          **19.**
degree, and since then, I <u>have been working / was working</u> in a small law firm where I am very
**20.**
happy. I know the partners of the firm quite well, as I <u>used to work / have worked</u> here in the
**21.**
summers when I was in law school. I was single at age twenty-four. Unlike my parents, whose marriage had been arranged by their parents, I didn't have any arrangement or even a boyfriend. But that summer, while I was working here at the law firm, I met a wonderful guy, Carl, who was working at another law firm. We <u>were getting / got</u> married the following year. He doesn't work there
**22.**
anymore; he <u>was becoming / has became</u> a judge and is well respected in the community.
**23.**

My family and I faced some difficulties when we first <u>arrived / were arriving</u> in this country
**24.**
because we <u>hadn't expected / haven't expected</u> things to be as difficult as they in fact were. We didn't
**25.**
know then what we know now: that ultimately we <u>used to succeed / would succeed</u> beyond our
**26.**
wildest dreams.

## EXERCISE 5: Verb Forms

*Read the excerpt from Lila's diary on the next page. Complete the excerpt with the words or phrases from the box.*

| | | |
|---|---|---|
| buy | fix | is |
| call | going to | promises |
| came | has | will |
| ~~cut~~ | hasn't | would |
| didn't | | |

*July 22nd*

That Craig! My husband never does what he promises.

Last week he told me that he would _____cut_____ the grass, but he
1.
hasn't done it yet. Then he said that he was going to _____ the
2.
leaky faucet in the kitchen, but it _____ still dripping. He promised
3.
that he would _____ my mom to wish her a happy birthday, but
4.
he _____ done that either. He thinks I'll feel better if he
5.
_____ to buy me an expensive gift. He told me that he was going
6.
to _____ me a big surprise for Valentine's Day, but he
7.
_____ give me anything at all, not even a card. Our anniversary is
8.
next month, and he said that he _____ make reservations at a fancy
9.
hotel to spend the weekend, but I'll bet that he _____ forgotten all
10.
about it. He even _____ up with the idea to give me a car for my
11.
birthday, but he didn't say which birthday.

There is one thing I know that he will do: nap. He told me that he was
_____ take a nap this afternoon, and I'm sure that he
12.
_____ take one!
13.

## EXERCISE 6: Past-Time Verbs

*Al and Bob are at their high school reunion. Complete their conversation. Circle the letter of
the correct answer.*

1. **AL:** Hi, Bob! Great to see you!

   **BOB:** Great to see you too, Al. What _____ for these past 10 years?

   **a.** did you do          **c.** have you been doing

   **b.** have you done       **d.** had you done

2. **AL:** Well, I'm a doctor. I _____ a pediatrics office last month.

   **a.** have just opened    **c.** was just opening

   **b.** just opened         **d.** had just opened

*(continued on next page)*

**3. Bob**: Oh, a doctor! I thought you _____ law.

    **a.** study                          **c.** are studying

    **b.** have studied                 **d.** were studying

**4. Al:** You have a good memory. I _____ law, but I decided to go into medicine instead. What about you?

    **a.** studied                        **c.** would study

    **b.** have studied                 **d.** was going to study

**5. Bob:** I write TV scripts. I _____ in advertising for 10 years, but I _____ my resignation two months ago.

    **a.** had been working / turned in     **c.** have worked / turned in

    **b.** worked / had turned in           **d.** worked / had been turning in

**6. Al:** How come?

    **Bob:** Comic Productions _____ me a great job, so I took it. I really like it.

    **a.** has offered                  **c.** offered

    **b.** has been offering             **d.** would offer

**7. Al:** That's great. You always were very funny. I remember that you _____ the funniest guy in our class. Whenever you made a joke, everybody _____ laugh so much.

    **a.** had been / used to           **c.** would be / used to

    **b.** used to be / would            **d.** have been / was

    **Bob:** Aw, gee.

**8. Al:** By the way, do you remember Mary Rush? She writes too. In fact, her first novel _____. Finally!

    **a.** just came out                 **c.** was just coming

    **b.** had just come out             **d.** had just been coming out

    **Bob:** Finally?

**9. Al:** Yes. By the time Brown-Smith Publishing _____ it, 11 other publishers _____ it.

    **a.** had accepted / had rejected     **c.** accepted / had rejected

    **b.** accepted / rejected             **d.** had accepted / rejected

    **Bob:** Oh, wow.

10. **AL:** Now, tell me about you and Sophie. Do you have any children?

   **BOB:** Oh, Sophie and I _____ married for only two years. We split up.

   **a.** have been          **c.** used to be

   **b.** were               **d.** would be

11. **AL:** You _____ divorced from Sophie? I'm sorry.

   **a.** get                **c.** were getting

   **b.** got                **d.** had been getting

   **BOB:** Yeah, I did. It's OK.

12. **AL:** We should get together sometime and talk about our carefree past.

   **BOB:** Right. Those days in the past _____ the good old days.

   **a.** were being          **c.** were going to be

   **b.** have been           **d.** were

## EXERCISE 7: Editing

*Read the blog by a teenager from another country. There are fifteen mistakes in past-time verbs. The first mistake is already corrected. Find and correct fourteen more.*

I am writing this blog now, during my last week in this country. I ~~am~~ *have been* here as an exchange student since January 1st of this year, and I'm leaving on Friday. When I first have come to this country last January, I knew that I will find things very different than they were at home. And that's good, because the reason I had decided to come here was to experience a completely different culture. I have been studying English for six years when I left home, and I wanted to know first-hand about life in an English-speaking culture.

On January 1st, my host family was meeting me at the airport. I like them immediately and they were liking me too. Two days later, I started going to school with my host sister. I made a lot of new friends. All year, I studied hard for my classes, played on the soccer team, and went to parties, just like American students. Many of my American friends were having boyfriends or girlfriends. I would always be interested in them and the people they were dating, but I didn't dated anyone. I never wanted to have a boyfriend myself partly because of all the drama and heartache and anxiety,

*(continued on next page)*

but mostly because I knew that I was go to have an arranged marriage. In my country, we don't have the custom of dating like here. There, parents arrange marriages for their children.

Of course, everyone in school knew about the arranged marriages in my country, and they had a lot of questions for me. They felt sorry for me because they couldn't imagine marrying anyone they didn't loved, or that their parents would forced them to marry. But it isn't like that at home! There, the parents introduce their children to each other, and if the couple like each other enough, they marry. If not, if either of the couple doesn't want the marriage, their parents look for someone else. By the time I left home, my parents have not yet found anyone for me, but I knew that they were looking, and I knew that they were going to continue to look until they found the right husband for me.

Before I came here, I was used to wonder about the system of choosing your own spouse. The divorce rate here is very high. At home, most marriages last, partly because experienced and loving family play an important part at the beginning when they choose the spouse. I see, though, that it is possible—very possible—to have a happy marriage, arranged or not. My host family is an example. The parents had been married for 25 years, and they have a wonderful life and a great family. I have learned a lot during my time here: that there is more than one way to live, and more than one way to find a good spouse.

## EXERCISE 8: Personal Writing

*On a separate piece of paper, write two or three paragraphs about how your parents (or another couple that you know) met. Use some of the phrases from the box.*

> My parents met in the year . . .
> My mother was . . .
> She had been . . .
> My father was . . .
> He had been . . .
> They got married after . . .
> Their wedding took place . . .
> When I was born, they . . .

# Future Time

## EXERCISE 1: Ordering Actions in Future Time

*Read the email. In each set of two sentences, write **1** in front of the action that happens first, and **2** in front of the action that happens second. If the actions are going to happen at the same time, write **S** on both lines.*

Dear Mom and Dad,

As you know, Kim and I are leaving for Europe next week. We did a lot of research to maximize the amount of time and money that we have. Here's what we have planned:

1. We arrive in London eight hours after we leave from Ottawa.

    __2__ We arrive in London.

    __1__ We leave from Ottawa.

2. When we get there, our friend Jamie will pick us up.

    _____ We get there.

    _____ Jamie will pick us up.

3. We'll be staying with Jamie for three days, until we leave for France.

    _____ We leave for France.

    _____ We stay with Jamie.

4. Before we leave London, we will have seen all the important landmarks there.

    _____ We see all the important landmarks.

    _____ We leave London.

5. In France, we'll chart our own course as we bicycle around the countryside.

    _____ We bicycle around the countryside.

    _____ We chart our own course.

6. We'll be staying at hostels and inexpensive hotels as we travel around.

    _____ We stay at hostels.

    _____ We travel around.

*(continued on next page)*

**7.** After we spend about 10 days in the countryside, we're going to Paris.

_____ We go to Paris.

_____ We spend 10 days in the countryside.

**8.** I'm excited about Paris. People say that after you've seen Paris, life is never the same.

_____ Life is never the same.

_____ You see Paris.

**9.** We're going to go the Chez Moi Hotel as soon as we arrive in Paris. It's an inexpensive one that Jamie has recommended.

_____ We arrive in Paris.

_____ We go to the Chez Moi Hotel.

**10.** If we have some money left over at the end of our trip, we'll go to one really nice French restaurant on the night before we come home.

_____ We go to a really nice French restaurant.

_____ We have some money left.

**11.** We're returning home on August 21, after we will have been away for three weeks.

_____ We are away for three weeks.

_____ We return home.

**12.** I'll call you as soon as we get off the plane.

_____ I call you.

_____ We get off the plane.

Love, Pat

## EXERCISE 2: Actions in the Present and Future

*Read the email. Write **P** for **present time** or **F** for **future time** over each underlined phrase.*
*Add a checkmark (✓) if the time includes a reference to the past.*

Hi, Thelma,

      P                                         P ✓                                                  F

<u>I'm updating</u> my resume right now. <u>I've been working</u> on this for the past week! <u>I'm sending</u> it

out as soon as possible—along with a cover letter—to about 50 advertising firms.

    A draft of the cover letter is attached. <u>I don't think</u> it has enough pizzazz, so <u>I'm sending</u> it to

you right now in the hopes that <u>you will improve</u> it. As you can see, <u>I haven't finished it</u>—I am

really stuck. <u>I've written</u> two previous drafts of this letter, and I am still not satisfied with it.

    <u>I'm also thinking</u> about posting my resume on one of those job sites on the Internet. What

<u>do you think</u> about that? It's very difficult—excruciatingly difficult—to find a job these days. Very

few companies <u>are hiring</u> new people; the mindset of corporations is to downsize now, not to take

on new people. I want to give myself as much exposure as possible. <u>If I post</u> my resume on the

job site tonight and send emails to 50 companies, <u>I'll get</u> some response by the end of the week,

don't you think? In fact, by this time next week, <u>I probably will have heard</u> from 10 or 15

different firms.

    <u>I'll redo</u> the resume and the letter with your suggestions as soon as <u>I hear</u> from you. I know

that you have a really hectic life, balancing your job and your family and all. But I hope you'll get

in touch with me right away. <u>I'll be sitting</u> here at my computer and <u>waiting</u> for your reply!

    I hope that something will happen very soon. As you know, next month <u>I'll be going</u> to Canada

for my cousin's wedding, and maybe by then <u>I will have received</u> some good news.

Thanks in advance for your help.

—Lucia

## EXERCISE 3: Verb Forms

*Read the coach's talk to his team before the season starts. Circle the correct verb forms to complete the talk.*

You guys, our team didn't win the championship last year, but we <u>are going to win</u> / are winning
**1.**
this year, in the season that <u>is just starting / that just starts</u> now. We're <u>traveling</u> / have traveled to
**2.**                                                                                    **3.**
Ohio next Saturday, and we <u>win / will win</u> that game! Here's why:
**4.**

First, you guys are in excellent physical shape. You <u>are seeing / will see</u> the great results from our
**5.**
serious training very soon. Second, you've practiced hard and long. You know what to do. You

<u>are taking / will take</u> possession of the ball at every opportunity. Third, the guys who were injured
**6.**
have recovered, and they <u>will be playing / play</u> in all of the games this year. Even Ruiz, who was in
**7.**
excruciating pain from his broken knee, and Wolfson, whose back was out of whack all last season,

are now in tip-top condition.

But the most important thing is our mindset. We're good physically, but we are even stronger

mentally. We train hard every day, and we <u>are training / will train</u> hard every day until the season
**8.**
<u>is / is going to be</u> over. We <u>have / are having</u> a tough schedule this year. We <u>go to play / play</u> the
**9.**                        **10.**                                                      **11.**
Flames next weekend and the Bears the following weekend. They're good teams, but we <u>are winning /</u>

<u>are going to win</u>. Will we beat the Flames? Yes, we will! Will we beat the Bears? Yes, we will! Are
**12.**
we psyched to win? Yes, we are! I'm pretty sure that we <u>travel / will be traveling</u> to the National
**13.**
Championships in Omaha after the season <u>is / will be</u> over.
**14.**

## EXERCISE 4: Future Verb Forms

*Read the conversations. Cross out the incorrect ways to complete them. More than one way may be correct.*

1. **A:** Let's go to the beach tomorrow.

   **B:** I don't think so. I just heard the weather report. It _____ tomorrow.

      **a.** ~~is rain~~           **c.** ~~is raining~~

      **b.** is going to rain    **d.** ~~rains~~

2. **A:** My computer crashed again. I can't do my work!

   **B:** OK. Don't panic. I _____ it for you again. You know I fix it every time it crashes.

      **a.** ~~'ll fix~~           **c.** am fixing

      **b.** would fix        **d.** ~~fix~~

3. **A:** Would you like to join us for dinner on Saturday?

   **B:** Thanks, but we can't. We _____ a play that night. We got the tickets two months ago.

      **a.** will see        **c.** are seeing

      **b.** are going to see    **d.** see

4. **A:** So you're leaving on vacation tomorrow?

   **B:** Yes, tomorrow afternoon. The plane leaves at 4 P.M., and tomorrow night at this time, I _____ over the Pacific Ocean.

      **a.** will fly        **c.** am flying

      **b.** am going to fly    **d.** will be flying

5. **A:** Will you finish writing that report today?

   **B:** I don't think so. By the end of the day, I _____ about half of it. I need another full day to complete it.

      **a.** will be writing      **c.** will have been writing

      **b.** will have written    **d.** will write

*(continued on next page)*

**6. A:** Is Dr. Wills ever going to retire?

    **B:** I don't think so! At the end of this year, he _____ medicine for 35 years. I think he is

    going to practice for another 35 years.

        **a.** will practice          **c.** will be practicing

        **b.** is going to practice     **d.** will have been practicing

**7. A:** Look, Mom! I can stand up in the canoe!

    **B:** Don't stand up in the canoe, Danny! You _____ !

        **a.** 'll fall out          **c.** fall out

        **b.** are falling out      **d.** are going to fall out

**8. A:** Sorry, I can't talk to you now. I'm watching my favorite program. I'll call you as soon as it

    _____ over.

    **B:** OK.

        **a.** will be          **c.** is

        **b.** is going to be     **d.** will have been

**9. A:** How late is Aunt Emma's plane?

    **B:** Very late. It _____ at midnight.

        **a.** will arrive         **c.** is arriving

        **b.** is going to arrive     **d.** arrives

*Read the letter from a tour director to her tour group. Complete the letter. Circle the correct verb forms.*

# ANTARCTIC ADVENTURE CRUISES, INC.

Dear Traveler:

Enclosed are your tickets, your itinerary, your luggage tags, and the passenger list for your trip to Argentina and Antarctica on the 30th of this month. We know that this is going to be the trip of your life!

We are meeting / will meet / will have been meeting you in Miami before we start / are starting / will start
**1.** **2.**
our actual trip to the Southern Hemisphere. As soon as you arrive / will arrive / will be arriving at the airport,
**3.**
go to the GlobeAir lounge, on Concourse F. Antarctic Adventure Cruises has arranged for a private room there, at the back of the lounge, where we can all relax, away from the hectic atmosphere of the airport terminal. After we are introducing / introducing / introduce ourselves to each other and enjoy drinks and a snack, we
**4.**
will board / are boarding / will have boarded the plane for the overnight flight to Buenos Aires.
**5.**
We have a one-day stopover in Buenos Aires, and then we continue on to Antarctica. When we
sail / will sail / are going to sail near the world's most unspoiled continent, you see / are going to see / will be
**6.** **7.**
seeing spectacular scenery. There are no man-made landmarks there, like the pyramids of Egypt or the Eiffel
Tower in Paris. There are only natural wonders—awesome glaciers, large groups of penguins, and clear, cold
air. Our experienced naturalists are describing / will described / will describe the area before we
**8.**
stop / will stop / are going to stop to explore. If the weather permits / will permit / will have permitted,
**9.** **10.**
we will explore around the bays in Zodiacs—small landing craft—and walk for a while on the actual
Antarctic continent.

When we are going to return / will return / return to Buenos Aires on the 15th, you feel / will feel / are feeling
**11.** **12.**
gratified that you have been to the most exciting place on Earth. You will have lots of happy memories. Many
of you will be making photo scrapbooks to email to your friends and family. I know that you remember / are
going to remember / are remembering the details of our trip together when you look / will look / are going to
**13.** **14.**
look at these photos, but you won't need the photos to remember your exciting trip.

I look forward to meeting you all and to our adventure together.

Truly yours,

Margaret de Bono, Tour Director

## EXERCISE 6: Future Verb Forms

*Read the predictions about these graduating seniors in the Central High School blog.*
*Complete the blog with the correct forms of the verbs.*

| TITLE | WINNER |
|---|---|
| Most Likely to Succeed | Al Albert |
| Funniest | Bob Bradley |
| Most Athletic | Fred Fenson |
| Best Dressed | Gail George |
| Most Popular | Harry Hernández |
| Best Natured | Jenny James |
| Cleverest | Katherine Klumper |

**HERE'S WHAT WE CAN EXPECT FROM OUR GRADUATING SENIORS
IN THE NEXT DECADE**

Several of our classmates are sure to make it big. Al Albert has always had a passion for the

law and great skill in debating. There is no doubt that Al will be a fine lawyer, and perhaps he

_____*will become*_____ a governor or a senator one day.
        **1. (become)**

Our class comedian, Bob Bradley, will certainly be a very successful stand-up comic. When they

_____ the prizes for the best television comedy star in 10 years, Bob is
        **2. (award)**

going to win one, for sure.

And what about our star athlete, Fred Fenson? Fred has won a football scholarship to State

University. We think that he will be a star there and that before he _____
                                                                        **3. (graduate)**

from State, he will have received several lucrative offers from professional football teams. Next,

it should come as no surprise that the best-dressed person in our graduating class, Gail George,

has accepted a job at *Glamourama Magazine*; we fully expect that by the time five years have gone

by, everyone in the fashion world _____ her name. Harry Hernández
                                        **4. (hear)**

will have tons of friends, wherever life leads him. As the most popular person in our class, Harry

_____ in any career he undertakes.
        **5. (succeed)**

Jenny James, with her warm and caring personality, is going to become a fine social worker.

She already has plans to start her career very soon. Next year, she _____
                                                                        **6. (take)**

some time off from school in order to work in a brand new program with underprivileged children.

The program _____ for just two weeks when Jenny starts next month. The
                    **7. (operate)**

following year, Jenny will enter City College of Social Work. Jenny is a very independent person, and

she will chart her own course, as usual.

And our clever Katherine Klumper? We predict that she _____
                                                                    **8. (become)**

president of a big company. About to enter Cornell University as a sophomore, she

_____ both her BA and MBA within four years.
        **9. (get)**

We have so many pictures of our school years in our scrapbooks. All this will be part of our past.

But, during the next 10 years, what will we be doing? What careers _____
                                                                            **10. (follow)**

during that time? How will we do as spouses and parents? Stay in touch, and come to our

10-year class reunion. By that time, we _____ or studying for 10
                                              **11. (work)**

years. By then, many of us _____ to other countries, and some of us
                                    **12. (travel)**

_____ the whole world. A lot of us _____ parents
        **13. (see)**                                          **14. (become)**

by then, and we certainly _____ a lot to talk about on that reunion night 10
                                  **15. (have)**

years from now.

*Look at the table of population estimates for big cities in the future. In the passage that relates to it, there are eighteen mistakes in the verb tenses that refer to future time. The first mistake is already corrected. Find and correct seventeen more.*

**Top 10 Largest Urban Areas**

| 2000 | Million | 2025 | Million |
|---|---|---|---|
| 1. Tokyo, Japan | 34.5 | 1. Tokyo, Japan | 36.4 |
| 2. Mexico City, Mexico | 18 | 2. Bombay, India | 26.4 |
| 3. New York City / Newark, USA | 17.9 | 3. Delhi, India | 22.5 |
| 4. São Paulo, Brazil | 17.1 | 4. Dhaka, Bangladesh | 22 |
| 5. Bombay, India | 16.1 | 5. São Paulo, Brazil | 21.4 |
| 6. Shanghai, China | 13.2 | 6. Mexico City, Mexico | 21 |
| 7. Calcutta, India | 13.1 | 7. New York City / Newark, USA | 20.6 |
| 8. Delhi, India | 12.4 | 8. Calcutta, India | 20.6 |
| 9. Buenos Aires, Argentina | 11.9 | 9. Shanghai, China | 19.4 |
| 10. Los Angeles / Long Beach / Santa Ana, USA | 11.8 | 10. Karachi, Pakistan | 19.1 |

In 2000, the most populous urban area in the world was Tokyo, and in 2025 it will still ~~is~~ *be* Tokyo. By that time, the population of Tokyo will gain 4 million people, but the population of two cities in India—Bombay and Delhi—have grown a lot more, by more than 10 million people each. In 2025, Bombay will has more than 26 million people.

In 2000, the second most populous urban area was Mexico City. In 2025, Mexico City has more people than it did in 2000, but it not be in second place any longer; it will be in sixth place.

The same going to happen in regard to New York City. In 2000, 18 million people are living there; in 2025 about 2 million more people are living there. However, New York will drops down from third place to seventh place.

The newest big city in 2025 will have been in Bangladesh. Its capital, Dhaka, have 22 million people at that time, and it will has become one of the largest urban areas in the world.

Cities that once were among the largest of the world—Shanghai and Calcutta—are going remain on the list, but they don't will be at the top of the list anymore. Buenos Aires and Los Angeles will have dropping from the list entirely. When 2025 will arrive, there be more people in large cities in Asia than on any other continent.

## EXERCISE 8: Personal Writing

*On a separate piece of paper, write two or three paragraphs about what you think your life will be like five years from now. Some things you could mention include your job, future education, your family, your hobbies, or travel. Use some of the phrases from the box.*

> Five years from now, . . .
>
> In five years, I . . .
>
> I will have completed . . .
>
> I'm going to . . .
>
> I will . . .
>
> If I have enough money, I'll . . .
>
> I will have been . . .
>
> I will have traveled to . . .
>
> By this time in 20__, I . . .
>
> In 20__, I . . .

# UNIT 4  Modals to Express Degrees of Necessity

## EXERCISE 1: Understanding Modal Expressions of Necessity

*Read the Q and A (Questions and Answers) from the website of a study-abroad program. In the numbered phrases following each paragraph, circle the letter of another way to say the same idea expressed in the corresponding numbered phrases within the text.*

STUDY ABROAD PROGRAM

# Why study abroad?

Because you are vitally interested in other ways of life, you **(1) should study** abroad. In a study-abroad program, you **(2) have to live** with a family in another country, live in the same way they do, and most importantly, speak their language.

**(1) a.** you have got to study          (b.) it's a good idea for you to study abroad
**(2)** (a.) you must live          **b.** you should live

You **(3) don't have to travel** to other countries to learn about them. You **(4) could read** about other cultures, watch travelogues, and interact with friends and colleagues from other countries. But the best understanding of another culture comes from being an actual part of it, a part in which you **(5) must speak** the language.

**(3) a.** you must not travel          **b.** it's not necessary for you to travel
**(4) a.** one idea is for you to read          **b.** you were able to read
**(5) a.** you ought to speak          **b.** you have got to speak

### Can I get credits toward my degree at my home university?

Yes, definitely. But you **(6) must make** arrangements with your advisor before you leave, and the university where you study abroad **(7) must officially confirm** that you have taken the courses.

**(6) a.** you have to make          **b.** you should make
**(7) a.** the university . . . has to          **b.** the university . . . is supposed to
     officially confirm               officially confirm

### What do I need to do before I leave home?

You **(8) have got to have** travel documents: a valid passport and in some countries, a special visa as well. You **(9) had better apply** early for your passport and any visas. Normal processing time for passports is **(10) supposed to be** four to six weeks, but sometimes it takes much longer.

**(8) a.** you ought to have          **b.** you must have
**(9) a.** you can apply          **b.** you should apply
**(10) a.** time is expected to be          **b.** time has got to be

You **(11) should also obtain** a student identification card, which you can get from your home university. This special card will identify your student status and may entitle you to discounts on anything from airline tickets to museum entrance fees.

**(11) a.** you ought to obtain          **b.** you had better obtain

### Will I be able to bring back souvenirs from abroad?

Souvenirs, yes, but you **(12) can't bring** back anything that's worth more than a few hundred dollars. Also, you are **(13) not allowed to bring** in food products.

**(12) a.** you are not supposed to bring          **b.** you are not allowed to bring
**(13) a.** you must not bring          **b.** you should not bring

### What can I expect when I return?

When you return, you will find that your views have expanded and that your life has been enriched. You will have an idea about how people think in other languages and about what their cultural values are. In order to keep up your language skills, you **(14) ought to practice** your improved language with native speakers from the country you have visited. You **(15) shouldn't let** your new language skills escape.

**(14) a.** you are allowed to practice          **b.** you should practice
**(15) a.** you must not let          **b.** you had better not let

If you don't take the opportunity to study in another country, you will probably be sorry later. You will say to yourself, "I **(16) should have studied** abroad when I had the opportunity. I **(17) shouldn't have declined** that opportunity."

**(16) a.** I didn't study abroad;          **b.** it was an obligation to study abroad
       that was a mistake
**(17) a.** I declined the opportunity;          **b.** I didn't decline the opportunity
       that was a mistake

## EXERCISE 2: Using Modal Expressions of Necessity

*Read Jackie's blog. Circle the correct modals to complete it.*

England and America are two countries separated by a common language. This is a remark that

George Bernard Shaw, an English writer, made early in the 20th century. I think that this is true. I

didn't think I (was supposed to) / was allowed to find any cultural differences when I came to the U.S.
1.

from England to study, but I was wrong. I found quite a few differences in the language.

*(continued on next page)*

As soon as I got here, I <u>must have rented / had to</u> rent an *apartment*, not a *flat*, as we say in
**2.**
England. To get to the sixth floor, where my apartment is, I <u>have to / should</u> take the *elevator*, not the
**3.**
*lift* as we do in England. If I am having trouble with my *car* (*automobile*, in England), I <u>must / ought to</u>
**4.**
look under the *hood*, not the *bonnet*, to find the problem and rectify it. And when someone helps me
put large items in the car, I<u>'d better / might</u> ask them to put them in the *trunk*. In England, the trunk
**5.**
is called the *boot*, and I<u>'d better not / am not supposed to</u> say *boot* or no one will understand me.
**6.**

When I first arrived here, I heard the robotic voice of telephone operators say, "When you are
finished, press the *pound sign*." But I couldn't find the pound sign on the phone because my image
of a pound sign is £, which represents money, the British pound. Here you <u>are supposed to / might</u>
**7.**
press the number sign, also called the pound sign: #, but I didn't know that. We call that a *hash*
*symbol*.

Surprisingly, even shockingly, some vocabulary has the opposite meaning in each of the countries.
In England, a *public school* is a school that a student <u>must / might</u> pay for, and a *private school* is
**8.**
one that a student <u>must not / doesn't have to</u> pay for because the government does. But in the U.S., a
**9.**
public school is one that is free, and a private school is one that a student <u>had better / has to</u> pay for.
**10.**

Another example of different meanings for the same expression is *to strike out*. In England, we
say *strike out* to mean *try to find success in something*, but in the U.S., people say *strike out* to mean
just the opposite: *fail*. One day I said to another student, "Good luck after graduation. I hope you find
success as you strike out." The student probably thought I was wishing him bad luck, but I meant
the opposite! What I <u>had to have / should have</u> said instead was "I know you'll do great things!"
**11.**

I <u>must not have had to / didn't have to</u> study American English as my second language, but I
**12.**
<u>have got to / am supposed to</u> learn the differences in vocabulary and phrasing if I want to
**13.**
communicate successfully here.

*Read the conversations between employees in an office. Circle the letter of the word or phrase that correctly completes each sentence.*

1. **A:** You weren't at the office picnic, Blanca. How come?

   **B:** Oh, I didn't have a ride. My sister _____ me there and come with me, but she never

   came to my house. Her car had a dead battery.

   **a.** drove         **b.** was supposed to drive      **c.** had to drive

2. **A:** Did you finish that report last night, Mike?

   **B:** No, I didn't. I _____ late, but I went home instead.

   **a.** had to work        **b.** should have worked      **c.** worked

3. **A:** Were you sick yesterday, Bob?

   **B:** Yes, I was. I _____ to the doctor. That's why I didn't come to work.

   **a.** should have gone      **b.** was supposed to go      **c.** had to go

4. **A:** Sacha, why weren't you at the meeting this morning?

   **B:** Oh, but I _____ at the meeting. I came in late and sat in the back.

   **a.** should have been      **b.** had to be         **c.** was

5. **A:** Ken, why weren't you at the meeting this morning?

   **B:** I'm sorry. I _____ there, but I was late to work today.

   **a.** had to be        **b.** should have been      **c.** was

6. **A:** Did you call Elizabeth to remind her of the meeting?

   **B:** I _____ her. She just called to remind me!

   **a.** didn't have to call      **b.** should have called      **c.** have got to call

7. **A:** Can you help me with my computer, Kim? It crashed again.

   **B:** I can't right now, Henry. I _____ fix Sally's machine. It's an emergency. I'll come down

   later, OK?

   **a.** should        **b.** have got to      **c.** had to

*(continued on next page)*

8. **A:** Attendance at the annual HR meeting is mandatory. Everyone _____ attend.

   **B:** Oh, gee. I was hoping to take the afternoon off.

   **a.** should                **b.** must                **c.** is allowed to

9. **A:** Going to lunch with us today, Sam?

   **B:** Hmm . . . _____. I have too much work to do.

   **a.** I'd better not         **b.** I don't have to        **c.** I'm not supposed to

10. **A:** My son is unhappy at school. Though he does excellent work, the teacher never praises him.

    **B:** That's a pity. A teacher _____ a child for doing good work. It's good motivation.

    **a.** could praise          **b.** is allowed to praise     **c.** should praise

11. **A:** My son's teacher is worse. He is always criticizing the children in front of the whole class.

    **B:** Yes, that's worse. Teachers _____ criticize the children. It discourages them from trying.

    **a.** could not             **b.** should not            **c.** might not

## EXERCISE 4: Using Modal Expressions of Necessity

*Look at the page from a traffic-law guide in the U.K. The guide is made especially for American drivers coming to England. Then complete the text in the guide. Cross out the modals and modal-like expressions in this memorandum that are NOT appropriate in the sentences. Cross out either one or two items in each underlined set.*

Be careful, American drivers! Many traffic laws in England are different from those in the United States. Here are some differences in traffic regulations in the two countries:

| U.S. | England |
|------|---------|
| Drive on the right side of the road. | Drive on the left side of the road. |
| In traffic circles, travel counter-clockwise. | In traffic circles, travel clockwise. |
| May make a right turn at a red light. It's OK. | May not make a right turn at a red light. It's illegal. |
| At airports, let the passenger exit on the right side of the car onto the sidewalk because it's safer. | At airports, let the passenger exit on the left side of the car onto the sidewalk because it's safer. |
| In most states, may use a hand-held phone while driving. It's not illegal. | May not use a hand-held cell phone while driving. It's illegal. |

1. First remember that in England, you ~~should~~ / must / have to drive on the left side of the road. You <u>can't</u> / <u>must not</u> / ~~don't have to~~ drive on the right side of the road.

2. When you come to a traffic circle, you <u>should / will have to / might</u> go around it by continually turning right because these circles go clockwise. And you <u>had better / should / could</u> enter these circles carefully; wait until there is an opening in the traffic before getting into the circle yourself.

3. In the U.S., you <u>should not / must not / don't have to</u> stay stopped at a red light if you want to turn right. However, there is no "right turn on red" here in England; you <u>can't / should not / aren't allowed to</u> turn right at a red light.

4. Airports are like big traffic circles. In England, you will be keeping to your left and driving clockwise at the airport. Here, when your passenger exits from the left of the car, he or she <u>should / has got to / ought to</u> exit into the outer left edge of the circle, onto the sidewalk. He or she <u>shouldn't / is not allowed to / might not</u> exit into traffic. There is no law about this, but it is much safer for the passenger.

5. In the U.S., most states still allow drivers to talk on their cell phones while driving, even though they <u>are not supposed to / shouldn't / must not</u>. In England, however, you <u>are not supposed to / are not allowed to / can't</u> talk on a phone while you are driving.

6. These are just a few basic pointers to help you get along more easily here. If you rectify your American ways of driving, you can probably avoid traffic incidents and you <u>must not have to / won't have to / were not supposed to</u> say, "Oh, I <u>might have / must have / should have</u> read the rules first, but I didn't."

## EXERCISE 5: Using Modal Expressions of Necessity

*When you are invited to someone's home for dinner, do you take a gift? If so, what kind of gift is appropriate? Read this story of a Japanese student who faced this dilemma when he was in the United States. Complete the story. Use the modal expressions from the box.*

| | | |
|---|---|---|
| are supposed to say | had better be | should I have bought |
| could have been | have to pay | shouldn't have bought |
| could have brought | might have turned out | was supposed to do |
| could have gotten | ~~must take~~ | will have to come |
| didn't have to bring | should I buy | |

### WHAT'S THE RIGHT THING TO DO?

Tetsuya is a Japanese student who has been studying English in the United States for about six months. Last Saturday, he went to the home of one of his American friends, Jason. Jason wanted to have Tetsuya over to his house to have dinner with him and his family.

Since this was Tetsuya's first dinner with an American family, he was a little nervous. He thought to himself, "As a guest, I _____ must take _____ a gift
 **1.**
to the family, as we do in Japan. What _____?" he wondered. He decided
 **2.**
to buy a watermelon, which is a very desirable and prestigious gift in Japan. He chose the most delicious-looking watermelon that he was able to find. To Tetsuya, American watermelons seemed big—much bigger than Japanese watermelons, which are round, not long and oval as they are in the United States. In Japan, watermelons are quite expensive; you _____ $15 to
 **3.**
$20 for a nice one.

He took his watermelon home and placed it in a nice box, which he then wrapped with pretty paper. He left his apartment at 6:30, carrying his heavy gift. As he walked to Jason's house and his arm began to hurt, he began to wonder about the watermelon. "_____ the
 **4.**
watermelon?" he asked himself. "Maybe I _____ it because it is really too
 **5.**
heavy to carry all this way."

Tetsuya arrived at Jason's house at 7:00 sharp. Jason had told him, "My mom is a very punctual person who doesn't like late people, so you _____ on time at 7:00, or she'll
 **6.**
get angry!" Of course, Jason was just joking, but he wanted Tetsuya to arrive as close to 7:00 as possible.

When Tetsuya arrived at Jason's home, the family welcomed him graciously. When he gave the beautifully wrapped watermelon to Jason's mother, Jason's mother opened the box and said, "Oh, isn't this—umm—interesting . . . a watermelon. What a nice gift! Well, Tetsuya! You _____ anything—it wasn't necessary, really—but we do thank
**7.**
you very much for your gift." Actually, though, she was perplexed; she didn't know what she

_____ with the watermelon. Serve it? She had already prepared a lovely
**8.**
dessert to serve, and besides, there was no time to chill the watermelon in the refrigerator.

   Tetsuya quickly replied, "It's just a small uninteresting gift," which is a translation of a Japanese expression that you _____ whenever you give a gift to someone. Jason's
**9.**
mother smiled at Tetsuya and put the watermelon in the kitchen. "We'll enjoy this tomorrow," she said politely. "You _____ back to eat it with us then."
**10.**
   Tetsuya then realized that the watermelon was not a very good gift idea because watermelons are not considered special in the United States. He still didn't know, however, what sort of gift

_____ better. But it really didn't matter. The evening turned out to be
**11.**
a great success. Jason's family was very welcoming, and Tetsuya appreciated their hospitality.

Perhaps Tetsuya _____ something else, and perhaps Jason's family
**12.**
_____ more pointers about Japanese customs beforehand, but the
**13.**
warmth and good feelings that were exchanged were more valuable than any material gift

_____.
**14.**

---

## EXERCISE 6: Editing

*Read this story by an English teacher. If the underlined phrase is wrong, write the correction above it. If it is correct, write C above it.*

   This is a true story about one of my students, Ana. I remember the first day she came to
                  *couldn't speak*
my class: She <u>couldn't to speak</u> any English at all. She spoke only Spanish. All the students
          *C*
<u>were supposed to speak</u> only English in class, but Ana was able to say only a few words.

She felt uncomfortable, but she <u>shouldn't have felt</u> that way. The situation was not unusual, and

several students were in the same situation.

*(continued on next page)*

One time during the holidays between school terms, the dorms were closed, so the students have to find a place to live during the break. Ana stayed with an American host family, and after the vacation, she asked me what she might to do to thank her new friends for their hospitality.

"Well, you could send them a gift," I told her. "Or you must just send them a nice card."

Ana decided that she will send a card. She asked, "Am I supposed to get a separate card for each member of the family?" "No, you haven't to do that. What you ought to do is get a nice card for the family and write a thoughtful message inside."

"But my English is not so good," she protested.

"OK, bring me the card, and I'll help you write your message," I offered.

Ana was extremely busy and easily could had forgotten her good intentions, but she didn't. The next day after class, she showed me a beautiful card. On the front of it were the words "In sympathy." On the inside were the words "You have my deepest sympathy. You are in my thoughts at this time."

This was a big mistake! The card that Ana had bought was a sympathy card, a card that you send when someone has died. Ana had confused the Spanish word *simpatico*, which translates to "nice" in English, with the English word *sympathy*, which expresses the emotions of feeling sorry about someone's death.

When Ana realized her mistake, she had a good, long laugh, and I chuckled too. She said that she must have asked someone to help her pick out the right card. Now Ana's English is excellent, and she must not need any help any more.

## EXERCISE 7: Personal Writing

*Have you ever been away from home in a different culture? Have you ever felt uncomfortable, or have you ever done something that you thought was correct but was incorrect in that culture? How did you feel when that happened? On a separate piece of paper, write two or three paragraphs about the cultural mistake you made. Use some of the phrases from the box.*

| | |
|---|---|
| I shouldn't have . . . | Because of that missed opportunity, I had to . . . |
| Instead, I should have . . . | In the future, I have to . . . |
| I could / might have . . . | In the future, I should . . . |
| I didn't realize that I was supposed to . . . | I have learned that I'd better . . . |

# Modals to Express Degrees of Certainty

## EXERCISE 1: Using Modal Expressions of Certainty

*Read the introductions to online news stories. What can you conclude about the missing information? Complete the sentences. Use the phrases from the box.*

| | | | |
|---|---|---|---|
| be operating well | have been a meteor shower | have taken the objects | speak Japanese |
| be very brave | ~~have been bad~~ | have won a big victory | want to anger the voters |
| be very effective | have snowed recently | like skiing | |

### Today's Top Stories

1. <u>Food Poisoning at Seafood Heaven.</u> Forty-six people who ate the shrimp at Seafood Heaven, a restaurant on the western shore, last Thursday night became ill with food poisoning. Other people who ate at the restaurant were unaffected.

   The shrimp must _____ *have been bad* _____.

2. <u>Pennsylvania Players Celebrate in Philadelphia.</u> The Pennsylvania Men's Soccer Team came home to a wild celebration in downtown Philadelphia yesterday. Pictured are . . .

   The soccer team from Pennsylvania must _____.

3. <u>New Anti-Headache Medicine.</u> A new medication used to treat severe and frequent headaches has relieved symptoms dramatically in 86 percent of patients . . .

   The new medication must _____.

4. <u>Hurricane Lashes Coast.</u> Winds of 120 miles per hour and tides as high as 10 feet whipped the shores of North Carolina early this morning. We cannot confirm the reports, but it is believed . . .

   Communications in the storm area must not _____.

5. <u>Artifacts from Indian Museum Are Missing.</u> Several small statues and pieces of very old pottery were stolen from the Indian Museum in the Great Desert. Authorities believe that only someone with an intimate knowledge of the museum could have committed the robbery. Because the museum is well-guarded 24/7 . . .

   The police believe that one of the guards, perhaps with a cohort, must

   _____.

*(continued on next page)*

6. <u>Heavy Response to Request to House International Tennis Players.</u> Sixteen students from various countries arrived in Springfield today to be contenders in the annual International College Tennis Championships. A call had gone out especially for hosts who can speak Japanese, and eight households responded with offers of hospitality for . . .

The people in these households must _____.

7. <u>Monks Join in Earthquake Rescue Efforts.</u> Monks from nearby monasteries are assisting in rescue efforts of victims of the massive earthquake that hit China. The monks put their own lives in danger to carry out their efforts and . . .

The monks must _____.

8. <u>Congress at a Standstill.</u> A proposal to enact new legislation to raise income taxes has not gone very far in the House of Representatives. Although everyone agrees that more money is necessary to run government programs, very few legislators want to go on record as supporting higher taxes . . .

The legislators must not _____.

9. <u>Odd Ball of Fire Lights Up Texas Sky, Astonishing Residents.</u> At first, officials believed the cause of the fireball was debris stemming from a satellite collision in space. But further investigation showed that there were meteors in the atmosphere at the time, and federal aviation officials have concluded that the fireball must _____.

10. <u>Unseasonable Heat in Europe.</u> An unseasonable December heat wave is lingering in Switzerland, Italy, Austria, and France, causing the cancellation of thousands of hotel bookings for the holiday ski season and . . .

It must not _____.

The people who canceled must _____.

## EXERCISE 2: Using Modal Expressions of Certainty

*Take this quiz in* Geo Trivia Magazine. *Complete the hints by circling the correct modal.*
*Then circle the letter of the correct answer. Answers are at the bottom of the page.*

## GEO QUIZ

1. The longest river in the world is the _____.
   HINT: The river is in Africa, so it might /(has to) be the Nile.
   (a.) Nile          b. Mississippi      c. Danube

2. The highest waterfalls in the world are _____.
   HINT: The falls are in South America, so the answer might not / can't be Niagara Falls or Victoria Falls.
   a. Niagara Falls  b. Victoria Falls   c. Angel Falls

3. The highest mountain in the world is Mt. Everest. It's located in _____.
   HINT: Turkey does not have extremely high mountains, so the answer might / must be India, or
   it could / must be Nepal and Tibet. FURTHER HINT: This area does not have a coastline.
   a. India          b. Turkey          c. Nepal and Tibet

4. The country with the longest coastline in the world is _____.
   HINT: The country is in the Western Hemisphere, so it might / must be Canada.
   a. Australia      b. Canada          c. the Philippines

5. The country with the largest land area is _____.
   HINT: The country has, mostly, a cold climate, and it is in the Northern Hemisphere. It could / should be
   Russia, or it could / should be Canada. FURTHER HINT: This country is not in the Western Hemisphere.
   a. Russia         b. Canada          c. Brazil

6. Early in the 21st century, the country with the largest population was _____.
   HINT: This country's capital is Beijing. According to projections, in 2028 this country must / should no
   longer have the largest population in the world because of its strong efforts to limit the size of its
   families.
   a. China          b. India           c. the United States of America

7. This country has won the World Cup more times than any other country: _____.
   HINT: The people in this country don't speak Spanish, so it might / should be Brazil, or it might / should
   be Italy. FURTHER HINT: This country is not in Europe.
   a. Brazil         b. Argentina       c. Italy

8. The country where they drink the most coffee per person is _____.
   HINT: This is a cold country, so here people can / must drink a lot of hot coffee—1,581 cups per year
   per person—in order to keep warm!
   a. Guatemala      b. Finland         c. Egypt

1.a 2.c 3.c 4.b 5.a 6.a 7.a 8.b

## EXERCISE 3: Using Modal Expressions of Certainty

*Two teachers in an English language program are talking about their students. Complete the teachers' statements. Circle the correct modals. You will have to use the information in the chart to complete some of the statements.*

| NUMBER OF CLASSES IN THE PROGRAM | | | |
|---|---|---|---|
| | **Beginning–1** | **Intermediate–2** | **Advanced–6** |
| **STUDENT NAME** | **COUNTRY** | **CLASS** | **EMPLOYMENT GOAL** |
| Beyhan Nurev | Turkey | Intermediate | to be an accountant |
| Hiba Rashid | Jordan | Beginning | to work in an international bank |
| Jared Larson | Sweden | Beginning | to be a chemical engineer |
| Jenny Chan | Singapore | Advanced | to teach English in Singapore |
| Mario Rivas | Mexico | Intermediate | to be a computer engineer |
| Roberto Beltran | Colombia | Advanced | to work in public relations |

1. Some of the students have cars. Beyhan **must /**(**might**) have a car, but I'm not sure.

2. Mario **might / must** speak English better than Jared.

3. Jenny **might / must** be older than Hiba.

4. Jared **might / must** know who Hiba is.

5. Roberto **could / couldn't** know Mario.

6. Jenny speaks Chinese and English. Hiba speaks Arabic and English. They had lunch together yesterday. They **could / must** have spoken to each other in English.

7. Mario **may / must** have traveled to France and England.

8. Jenny is only eighteen years old. She **must / could** not have taught English in a high school.

9. Mario **must / might not** know something about computers already.

10. Beyhan **might / must** be interested in numbers.

11. Jared **might / must** have seen snow.

12. Mario isn't very happy at this school. He thinks that it **might / might not** have been a mistake to attend this college.

13. Jenny and Roberto are both advanced students, but they **may / may not** be in the same class.

14. Hiba and Roberto **can't / might not** be in the same class.

**15.** Beyhan failed the last test, but all of the other students passed it. Beyhan admits that the test was actually quite easy. She **must / must not** have studied very much.

**16.** Jared is really interested in chemistry. Both his parents are chemists. He is a hard worker with great potential and is a contender for the National Merit Scholarship. He **should / must** be very successful in this field in the future.

## EXERCISE 4: Using Modal Expressions of Certainty

*Read the excerpts from different conversations heard in the halls of a high school. Circle the letter of the modal expression that completes each statement correctly.*

**1. A:** I need an easy math class. Which teacher's class is easy?

   **B:** Take Mr. Pembroke's class. It _____ be very easy. He usually teaches children.

       **a.** may                     **b.** could                    **c.** should

**2. A:** How old is Mr. McKenna?

   **B:** Oh, he _____ over fifty. He's been teaching here for 30 years!

       **a.** 's got to be           **b.** could be               **c.** might be

**3. A:** Juan said he missed 12 questions on the test.

   **B:** He _____ missed 12 questions! The test had only 10 questions.

       **a.** couldn't have         **b.** might not have        **c.** must not have

**4. A:** Where's Ms. Fowler? She's not in her office!

   **B:** She _____ in class or she _____ at a meeting.

       **a.** might be; might be      **b.** must be; must be      **c.** should be; should be

**5. A:** Where's Mr. Lamar? It's 11:00 and he's not here yet.

   **B:** He _____ be here soon. He's never more than 5 minutes late.

       **a.** must                  **b.** could                **c.** ought to

**6. A:** Franco looks really sad today. What do you think happened?

   **B:** He _____ passed his chemistry exam. He was really worried about it.

       **a.** couldn't have         **b.** must not have        **c.** can't have

*(continued on next page)*

**7. A:** I hear that school's going to be closed for a holiday tomorrow. It's the principal's birthday.

   **B:** That _____ be true! School is never closed for a reason like that!

   **a.** may not          **b.** might not          **c.** can't

**8. A:** Do you know where Ms. Banta is? She's not in her office.

   **B:** She _____ home sick. I know she wasn't feeling well this morning.

   **a.** must have gone          **b.** has to go          **c.** ought to go

---

## EXERCISE 5: Using Modal Expressions of Certainty

*Two friends have just arrived at a restaurant. Complete the conversation with the correct phrase from the box. There is one extra phrase in each box.*

| | |
|---|---|
| could be | ~~must have~~ |
| could have eaten | should have been |
| might have put | shouldn't have put |

<table>
<tr><td colspan="2" align="center">SPECIALS</td></tr>
<tr><td colspan="2" align="center">SOUPS</td></tr>
<tr><td colspan="2" align="center">Onion soup</td></tr>
<tr><td colspan="2" align="center">Vegetable soup</td></tr>
<tr><td colspan="2" align="center">Mystery soup of the day</td></tr>
<tr><td colspan="2" align="center">SANDWICHES</td></tr>
<tr><td colspan="2" align="center">Jumbo burger, fries, salad</td></tr>
<tr><td colspan="2" align="center">Tuna salad with relish</td></tr>
<tr><td colspan="2" align="center">Roast chicken with cream cheese and pimento</td></tr>
</table>

**DAVID:** I wonder what the soup of the day is.

**CAROL:** They always have a mystery soup. It ___*must have*___ stuff in it that's left over from the
                                                  **1.**

   day before. It almost always does. It _____ delicious.
                                              **2.**

**DAVID:** How is that? Are you saying that they _____ leftover meat and vegetables in
                                                      **3.**

   the soup? Is that healthy?

CAROL: Of course! At home, we do it all the time. We use leftover meat and vegetables. Last night,

for example, we _____ the same chicken and vegetables from the night
                           4.

before, but we didn't.

DAVID: So what did you eat instead?

CAROL: I made a delicious soup. I had some clear soup in the freezer, so I used that, and added the

chicken and vegetables with some spices and rice. I used too much pepper for my father,

though. I _____ in so much pepper.
              5.

DAVID: Very creative. I don't cook much, as you know.

| | |
|---|---|
| has to be | must have been |
| might have | shouldn't eat |
| must have | should become |

CAROL: Well, you ought to learn. You like to eat, and you're creative, so you _____
                                                                                    6.

a good cook in no time, if you want to. In fact, I think that you have the potential to be a

great cook.

DAVID: Maybe. It's true that I love to eat, but I don't have the time or the patience to cook. I do

want to find out about the mystery soup, though.

CAROL: Let's ask the server. Here she comes. What's the "mystery soup of the day"?

SERVER: It's really not a mystery. It's corn soup with potatoes and vegetables. The only mysterious

thing is the special way the chef makes it. He never tells anyone his recipes.

DAVID: Does it have onions?

SERVER: I'm not sure. It _____ onions. I'll ask.
                          7.

CAROL: Why are you asking about onions? Don't you like onions?

DAVID: I'm allergic to onions. I _____ them.
                                    8.

CAROL: I think the soup _____ onions in it. Good soups usually have onions.
                           9.

DAVID: I'll have the mystery soup anyway, even if it does have onions. It sounds good.

SERVER: I'm sure it's good. It _____ good if our chef made it.
                              10.

## EXERCISE 6: Using Modal Expressions of Certainty

*Read the information about a crime. Write whether the sentences below it are* **True** *or* **False***.*
*Then write short explanations for your answers.*

There was a murder at the Nelsons' house last night. Mr. Nelson, a very wealthy eighty-year-old man, was murdered. The police are investigating, and they believe someone in the house was the murderer. The murder happened at about 10 P.M. The police found the body in the living room. The police are sure only one person committed this crime.

| PERSONS IN THE NELSONS' HOUSE | | |
|---|---|---|
| Mildred | wife | She is old and walks with a cane. She was asleep by 9:30 P.M. |
| Belinda | cousin | She is thirty-five years old. She was envious of the Nelsons' wealth. |
| Mark | cousin | He is Belinda's husband. He didn't come home until 11 P.M. |
| Georgia | cousin | She is Belinda and Mark's baby. She is only six months old. |
| Frank | brother | Frank is visiting from New York. He loved his brother very much and is sincerely upset over his death. |
| Karla | the maid | Karla has been with the Nelsons for over 30 years. She usually goes to bed at 10 P.M., but last night she was awake in her room until midnight. |

___True___ 1. Karla could have heard the murder.

   *It's possible. She was awake at the time.* _____

_____ 2. Georgia could have killed Mr. Nelson.

   _____

_____ 3. The murderer might have used poison to kill Mr. Nelson.

   _____

_____ 4. Belinda might have killed Mr. Nelson.

   _____

_____ **5.** Mildred must have killed her husband.

_____

_____ **6.** Frank must not have been the killer.

_____

_____ **7.** The killer must have shot Mr. Nelson with a gun.

_____

_____ **8.** Mr. Nelson must have had more money than his cousin Belinda.

_____

## EXERCISE 7: Editing

*Read this response from Ricardo to his friend Marco's email. There are ten mistakes in the use of modals of certainty. The first mistake is already corrected. Find and correct nine more.*

Marco,

I guess you must not ⨉ be entirely happy over there. Are you lonely? It should be that you're not trying hard enough to make friends. Go out and socialize with people! At first, they must not be so friendly, but after people get to know you, they should liked you. You're a cool guy, even though you are a little shy.

I think that you may be not going out enough. It can't be good for you to stay home all the time. If you study at the library, for example, you may have met some nice people there. It's possible. And how about going off-campus to meet people? It could happened that you will meet another Ms. Right at an international movie group or a tango group.

But enough about you. Let's talk about me now. You think you've got problems? Last week Emilia left me, right after I got fired. That's right. I lost my job. Emilia must had decided I wasn't going to be a good provider. I admit I must have shown up on time every day, and I didn't, so that's probably why they fired me: because I was late to work a lot. I must have been crazy to be so lazy on that job at the software company. I could had a nice future at that company, but I blew it.

Anyway, here I am—no job, no girlfriend. I'm feeling pretty down myself. Let me hear from you, friend.

—R

## EXERCISE 8: Personal Writing

*Has something like this ever happened to you: Someone or some people are suddenly angry with you, and you have no idea why? Write two or three paragraphs about this incident, or about how it might feel to experience something like this. Use some of the phrases from the box.*

I may have . . .

I could have . . .

Maybe I didn't . . .

I should have . . .

I shouldn't have . . .

I must have . . .

But I am going to find out. But how?

I could ask . . .

I might talk to . . .

I should . . .

I have to know . . .

# UNIT 6 Count and Non-Count Nouns

**EXERCISE 1: Identifying Count and Non-Count Nouns**

*Read the introduction to a brochure from a gym. Underline the count nouns and circle the non-count nouns.*

## ━ PENFIELD ATHLETIC CLUB ━

Have you ever heard anyone say, "Use it or lose it"? It's true! If you don't *use* your body, it will surely *lose* some strength and flexibility. Your muscles will become weak. Your heart and lungs won't function efficiently. And your joints will be stiff and easily injured. Inactivity is as bad for your health as cigarettes are.

But when we exercise, we can become stronger and healthier. Research shows that regular exercise not only keeps us from becoming obese, but it lowers our BMI* and reduces the risk of heart disease, cancer, high blood pressure, and other diseases. And there is evidence that physical activity actually keeps the brain in good condition.

Furthermore, as you exercise, you can look better and younger. People who exercise regularly tend to have better skin and better posture. Exercise reduces stress, lifts moods, and helps you have better sleep. All in all, if you exercise with regularity, you will have a better quality of life.

Join our gym today. You will have fun getting healthy, and you will like the results.

* **BMI:** Body Mass Index

## EXERCISE 2: Recognizing Non-Count Nouns

*Read the article about Vancouver. There are twenty-nine non-count nouns. The first one is circled. Find and circle twenty-eight more.*

What does it take for a city to be voted the "Best City in the Americas"? It takes top scores in a poll that includes (friendliness), culture, restaurants, lodging, and shopping. This year the city that ranked highest in all areas was Vancouver, British Columbia.

Located on the west coast of Canada, Vancouver has a wonderful climate, with mild weather and clean air. Although it is far north—at latitude 49° 16' N—the winters are not cold because of the warm Pacific currents that flow by. Wherever you look in the area, you see spectacular scenery: The city is surrounded by mountains capped with snow, and you are never far from the sea.

The water and the nearby wilderness provide plenty of opportunities for people who are devoted to outdoor recreation: hiking, camping, skiing, and water sports are popular all year round. Because of its natural attributes, the area attracts outdoor enthusiasts, and tourism is important here.

In addition, Vancouver has a large number of cultural events, especially in the fields of music, art, and dance. There is plenty of entertainment —theaters, concerts, art shows, and festivals— as well as many fine shops and restaurants.

The economy is usually strong. Vancouver is a major port, and it offers easy transportation to all parts of Canada. Because of its ideal location and multicultural community, Vancouver is the gateway of commerce to the entire Pacific Rim. Downtown Vancouver is the headquarters for many businesses in the fields of forestry and mining, as well as in software, biotechnology, and most recently, movies.

Vancouver seems like the perfect city for livability, and for many of its residents, it is. They take pride in their city. Vancouver looked good when the winter Olympics were held there in 2010. And you didn't have to be an Olympic champ to appreciate the charms of the city. Many thousands of visitors to the Games came away from them impressed not only with the beauty of the city, but with the hospitality of its residents.

## EXERCISE 3: Matching Phrases with Non-Count Nouns

*Match the non-count nouns on the left with the correct phrases of measurement on the right.*

| | | | |
|---|---|---|---|
| __j__ | 1. equipment | **a.** | a bolt of |
| _____ | 2. electricity | **b.** | a different branch of |
| _____ | 3. French bread | **c.** | a few drops of |
| _____ | 4. gasoline | **d.** | 12 gallons of |
| _____ | 5. iced tea with lemon | **e.** | a nice game of |
| _____ | 6. news | **f.** | three glasses of |
| _____ | 7. rain | **g.** | a grain of |
| _____ | 8. brown rice | **h.** | an interesting item of |
| _____ | 9. science | **i.** | two loaves of |
| _____ | 10. tennis | **j.** | a heavy piece of |

## EXERCISE 4: Using Phrases with Non-Count Nouns

*Read the email to Mary from her friend LeAnn. Complete the letter with the phrases from the box. Some phrases will be used more than once, and in some places, more than one phrase is appropriate.*

| | | |
|---|---|---|
| a clap of | a drop of | a flash of |
| a game of | a glass of | a period of |
| a piece of | a serving of | a slice of |

Hi, Mary,

You know how much I dislike picnics. But Ted insisted that we go on one before the summer ended, and so we did. We went yesterday, and we had a lot of fun.

In the morning, we drove to Grover's Cove, which is a pleasant, secluded area. There we met some friends, three other couples. At first, the weather was fine. We decided to have

_____*a game of*_____ volleyball before lunch. But our friends had forgotten the volleyball net, so
     **1.**

we forgot about the volleyball game and sat down to play _____ cards instead. It
                                                           **2.**

was hot, and the sun was strong, so we all put on sunblock.

At lunch, as usual, I ate too much. I should really get in the habit of eating in moderation, but it's difficult! I've gained a little weight around my middle, which is telling about the fact

that I love to eat good food. I had _____ Sheila's special seven-grain bread,
                                                    **3.**

_____ Ted's delicious chicken salad, _____ Saga bleu
       **4.**                                                 **5.**

cheese, _____ Sheila's famous apple pie—brimming with calories—and
            **6.**

_____ lemonade. Sandy had brought her radio, and she turned on the classical
     **7.**

music station. Bob and Mia objected because they wanted to listen to rock, but all the others sided

with Sandy, so we listened to _____ music by Mozart, the Violin Concerto
                                        **8.**

Number 3. Everything turned out fine. It was like being together at an outdoor concert, with everyone listening to the same thing, and no one listening to their own iPods.

As soon as we were comfortable, almost falling asleep on our blankets, we heard

_____ thunder, which really startled us. Then we saw _____
     **9.**                                                 **10.**

lightning nearby, so we packed up really fast and left in a hurry. We felt just _____
                                                 **11.**

rain as we got into our cars, and then the rain came down really hard. When we turned on the car

*(continued on next page)*

radio, we heard _____ news: Tornadoes were in the area, and it was going to be

12.

dangerous to be outside for _____ time.

13.

We were quite anxious, but we got home safely and stayed together singing old songs for the

rest of the afternoon. You might think that the rain spoiling our picnic was a drag, but it wasn't. We

really had a wonderful day. I'm sorry you weren't with us. Next time.

Love, LeAnn

## EXERCISE 5: Using Count and Non-Count Nouns

*Read the article reporting the results of a survey that asked people what they valued most
in life. Complete the passage. Circle the word or phrase that is correct.*

### SURVEY RESULTS

As expected, (good health) / a good health was cited as the number one factor necessary to have a

1.

happy life. Devoted partner / A devoted partner to share the ups and downs of life with was the next

2.

most important factor. In describing what they valued or would value in the partner, people said they

wanted to spend their lives with someone who had integrity / an integrity, who wasn't afraid of

3.

work / a work, but at the same time was capable of having great fun / a great fun and who would

4.                                                                                          5.

give love / a love generously. Interestingly, more men than women mentioned that they wanted their

6.

partners to be intelligent. Women tended to mention practicality / a practicality as a feature they

7.

desired in a relationship.

The third factor—following a compatible companion / compatible companion in importance—

8.

was a strong family, cited equally by both sexes. Evidently, people yearn for connections and warmth /

a warmth. Also high on the list was having work / a work that is fulfilling and job / a job that

9.                                          10.                                     11.

provides satisfaction. Good salary / A good salary was not the only consideration; most people said

12.

that they also wanted to receive respect / a respect for their work.

13.

**A.** *Look at the menu, which contains selected items from the Mitsitam Native Foods Café. It includes many healthful foods that originated with the Native American peoples. Some of these foods are described in the sentences on the following page.*

## Mitsitam Native Foods Café
### National Museum of the American Indian, Washington, D.C.

**Authentic Soups and Chowders**
**made from . . .**

| | | |
|---|---|---|
| Peanuts | Cup $4.90 | Bowl $6.60 |
| Pumpkin | Cup $4.75 | Bowl $6.25 |
| Corn and clams | Cup $4.90 | Bowl $6.60 |

**Salads made with . . .**

| | |
|---|---|
| Wild Rice and watercress | $ 3.25 |
| Cabbage, peanuts, and pineapple | $ 3.25 |

**Main Dishes**

| | |
|---|---|
| Maple-roasted turkey | $ 9.95 |
| Taco made with chicken, lettuce, tomatoes, and cheese | $ 9.95 |
| Fire-roasted salmon | $12.50 |
| Chicken spiced with chili | $14.95 |

**Sides**

| | |
|---|---|
| Stewed pinto beans | $ 3.25 |
| Whipped potatoes | $ 3.25 |
| Grilled turnips with green onions | $ 3.25 |
| Roasted sweet potatoes | $ 3.25 |

**Sweets**

| | |
|---|---|
| Cookies made with dried cherries | $ 4.50 |
| Tart made with strawberries | $ 4.95 |
| Cake made with oranges | $ 4.95 |
| Chocolate tart | $ 4.95 |

**B.** *Complete the sentences. Use the nouns in the box. Add the indefinite article **a** or a plural ending when necessary. Some nouns are used more than once in an item.*

| | | |
|---|---|---|
| bean | peanut | strawberry |
| cheese | potato | tomato |
| chocolate | pumpkin | turkey |
| cookie | rice | |
| ~~corn~~ | salmon | |

1. This yellow vegetable has been basic to Native American cooking since about 6000 B.C.E. It is used to make tortillas, among other things. It's _____ *corn* _____ .

2. Used in cakes, pies, and to flavor ice cream, these red berries are also delicious to eat fresh from the vine. They're _____ .

3. This vegetable comes in many varieties and colors. It is high in carbohydrates, and it forms the basis of many Central American and Caribbean dishes. Each one is very small. We buy these packed together in cans or in packages, and they are called _____ .

4. This grain grows in warm moist places all over the world. It can be served with meat, vegetables, and even fruit. Native Americans grow a special wild kind. It is used a lot in Asian, African, and Central American dishes. It's called _____ .

5. Originating in Brazil and Peru, and then grown in the southeastern United States, we now use these as a snack and in candy. They are also used as the basis of many sauces in Southeast Asia. They're _____ .

6. Round and red, these are used in salads and as the basis of many pasta sauces. They're _____ .

7. This large brown vegetable originated in the New World, but is used in many European dishes. They are popular as "French fries," and we also bake them. These are _____ .

8. These round, flat items are made from sugar, flour, eggs, and often have added fruits or nuts. We eat them as a dessert or as a snack. They are _____ .

9. This product is made from milk. It is white or yellow. We often eat it on bread or crackers. It's _____ .

10. This delicious brown food comes in both liquid and solid form. It is a popular ice-cream

   flavor. It's _____.

11. This pink fish lives in cold water. As a main course, it is called _____.

12. This vegetable is large, round, and orange. It is used in soup, breads, and pies. One is

   called _____. When used in cooking, it is called _____.

13. This large bird is now part of the American Thanksgiving holiday. One of them is

   called _____. As a main course, it is called _____.

## EXERCISE 7: Editing

*Read the article from a health website. There are nineteen mistakes in the use of count and non-count nouns. The first mistake is already corrected. Find and correct eighteen more.*

                                                 *pounds*

The brain is a complex organ. It weighs only about 3 ~~pound~~, but it controls all our behavior, our motor functions, and the five sense: sights, hearing, taste, smell, and touch. Doctors have estimated that the brain has 100 billion nerve cells, called *neurons*. Piece of brain tissue the size of grain of sands contains 100,000 neurons.

As we get older, we tend to lose some brain cell. However, if you take care of your brain, you may reverse that process. You can do several things to increase your mental agility even when you are young.

How can we take care of our brains? Recent studies have found that the same things that keep your heart in good condition will also keep your brain in good condition. Here's what you can do:

- Even in your 40s, take care to keep your cholesterols down.
- Get rid of fat, belly fats in particular.
- Eat antioxidants, especially a berries and red grapes. A research shows that both protect against aging signs and can improve your learning and motor skills as well.
- Eat foods with a lot of fiber, such as bean, nut, and cereal but don't eat a sugar. (Too much sugars in the bloods actually can damage the memory center of the brain.)
- Get plenty of physical exercise.
- Get plenty of mental exercise: do puzzles, learn new language, practice brushing your tooth with your other hands.
- For the best sleeps, sleep in a cool room.
- Take a midday nap of at least one hours. Midday REM sleep is good for problem-solving skills.

*People differ greatly in their habits. How would you describe yours? Write two or three paragraphs describing your health habits. Use some of the phrases from the box.*

Some foods that I like are . . .

I should eat . . .

I (exercise / don't exercise) very often. For exercise, I like . . .

I (get / don't get) enough sleep at night. I need to . . .

When I have free time, I often . . .

My cholesterol count is . . .

My blood sugar reading is . . .

My BMI is . . .

I (am / am not) obese. My weight is . . .

I have got to . . .

# Definite and Indefinite Articles

## EXERCISE 1: Using Articles

*Read the text of an email in which Sara describes a family reunion to her cousin Elaine. Complete the email. Circle the correct articles, or — if no article is needed.*

Hi, Elaine—

Sorry you missed (the) / — family reunion last weekend! I'll try to bring you up to date.

**1.**

First, Uncle Jasper and Aunt Sue came all the way from Wyoming. You know that they moved

there about two years ago. They live on a / — small farm and raise organic vegetables. Sue takes

**2.**

care of a / the vegetables—she grows them, hauls them to market, and sells them— and they are

**3.**

building up a / — small business. Uncle Jasper is now — / a professor at a / — college out there.

**4.**                        **5.**             **6.**

(I forgot a / the name.) They seem very happy.

**7.**

Aunt Melissa was there. She has just retired. She doesn't have to worry about a / — money

**8.**

because she had been saving all her life, and now she is traveling all over — / the world. There

**9.**

used to be a big rivalry between her and her sister Maggie, remember? Well, now that they are

older, they are good friends, and Melissa takes Maggie with her on trips.

Cousin Bert is looking for the / a job, again. Poor Bert! He liked the / a good job he had at the

**10.**                                    **11.**

software company, but unfortunately, it went out of business last year. Things are bad with him,

and he's getting desperate for work. It's too bad because he's a / — really sweet guy. It's the / a

**12.**                                **13.**

pity that he's always out of a / — work.

**14.**

Cousin Jennifer is the one with a really satisfying job. She works for the Wildlife Association.

She raises a / — money to save endangered species. As you know, several species, like the / —

**15.**                                           **16.**

pandas, an / — elephants, and a / — tigers, are in danger of becoming extinct. Their numbers

**17.**             **18.**

have become drastically low, partly due to human actions. There is a program called "Adopt an

Animal." When people give money for an / — animal—one that is or will be in a zoo—it helps to

**19.**

keep that animal alive. She's very enthusiastic about her work.

You'll be at the / a next reunion, I hope. It's going to be in two years.

**20.**

Sara

## EXERCISE 2: Using Articles

*Read the job ads from an environmental jobs page on the Internet. Complete the ads. Circle the correct articles, or — if no article is needed.*

---

**ENVIRONMENTAL JOBS**

### Associate Zoological Veterinarian

Requires a degree in **—** / a veterinary medicine from a / the recognized university and two
　　　　　　　　　　**1.**　　　　　　　　　　　　　**2.**
to three years of an / — experience in a / the medical care of wild animals in a zoological
　　　　　　　　**3.**　　　　　　　**4.**
institute. Extensive knowledge of the / — wildlife and a / — wildlife behavior is highly
　　　　　　　　　　　　　　　　　**5.**　　　　　　　**6.**
desirable. The / A salary is above average. Excellent benefits.
　　　　　　**7.**

---

### Coordinator of Endangered Species

This is — / a unique opportunity for an / — experienced and highly motivated professional
　　　**8.**　　　　　　　　　　　**9.**
to deal with issues regarding endangered species. Three years in a / the program or institute
　　　　　　　　　　　　　　　　　　　　　　　　　　　　**10.**
protecting endangered species is necessary and one year at a technical or professional level
in the / — researching and analyzing data. A master's degree or higher is desirable. Salary:
　**11.**
$4,016 per month, plus generous benefits.

---

### Fisheries Biologist

Our small commercial company needs a / the field biologist to test fish on commercial
　　　　　　　　　　　　　　　　**12.**
fishing boats off a / the coast of Alaska. A / The position requires a master's degree in
　　　　　　　**13.**　　　　　　　　**14.**
— / the biology or another natural science, a / — college-level statistics course, and the / a
**15.**　　　　　　　　　　　　　　　　**16.**　　　　　　　　　　　　　　　**17.**
flexible attitude. Applicants can expect strenuous working conditions, but a / the good
　　　　　　　　　　　　　　　　　　　　　　　　　　　　　　**18.**
salary commensurate with their experience. Apply to a / the head office in Juneau.
　　　　　　　　　　　　　　　　　　　**19.**

---

### Environmental Microbiology

A / The Department of the / — Civil Engineering at the / — University of Atlantis invites
**20.**　　　　　　**21.**　　　　　　　　　**22.**
the / — applications for an / — associate professor position. We are particularly interested
**23.**　　　　　　　**24.**
in candidates with an / — extensive experience in the / — research. The successful candidate
　　　　　　　**25.**　　　　　　　　　　**26.**
will demonstrate a background of high-quality teaching at the undergraduate and
graduate levels and must have a Ph.D. The / A highest possible salary is offered.
　　　　　　　　　　　　　　　　　**27.**

## EXERCISE 3: Using Articles

*Read the text of a chat between Marco and Ricardo. Complete the conversations. Circle the correct articles, or — if no article is needed.*

**M:** Hey, Ricardo. Things have gotten better since I last wrote to you. First, I received **a** / — letter from my
**1.**
family with <u>the / a</u> very nice surprise in it: <u>the / a</u> check for $200. <u>A / The</u> letter made me feel good because I
**2.** **3.** **4.**
thought my family had forgotten me, and <u>the / —</u> check made me feel even better. Then, with <u>the / a</u>
**5.** **6.**
money, I went to <u>an / —</u> expensive restaurant downtown with <u>a / —</u> new friend.
**7.** **8.**

**R:** <u>A / —</u> new friend? Who's <u>a / the</u> new friend?
**9.** **10.**

**M:** She's <u>a / the</u> beautiful young woman. If our relationship develops, I'll tell you more.
**11.**

**R:** Hey, no fair. Who is she? You have to tell me something.

**M:** OK. What I will tell you for now is that she is <u>an / the</u> only daughter of <u>the / —</u> president of my university.
**12.** **13.**

**R:** Oh, wow. Way to go, What else is new?

**M:** Well, we haven't had <u>the / —</u> rain for three days now. I've seen <u>the / a</u> sun every day, and over the
**14.** **15.**
weekend, I went to <u>the / —</u> beach and got <u>a / —</u> bad sunburn.
**16.** **17.**

**R:** So now we're talking about <u>a / the</u> weather?
**18.**

**M:** OK. Then I'll tell you about my classes. I like <u>the / —</u> organic chemistry and computer science. I even like
**19.**
<u>the / —</u> history now; the course I am taking covers <u>the / —</u> history of the 20th century. And I like <u>the / —</u>
**20.** **21.** **22.**
English too, even though, as you know, I am just not very good in <u>the / —</u> languages.
**23.**

**R:** Boring!

**M:** Here's more boring stuff. Have you seen my university in the news? <u>The / A</u> president—George
**24.**
O'Day—was on TV, talking about saving the rainforests. He— <u>the / —</u> President O'Day—is a world-famous
**25.**
expert in ecology. He said that we can't hide our heads in the sand any more—ostrich-like—and that we have
to cut our carbon emissions drastically.

**R:** Fascinating. Let's chat again when you have more to tell me about <u>a / the</u> president's daughter, OK?
**26.**

## EXERCISE 4: Using Articles

*Read an archaeologist's description of an abandoned city on the planet Green. Complete the description. Write the articles* **a, an,** *or* **the** *where appropriate. Write — if no article is needed.*

<u>SITE</u>: **Planet Green**

<u>YEAR</u>: C.E. **3005**

<u>NOTES: Abandoned City</u>

Remains were found of what appears to be ___*a*___ large city on _____ island in _____
                                                    **1.**                    **2.**              **3.**

Northern Hemisphere. It seems that _____ city was part of _____ advanced civilization.
                                              **4.**                    **5.**

What we had thought was _____ sophisticated canal system has turned out to be something
                                 **6.**

else entirely. _____ canals that we thought we saw contained no water but were covered with
              **7.**

_____ hard surface. We think these were actually _____ roadways that _____ vehicles
**8.**                                              **9.**                  **10.**

traveled on. _____ vehicles had four wheels, and we saw _____ pieces from thousands of
            **11.**                                        **12.**

them.

_____ shadows that we had previously seen by telescope were actually _____ very tall
**13.**                                                                 **14.**

buildings, which _____ population probably lived in.
               **15.**

We found no agricultural areas, although we did find _____ large open space in _____
                                                    **16.**                       **17.**

middle of _____ island. Perhaps it was used as _____ large park. We are not sure how the
         **18.**                                  **19.**

inhabitants obtained their food; probably they brought it by boat from _____ mainland, or over
                                                                      **20.**

_____ bridge. We also found _____ parallel rows of _____ iron, perhaps used as a form
**21.**                        **22.**                    **23.**

of _____ transportation. We suspect that the inhabitants traveled by air too, but we didn't find
  **24.**

_____ evidence of any airport or air transportation vehicles.
**25.**

We are not sure why _____ area was abandoned, but it may have been because _____
                   **26.**                                                            **27.**

entire planet was suffering from _____ severe pollution.
                                **28.**

*Read the page from a program from an environmental conference. Complete the page. Write*
*the where necessary. Write — where the article should be omitted.*

### The 7th Annual International Environmental Conference
### New York, New York • March 4–9

**Highlighted Sessions**

Clara Aguilar, Ph.D., of ___*the*___ University of Santo Domingo in _____ Dominican Republic
     **1.**                                        **2.**

    **Topic:** *Better Systems of Waste Disposal in* _____ *Caribbean*
                                               **3.**

Dr. Tarek Maher, of _____ Cairo University in _____ Egypt
            **4.**                    **5.**

    **Topic:** *Preserving the Ecosystem of* _____ *Nile River*
                                       **6.**

Henry Clayton, Ph.D., of _____ Yale University in _____ United States
            **7.**                      **8.**

    **Topic:** *Air Pollution Reduction in Cities in* _____ *Rocky Mountains*
                                        **9.**

Professor Renu Gupta, of _____ University of Mumbai in _____ India
            **10.**                      **11.**

    **Topic:** *Solar Energy in* _____ *Southern Asia*
                          **12.**

Professor Richard Chan, of _____ Queensland College in _____ Australia
            **13.**                      **14.**

    **Topic:** *Climate Change and* _____ *Philippine Islands*
                            **15.**

**Housing Reminder**

You must make your hotel deposits no later than February 8th. _____ Hilton and _____ Sheraton
                                                  **16.**            **17.**

are the official convention hotels. Consult the map of _____ New York City on page 3 to find other
                                                 **18.**

hotels nearby. All the hotels are centrally located, five minutes by taxi to train stations, one-half hour

from _____ LaGuardia Airport, and less than one hour from _____ Kennedy International Airport.
     **19.**                                                **20.**

**Tours**

You may arrange guided tours to see some of New York's famous landmarks: _____ Fifth Avenue,
                                                    **21.**

_____ Empire State Building, _____ New York Public Library, and _____ Central Park,
**22.**                         **23.**                               **24.**
for example.

You can take advantage of three special post-convention tours.

1. A one-day cruise on _____ Hudson River on _____ *Lady Sunbeam*, a boat that the
                             **25.**                      **26.**

conference has chartered. You will be able to observe the successful clean-up of the river, as well as

spectacular views of the city along the way.

2. A two-day bus trip to areas near the city of _____ Boston and to _____ Nantucket Island to
                                      **27.**                      **28.**

observe a wind farm on _____ Atlantic Ocean.
                     **29.**

3. A three-day bus trip to _____ Adirondack Mountains, the largest wilderness area east
                         **30.**

of _____ Mississippi.
  **31.**

## EXERCISE 6: Using Articles

*Read the FAQs (Frequently Asked Questions) on a website about ecology. Circle the correct articles, or — if no article is needed.*

# What is a rainforest?

Rainforests are very thick and wet forests.

Millions of different kinds of <u>the / — </u> plants
                   **1.**

and <u>the / — </u> animals live in rainforests.
   **2.**

**Where are rainforests?**

Tropical rainforests cover about 7 percent of the Earth's surface. They are found in a band around

<u>an / the</u> equator of the Earth, which is <u>an / —</u> imaginary circle halfway between <u>the / —</u> North Pole
  **3.**                        **4.**                        **5.**

and <u>the / —</u> South Pole. Here the temperatures are high. These high temperatures cause <u>— / a</u> water
   **6.**                                                                 **7.**

to evaporate quickly, and as a result, there is <u>a / —</u> frequent rain in these areas of <u>the / —</u> tropics.
                                      **8.**                           **9.**

<u>The / —</u> largest tropical rainforests are near <u>the / —</u> Amazon River, <u>the / —</u> Congo River, and
  **10.**                          **11.**                **12.**

throughout much of <u>the / —</u> Southeast Asia. Three countries— <u>the / —</u> Brazil, <u>the / —</u> Indonesia, and
           **13.**                             **14.**       **15.**

<u>the / —</u> Democratic Republic of Congo—contain almost half of the world's tropical rainforests.
  **16.**

**Why are rainforests important?**

Rainforests are extremely important to <u>the / —</u> ecology of the Earth. The plants of the rainforest
                                    **17.**

generate <u>the / —</u> oxygen and store <u>the / —</u> carbon dioxide in their leaves, roots, and trunks. These
       **18.**                 **19.**

plants are also important to people in other ways too. Scientists have used them to make <u>a / —</u>
                                                                                 **20.**

medicines to fight <u>a / —</u> diseases. For example, quinine—used against <u>the / —</u> malaria—comes from
                **21.**                                        **22.**

the bark of <u>a / the</u> tree found in <u>the / —</u> South America and in <u>the / —</u> Africa. And rainforests fight the
         **23.**               **24.**                       **25.**

greenhouse effect, which traps <u>a / —</u> heat inside the Earth's atmosphere.
                         **26.**

**What's happening to the rainforests?**

The rainforests have decreased in area over the last 50 years because of the human demand for their

<u>a / —</u> wood and <u>an / —</u> land for <u>an / —</u> agriculture. In addition, urban development has spread into
 **27.**         **28.**        **29.**

some areas near rainforests. Scientists have predicted that a lot of the rainforest areas will continue

to disappear in the next 50 years, but some countries and organizations are making serious efforts to

stop this decline.

*Read the flyer. There are twenty-seven mistakes in the use of articles. The first mistake is already corrected. Find and correct twenty-six more. Add articles where needed and cross out or replace incorrect ones.*

# HELP THE METROPOLITAN ZOO!

Your Metropolitan Zoo needs you! Would you like to "adopt" ^an^ animal? You can "adopt" one by contributing a money, which will be spent for its care. With your adoption, you will have a satisfaction of knowing that your support is keeping "your" animal alive and well. A money pays for a food that your animal needs, a special equipment, and an extra time and a specialized attention from designated zoo employee.

In need of adoption right now are two tigers, one lion, two camels, family of four chimpanzees, and one gorilla. Which animal would you like to adopt?

Both our tigers are females; we are hoping to obtain male from Pakistan or China next year. A lion, recently named Mufasa by a group of the schoolchildren, is three years old. Both camels are Arabian kind, with one hump, not Bactrian kind, with two humps. Chimpanzees in our zoo act just like human family. They take care of each other, play, and sometimes even have a little fights. Sometimes, the two little ones push each other until one of them topples over. Our gorilla is most popular animal at zoo and also most expensive to maintain. He needs several sponsors. He puts on a show every afternoon by interacting with a visitors. He loves an applause that he gets.

As a sponsor, you will receive free admission to a zoo and receive a news and updates about your adopted animal regularly. In addition, your name and name of your animal will appear on the program at our annual banquet. Please find it in your heart to contribute to well-being of our animals. Become sponsor today!

*Write a short essay describing an environmental issue or crisis. Write two or three paragraphs to describe a phenomenon such as global warming, loss of the rainforests, an earthquake, a volcanic eruption, a tsunami, or a hurricane. You may find it helpful to use some phrases from the box.*

The temperatures of the Earth . . .

Tropical rainforests throughout the world . . .

Endangered species are . . .

The huge earthquake in China / Haiti / Japan . . .

A volcanic eruption in the summer of 2010 . . .

Hurricane Katrina . . .

An enormous flood in Pakistan / the American Midwest . . .

A disaster that happened in my hometown / country was . . .

The environmental situation has improved in . . .

# UNIT 8 Quantifiers

## EXERCISE 1: Recognizing Quantifiers

*Read the online ad from a graduate business school. Underline the quantifiers, and draw an arrow from the quantifier to the word it modifies.*

# Earn an International MBA from Global University

What do all executives need to understand today's business world? They need the kind of cutting-edge education that Global University provides: an overview of the international business environment, analyses and strategies for a great many markets, and plenty of personal interaction with experienced business people from many countries throughout the world. Global University offers this education.

- Earn enough credits to get your MBA degree in one year (full-time), or in two years (part-time). Both courses cover the same material, and each course confers the same prestigious degree.

- Students will intern for one month with a local international company. Some students work abroad for this internship.

- All our students must be proficient in two languages: English plus one other.

If you want to know how to function effectively in the business world, and to be able to make a lot of money while doing it, apply to Global University now.

Comments from a few graduates:

"I gained a lot of confidence. I know that I have a great deal of the knowledge I need to succeed in business." *JS from Shanghai*

"I had little real knowledge of how the business world works before I came to Global. Now I can identify most problems and approach solutions in a systematic way." *JLB from Paris*

"There are few graduate business programs that can match Global's. There's not much information that they don't offer about business, every aspect of it." *RL from Kuala Lumpur*

*(continued on next page)*

**65**

"After graduating, I joined a financial firm at a good salary. I am gaining the expertise needed to solve most problems. In a few years, I expect to become a partner." *BB from New York*

"At first, I had a little anxiety about competing in the business world. But I've become confident. I'm now well established in a consulting firm, and I have no worries about my future. Thank you, Global!" *FA from Dubai*

## EXERCISE 2: Using Quantifiers

*Read the text of an email from Ricardo to Marco. Complete the email. Circle the correct quantifiers.*

Marco,

Well, you certainly seem to be having (a lot of) / many fun in the United States now. I see that
**1.**
a few / a little friends in your life makes a number of / a great deal of difference to your state of
**2.** **3.**
mind. You should send a little / a few news about the lady you wrote about. Is she special, or do
**4.**
you have many / much girlfriends? You never used to have any / no girlfriends at all, Marco. What
**5.** **6.**
happened? Did you have a couple of / a bit of luck suddenly? Did you suddenly get handsome? Do
**7.**
a great deal of / all the girls call you up every day? If you think that I sound jealous, I am.
**8.**
A little / A couple of weeks ago you were complaining that either / every person you had met was
**9.** **10.**
ignoring you; now it seems that you have an amount of / a bunch of friends and that you are even
**11.**
doing well in a couple of / a bit of your classes.
**12.**
I, on the other hand, may fail a great deal of / most of my classes. Besides that, I lost a great many /
**13.** **14.**
a lot of money last month when I invested in a "get-rich-quick" scheme. I borrowed money from
everybody, and now I owe many / a great deal of money to a bit of / a few of our friends. Besides
**15.** **16.**
that, I had run up quite a bit of credit-card debt—everyone takes plastic these days—and I was really
living way beyond my means.

Marco, do you think that you could lend me a little / a few money? I'll pay you back in a little / a
**17.** **18.**
couple of months, I promise.

Ricardo

## EXERCISE 3: Using Quantifiers

*Aunt Madeline has taken her sister's four children to Big Frank's Franks for a treat. The boys are Adam and Barry, and the girls are Nicole and Zoe. The Xs in the chart below show what each child is having to eat. (XXX = a very large quantity.) Using the information in the chart, complete the sentences below. Use each quantifier from the box only one time.*

|  | ADAM | BARRY | NICOLE | ZOE |
|---|---|---|---|---|
| hot dog | XXX | X | X | |
| hamburger | | | | X |
| fish sandwich | | | | |
| fries | X | X | X | X |
| mustard | | X | X | X |
| ketchup | X | XXX | | X |
| salad | | | | X |
| soda | X, extra large | | X, small | |
| chocolate milkshake | | X, medium | | X, extra large |

| | | | | | |
|---|---|---|---|---|---|
| a couple of | a few of | a lot of | all | any | both |
| ~~every~~ | many | much | no | one | |

1. _____Every_____ child is having meat for lunch.

2. _____ child is having a fish sandwich.

3. _____ boys are having hot dogs.

4. _____ girl is having a hamburger.

5. _____ the children are having fries.

6. _____ children are having soda.

7. _____ the children are using mustard.

8. Adam is having _____ hot dogs.

9. Nicole isn't drinking _____ soda.

10. Barry is using _____ ketchup on his hot dog.

11. Adam, Barry, and Nicole aren't having _____ salad.

*Read the passage from a professor's lecture on the topic of changing language. Complete the passage. Circle the correct quantifiers.*

Is the English language changing? Yes, and so is (every)/ a / one language. A great deal of / A little / All
 **1.**                                                                    **2.**
languages change and adapt to the needs of their users. A language does not change by fiat; rather,

it evolves through usage. For example, a hundred years ago, many / much / any expressions used
                                                                **3.**
today—such as *the bottom line* and *at the end of the day* (both / a couple of / each expressions meaning
                                                                         **4.**
*the only important result*)—did not exist. In the 1950s, there were any / no / a little words in English
                                                                              **5.**
to refer to modems, fax machines, or cable TV, but one / each / every of these items had become
                                                                   **6.**
common by the 1990s. Several / A great deal of / Enough years ago, there weren't any / no / some
                        **7.**                                                            **8.**
words to describe social networking or activities on social networking sites, e.g., *friending and*

*tweeting*, but these words have entered newer editions of a number of / every / a great deal of dictionaries.
                                                                         **9.**

Because the needs of language users continue to change, language will change correspondingly.

Sometimes a word needs only a little / a few / any time to enter a language. For instance, after the
                                **10.**
terrible *tsunami* in 2006, the word *tsunami* came into everyone's vocabulary right away. Most / A

great deal of / Much English speakers hadn't known it previously. But usually people have to hear a
    **11.**
word a great deal of / a great many / much times before it becomes part of the language.
     **12.**

We get new words from much / a great deal of / a lot of different places. We take many / much / a
                            **13.**                                                 **14.**
great deal of words from other languages (*sushi, macho, algebra*), we create some / any / every by
                                                                                **15.**
shortening longer words (*gym* from *gymnasium*, *lab* from *laboratory*, *exam* from *examination*) or by

combining words (*brunch* from *breakfast* and *lunch*, *smog* from *smoke* and *fog*, and *camcorder* from

*camera* and *recorder*), and we even make a little / a few / little new words out of proper names (*Levi's*,
                                            **16.**
*Fahrenheit*). Most / Much / A great deal of English speakers know the names of several / a great deal
              **17.**                                                                  **18.**
of / much other currencies* and a lot of them know how much / many / most dollars equal one / few /
                                                                    **19.**                        **20.**
much *euro* or much / a couple of / each *pesos*.
                    **21.**

Do the new words and phrases enhance or detract from the language? To some people, the jury

is out on the value of the new words. However, a great deal of / plenty of / every language lovers
                                                             **22.**
appreciate the contemporary additions to the language.

**\*Note:** a *dollar*, a *euro*, and a *peso* are examples of different kinds of *currency*.

## EXERCISE 5: Using Quantifiers

*Read the passage about choosing a financial advisor. Complete the passage. Use the words from the box above each section.*

Though sometimes it is profitable to manage your own finances, in many cases the advice of an experienced financial planner is in order.

| expertise | ~~financial planner~~ | paycheck | professional advice | time |
|---|---|---|---|---|

Who needs a ___*financial planner*___ to help plan finances? People whose
         **1.**

income and assets are more than just a _____ need one. If you
                                        **2.**

don't have any _____ because you're too busy, or if you have little
                   **3.**

_____ in the area of money, you will definitely benefit from some
      **4.**

_____.
    **5.**

| goals | professionals | vacation | year |
|---|---|---|---|

Do you want to improve your current financial situation? Do you want to plan for inevitable future expenses? What about retiring while you're young enough to enjoy it? How about being able to take a _____ or two every _____? For these and
                **6.**                          **7.**

many other _____, you could benefit from the advice of one of a number of
            **8.**

_____.
    **9.**

| experience | insurance | interests | money | specialty | stock market | trust |
|---|---|---|---|---|---|---|

What kind of professional? A financial advisor may have a(n) _____
                                                          **10.**

in one area, such as _____. Or he or she may have more
                    **11.**

_____ working in the _____, buying and selling
      **12.**                                **13.**

stocks and funds. Whatever the specialty, the advisor must have no financial _____
                                                                        **14.**

that conflict with your own. You shouldn't invest too much _____ with
                                            **15.**

an advisor at first. After you feel that the advisor is looking out for your financial welfare, you will

probably develop a great deal of _____ in him or her.
                                        **16.**

## EXERCISE 6: Using Quantifiers

*Read the restaurant review. Cross out the phrases that are NOT appropriate for the nouns they modify. Cross out either one or two answers for each item.*

### RESTAURANT REVIEW: *SAHARA*

Many / ~~Much~~ / A lot of people in our town
**1.**
have been looking for a good Middle Eastern
restaurant. We have a few / a little / some Italian
**2.**
restaurants in the family style, a couple of /
a great deal of / every French bistros,
**3.**
several / a few / a little Asian restaurants, and
**4.**
one / some / every Mexican restaurant, but we
**5.**
haven't had no / any / each good, authentic
**6.**
Middle Eastern restaurants—until now.

The new restaurant Sahara has excellent food
and service, along with some / any / a few
**7.**
exotic atmosphere: flowing red curtains,
plenty of / lots of embroidered pillows on the
**8.**
floor, and a great deal of / a great many / every
**9.**
colorful Moroccan lamps hanging from the
ceiling. As soon as we arrived, we were seated in
a roomy booth. Almost immediately, a waiter
brought some / a couple of / every hot pita
**10.**
bread—nice and soft, not crisp—and
some / one / any olive oil to dip it in.
**11.**
To begin, my companion and I chose
two / one / both different appetizers: She had
**12.**

a little / some / one stuffed grape leaves, and I
**13.**
had a plate of creamy hummus. Both / Two /
**14.**
A couple of them were delicious. Then, our main
courses: the lamb kabob, which consists of pieces
of lamb and a few / a little / much vegetables
**15.**
—onions, peppers, and mushrooms—which was
tender and tasty, and the chicken, which had
been cooked in a sauce made of a little / some /
**16.**
several mysterious spices, was out of this world.
We both had a side dish of yogurt with
lots of / several / much vegetables cut up in it.
**17.**
Of course, we wanted dessert, and we chose the
baklava, a delicate, flaky pastry filled with
some / a little / plenty of pistachio nuts and
**18.**
covered with a little / a few / a couple of honey.
**19.**
And, surprise! You will be pleased that the
restaurant is so affordable. You won't have to
spend much / some / a lot of money here. You'd
**20.**
better get to this restaurant soon. Before long,
there will be a long wait to get in.

Rating: ★ ★ ★ ★

*A "scam" is a scheme to cheat people. "Spam" is unsolicited email that goes out to large numbers of people. Read the text of an email that is both a scam and spam. There are fourteen mistakes in the use of quantifiers. The first mistake is already corrected. Find and correct thirteen more. Change only the quantifiers; do not change any other words.*

Dear Sir or Madam:

It gives us ~~many~~ *much* pleasure to write this letter to you. Our bank has any information which will benefit you enormously. We are in possession of a great many money in an account with your name on it!!! Yes, this is true. An unnamed person has designated these funds for YOU!

In order to withdraw the money from the bank, we need to request a few information from you:

1. What is your Social Security number? We need this in order to access all account of yours.

2. What is your date of birth and where were you born? We need this information to answer every questions about your identity.

3. Please send the name of your bank and your account number. We need this so we can transfer the money easily without no problems with international banking laws. Please write all number carefully.

4. What is the password for your bank account number? Please double-check this password, and make sure it is up-to-date. A great deal of people have lost out on receiving their money because of incorrectly written passwords.

5. Please take these steps immediately. If the account is not settled by the last day of this month, you will not be able to receive some money.

It has taken a while for us to find you. That's why you must respond quickly in order to meet the deadline for unclaimed funds. Do not take many time to respond or you will lose each of the money in your account!

Also, very important! Please keep this matter confidential. Even if only a little people find out about this, it could make many trouble with the authorities.

Very truly yours,

B. V. Jackson, President

Shady People's Bank, Inc.

*Imagine this: You enter a writing contest. You write a short novel about your life. The novel becomes a best-seller\* and you become rich! What will you do with all this money? Using this scenario, write two or three paragraphs. Use some of the phrases from the box.*

   **\*Note:** *best-seller* = a popular product, especially a book, which many people buy

> First, I will pay all . . .
>
> I might buy a couple of . . .
>
> Then I am going to put a little . . .
>
> I'll contribute to certain . . .
>
> I will invest in some . . .
>
> I will finally have enough . . .
>
> I will probably take a few . . .
>
> I should give some . . .
>
> I am going to buy many . . .
>
> I will relax and have a lot of . . .

# Modification of Nouns

## EXERCISE 1: Ordering Modifiers

*Read the review of a fashion show. Complete the review by putting the modifiers in parentheses in the correct order. Place commas where they are needed.*

Last week at the _____*annual fashion*_____ show in Paris, some
1. (fashion / annual)

_____ designers displayed their latest creations.
2. (young / bright)

Everybody had expected these _____ fashions
3. (spring / new)

to be similar to last year's rather ordinary and boring clothes; instead, the

designers delighted the audience with a brilliant presentation. Drawing on

_____ inspirations, they showed the first
4. (various / international)

_____ collection in a decade. Once again, Paris is living up to its reputation
5. (big / exciting)

as the fashion capital of the world. Maurice Isak's inspiration came from the Orient; his

_____ lines with only the _____ ornamentation,
6. (simple / straight)                          7. (added / smallest)

done in _____ fabrics, obviously recalled some
8. (expensive / silk)

_____ paintings. He translated these _____
9. (Japanese / old)                          10. (classic / beautiful)

images into _____ suits and gave them a _____
11. (elegant / business)                          12. (fabulous / modern)

touch. Another designer, Liliana Darrieux, exploited the Pacific island atmosphere of Tahiti, where she

lived for two years. She showed her _____ outfits, which bring to mind
13. (brightly colored / cotton)

images of _____ islands, and which are perfect for
14. (tropical / South Sea)

_____ clothes. But inspiration for the _____
15. (summer / casual)                          16. (liveliest / new)

clothes came from sunny Spain, in Guillermo Pérez's collection. His _____
17. (cotton / long)

skirts were the sensation of the show. They featured bright colors— _____
18 (pink / hot)

hues combined with several shades of purple, and woven together with

_____ strands. The gorgeous skirts were almost otherworldly in feeling. It
19. (silk / turquoise and orange)

has been a long time since we have seen such fresh styles from any _____
20. (well-known / contemporary)

designer; the show exceeded all our expectations.

*Read the passage from a memoir. Turn the phrases in the box into noun modifier constructions. Then complete the passage by writing the modifiers in the appropriate blanks.*

| | |
|---|---|
| a house for dogs | a night in the summer |
| a pie made of peaches | a sister who is a baby |
| a table in the kitchen | cats that live in the house |
| dogs that belong to a family | dreams from childhood |
| a garden where flowers grow | a garden where vegetables grow |
| horses shown in competitions | horses used for work |
| jam made of strawberries | memories of childhood |
| tea made of blackberries | ~~trees that grow apples~~ |

My happiest memories are of visiting my grandparents' farm every summer when I was a child.

There they had many _____ *apple trees* _____ that I used to climb to pick the apples.
**1.**

They had both _____, where roses and violets grew, and _____,
**2.** **3.**

from which we gathered the carrots and beans that we ate at dinner.

There were some horses—_____—which helped my grandfather
**4.**

and the men in the fields, and even a few _____, which won prizes in
**5.**

the state fairs. There were a lot of cats, but most of them weren't _____;
**6.**

they roamed outside, particularly in the barn area, hunting the mice. There were also the

_____ that patrolled the fields and protected us from intruders. They slept
**7.**

outside in the special _____ that Grandfather had made for them.
**8.**

My grandmother used to make her own jellies and jams; I loved to pick the strawberries

in the fields to make my contribution to her special _____. She also
**9.**

made a delicious tea from the wild blackberries growing nearby. I would have that wonderful

_____ at night, along with a piece of _____ that
**10.** **11.**

she made from her own home-grown peaches. We would sit at the _____
**12.**

after clearing off the dinner dishes and talk about life, about her childhood and how life used to be,

and about my _____ for the future. I'll never forget her advice to me one
**13.**

particular evening. She said, "Don't ever relinquish your dreams. Always carry the hope that they will

come true, but never the expectation." Then she would gently lead me to the small, cozy bedroom that I shared with my _____. I slept peacefully every

_____ that I spent at my grandparents' house, and I dreamed almost every
<br>15.

night in the intervening winters that I was back at the farmhouse, basking in my grandmother's

warmth. I will cherish these beautiful _____ forever . . .
<br>16.

## EXERCISE 3: Using Noun Modifiers

*Read Kevin's email to a friend. He wants this friend to live in the house he has rented for several people. Complete the sentences with the words from the box.*

| | | |
|---|---|---|
| absent-minded | gourmet | runner |
| ~~buff~~ | hand | surgery |
| cook | marathon | ~~tennis~~ |
| experienced | professor | wonderful |

Hey, Kim.

I found a big house to rent. There are five of us so far, and enough room for one more. How about

you? Here's a description of the others, so you know what to expect.

**1.** Lila's a lawyer. She plays tennis four times a week, and she loves to watch all the matches on TV.

She is a real _____*tennis*_____ _____*buff*_____.

**2.** Martina's a writer. She has a problem in her hands. When she is working on her computer, her

muscles get painful and tight. She will probably have to have _____ _____.

**3.** Jack's a financial advisor who runs a lot. He's an _____ _____

_____. He has run in 11 marathons!

**4.** Sam's an interior designer, and he loves to cook for all of us. He's a _____

_____ _____.

**5.** Then there's me, the _____ _____. Someday I would like to do

something besides teach mathematics at the local college, but I'm not ready to find a new career yet.

Why don't you drop by this week and meet everybody? I expect that you'll like them all.

Kevin

## EXERCISE 4: Forming Compound Modifiers

*Look at this list of items for sale at Joseph and Lillian's Antique Shop. Rewrite the items as nouns with modifiers. Each item will include a compound modifier.*

**Joseph and Lillian's Antique Shop**

1. 2 silver candlesticks       ninety-five years old

   *2 ninety-five-year-old silver candlesticks*

2. 1 dining room table       two hundred years old

   _____

3. 8 dining room chairs       covered in velvet

   _____

4. 2 Tiffany lamps       century old

   _____

5. 1 samovar       plated in silver

   _____

6. 2 rocking chairs       one hundred fifty years old

   _____

7. 1 Persian carpet       woven by hand

   _____

8. 1 manuscript       written by hand

   _____

9. 3 coffee tables       inlaid with ivory

   _____

10. 4 serving dishes       painted by hand

   _____

11. 2 mahogany beds       carved by hand

   _____

12. 2 vases       one hundred thirty years old / inlaid with gold

   _____

*Read the excerpt from a graduate school application. Turn the phrases in the box into noun modifier constructions. Then complete the excerpt by writing the modifiers in the appropriate blanks.*

| | |
|---|---|
| activities for students who are international | award from five states for volunteerism |
| award given for four years of service | ~~camp where boys go in the summer~~ |
| council for ethics of students | disorder that is a deficit in paying attention |
| houses that are old and dilapidated | local shop for coffee |

I hope to attend the John K. Smith School of Business in order to expand my business knowledge and build the skills I'll need to succeed. I offer significant leadership experience and my sincere eagerness to learn. During the past five years, I have served my university and community in the following ways. I have been:

1. a tennis coach at a _____boys_____ ____summer____ ____camp____.

2. the weekend manager at a _____ _____ _____.

3. the president of the _____ _____ _____ for ethical behavior at my university.

4. the coordinator of the _____ _____ _____ for foreign students at my university.

5. a volunteer who fixes up _____ _____ _____ for the Better Community Housing Commission.

6. a volunteer who works in the public school system with children who have _____ _____ _____.

7. the recipient of the _____-_____ _____ _____, in appreciation for service during four years of undergraduate school.

8. the recipient of the _____-_____ _____ _____ for contributions to volunteerism in five states.

If I am fortunate enough to be admitted, I expect to make the John K. Smith School of Business proud of me as a graduate.

I am looking forward to hearing from you soon.

Very truly yours,

*Edward T. Larson*

Edward T. Larson

## EXERCISE 6: Editing

*Read the passage about a writer's first days in Los Angeles. There are twenty mistakes in the use of noun modifiers. The first mistake is already corrected. Find and correct nineteen more.*

I moved to Los Angeles ten years ago. I had expected to love "sunny" Los Angeles right away.

However, my first months in the city were terrible. Here's what happened:

Moving from the ~~country fresh~~ *fresh country* air to the awful, polluted stuff that city people breathe presents a

shock to the body. Ten years ago, I had miraculously obtained a well-paying job in the television

glamorous world, and I moved with my wife and two daughters from southwest beautiful Kansas,

with its golden magnificent corn in the fields and blue clear skies, to Los Angeles, where there

appeared to us to be no skies at all, only gray dirty smog.

Within a week, my wife and children and I all came down with a respiratory mysterious illness.

Coughing and sneezing, with eyes and noses dripping, we suffered for ten days. A ten-days stay

inside a small four-room apartment felt like being in a cement, cold jail cell. We were accustomed

to being outdoors, in the open Kansas air. After only two weeks at my new prized job, I got sick.

And I was really sick! My 42-years-old, feverish body ached as it had never ached before. Iron

enormous hammers pounded in my head. My lungs felt like lead huge weights. I coughed

constantly, and I never had more than a two-hours rest, even though I took double the

recommended dose of the cough over-the-counter medicine we had bought at the drug corner store.

Finally, after ten days, we recovered physically, although not psychologically, from our Los Angeles

rude reception.

My first three weeks in Los Angeles gave me the feeling that I was living in a foreign and hostile

country—and it would be many months before I felt differently. The irony of all this is that I—the

person who had hated the big terrible city at first—now love Los Angeles. They have cleaned up the

air here, and we see sunshine almost every day. I am really enjoying my active exciting life in Los

Angeles, and I hardly miss Kansas at all.

*What kinds of stores do you shop in? What do you expect to see in stores? What do you want to see in stores? Write two or three paragraphs about the things that you are looking for and the things that you might buy. Include four or five phrases, each using two or more adjectives or compound modifiers.*

EXAMPLES:

1. I bought a <u>beautiful new</u> pair of shoes at the <u>shoe</u> store.

2. At the <u>indoor food</u> court, I didn't have change. I had to use a <u>fifty-dollar</u> bill to buy a <u>two-dollar</u> hamburger.

*Use words such as these—or any that you choose—in your description. Combine some of the words.*

| | | | |
|---|---|---|---|
| baby | cool | neighborhood | store |
| ball | denim | new | strawberies |
| beautiful | dress | nice | supermarket |
| black | eighty-year-old | old | tall |
| blue | girl | ripe | tennis |
| boy | great | salad | tuna |
| cell phone | ice cream | sandwich | two-year-old |
| cheese | jacket | shop | woman |
| chocolate | jeans | soccer | |
| computer | man | sports | |

# UNIT 10  Noun Clauses: Subjects, Objects, and Complements

## EXERCISE 1: Recognizing Noun Clauses

*Look at the conversation between student A and professor B. There are twenty-three noun clauses. The first one is already underlined. Find and underline twenty-two more.*

**A:** Is it really true <u>that a plant will grow better if you talk to it?</u>

**B:** Yes. Studies have shown how much better plants grow when they are talked to.

**A:** But plants don't have sound receptors or nervous systems, so can you tell us why

that is?

**B:** Scientists know that plants aren't responding to the specific words people say.

What happens is this: When you talk, you breathe out carbon dioxide and water vapor. That

plants need carbon dioxide and water in order to grow is basic knowledge. They get a

lot of these two vital nutrients from your breath. And soundwaves from your voice cause plant

cells to vibrate. Experiments have demonstrated that certain types and strengths of sound can

affect plants. These sounds can cause plants to grow better—or worse—than usual. For example,

something amazing is what plants have done after being exposed to classical music: They grew

thick, healthy leaves and developed good roots.

**A:** Only classical music? It makes a difference if the plants hear classical music or other kinds

of music?

**B:** Well, it's interesting that it does seem to matter. Plants seem to care about what kind of

music they "hear." Jazz has a beneficial effect too. And plants exposed to country music had

normal growth. But plants that were exposed to rock or rap music did very poorly. Their root

development was so terrible that the plants began to die.

**A:** No way! Do plants actually know who they are listening to—whether they are listening to Mozart

or to Eminem?

**B:** Not exactly "know." They have an inclination, in a way, to like classical music. What they do, apparently, is sense the vibrations and respond differently to different types of rhythm.

**A:** Hmm. Well, here's what I think: The fact that you talk to your plants is good because it means that you are paying attention to them. What you are doing is giving them the water and food and pruning they need and not letting them die of neglect.

**B:** That's true. The issue of whether plants live or die depends on their receiving nutrients. But the answer to your original question—whether or not plants actually *do better* when you talk to them—is definitely "Yes." In health and longevity, plants that you talk to definitely outdo plants that you don't talk to.

## EXERCISE 2: Forming Noun Clauses Beginning with *That*

*Read the text of an email from Marco to Ricardo. Complete the noun clauses in the email by putting the words in parentheses in the correct order.*

Hey, Ricardo,

   About your email—You are really direct, and you are also right. It's true

_____that I have to shape up_____. I know _____,
   **1. (have to / I / shape up / that)**          **2. (I / forget / have to / that / about Lisa)**

yet it seems clear _____. The problem is
          **3. (this / is / that / going to be easy / not)**

_____. I'm in a big dilemma, because I know that I should
   **4. (I / forget / about her / can't / that)**

forget her, but at the same time, I don't want to forget about her. I'm sure that you're right

when you say that somebody new might make me forget. But the big difficulty with this is

_____. I'm going to try, though. My goal now
   **5. (I / not / that / am / receptive to meeting people)**

is simple: _____, and this means
          **6. (I / get / my life in order / that)**

_____.
   **7. (about other things / that / I / should think)**

   And you, Ricardo—what's going to happen to you? You lost another job! You know

_____. It's obvious
      **8. (have to be / that / you / responsible on the job)**

*(continued on next page)*

_____. You must keep the next job that you

**9. (you / have / that / been / always / too casual about your work)**

get, if you actually get one. _____ is vital.

**10. (that / adopt / you / a better attitude)**

In fact, you ought to become exemplary in your work habits. You have to get to work

on time, be careful with the details, work late if necessary, and no complaining. And

_____ goes without saying.

**11. (invest / won't / you / that / in any more iffy deals)**

   With that advice, I'm signing off.

—Marco

P.S. I'm sorry if I am hard on you. But the fact _____ is

**12. (truthful / we are / that / with each other)**

one of the bases of our strong friendship, isn't it?

---

## EXERCISE 3: Forming Noun Clauses Beginning with Question Words

*Read the transcript from a TV game show. Complete the contestants' answers by writing noun clauses based on the host's questions.*

**Host:** OK, Contestant Number 1, Jerry. Answer this: When did Neil Armstrong walk on the moon?

**Jerry:** Hmm. I don't know when ___*Neil Armstrong walked* OR *he walked*___ on the moon.

**1.**

**Host:** Sorry, Jerry. It was in 1969. OK, Contestant Number 2, Mary, answer this: Where did the

summer Olympic Games of 2000 take place?"

**Mary:** Oh, I'm not sure where _____. Was it in China?

**2.**

**Host:** No, Mary, sorry. It was in Sydney, in Australia. All right, Contestant Number 3, Jose: In

chemistry—what is the symbol for ozone?

**Jose:** I know what _____. It's O³.

**3.**

**Host:** Correct! Now, Jose, you are eligible for the grand prize! Are you ready for the next

three questions?

**Jose:** Yes, I am.

**Host:** OK, Jose—for the grand prize, answer these three questions correctly: First—what does

*numeracy* mean?

**Jose:** What _____ is to be literate in basic mathematics.

**4.**

**Host:** Yes! You're absolutely correct! Now, to double your earnings, answer this: What is the largest

organ of the body?

**Jose:** I know what _____. It's the skin. The skin
<br>**5.**

covers the largest area.

**Host:** Right again! Now, if you get this last question correct, you will win the grand prize. Jose,

why do some fish swim upstream, that is, against the current of the river?

**Jose:** Hmm. Why _____ upstream is obvious: They
<br>**6.**

do it to breed. Like Pacific salmon—they swim for hundreds of miles upstream to lay their

eggs before they die.

**Host:** Excellent! You have won the grand prize of $75,000. How do you feel about this?

**Jose:** Great! My fiancée will be ecstatic. This means we can take a beautiful honeymoon.

**Host:** Well, congratulations and the best of luck to both of you!

## EXERCISE 4: Forming Noun Clauses Beginning with *Whether* or *If*

*The newscaster has just announced that because of a storm, schools in Casper County
will be closed today. The Mason family is reacting to the announcement. Read the family
members' questions. Then complete the sentences based on the questions. Use noun
clauses with* **whether (or not)** *or* **if.**

1. **Mother:** Is there going to be mail delivery?

    Mother wants to know <u>whether (or not) there is going to be mail delivery OR if there is</u>

    <u>going to be mail delivery</u> .

2. **Sally:** Will the stores be closed?

    Sally is uncertain _____.

3. **Dad:** Are the buses running?

    Dad needs to find out _____.

4. **Jack:** Is there enough food in the house?

    Jack is wondering _____.

5. **Mother:** Are the roads safe?

    _____ isn't clear to Mother.

*(continued on next page)*

6. **Sally:** Is the electricity going to go off?

   Sally wants to know _____.

7. **Jack:** Does anyone want to play Scrabble?

   Jack is asking _____.

8. **Dad:** Do I have to go to work?

   No one has told Dad _____.

9. **Mother:** Will the doctors be on call?

   It's unclear _____.

10. **Sally and Jack:** Are the schools going to be closed tomorrow too?

    The question is _____.

## EXERCISE 5: Forming Noun Clauses

*Read this office conversation. Complete the answers by writing noun clauses based on the questions.*

**Q:** Who told the boss about Marla?

**A:** I don't know _____*who told the boss about Marla (her)*_____.
                                              1.

**Q:** What did he say to Marla?

**A:** I don't know _____.
                                        2.

**Q:** Is it true that Marla is upset?

**A:** _____ is an understatement. She is furious!
                      3.

**Q:** Where is Marla now?

**A:** I can't imagine _____*where Marla is.*_____.
                                          4.

**Q:** Well, what's Marla going to do?

**A:** _____*what Marla is going to do*_____ is no concern of mine.
                      5.

**Q:** Is Marla going to get fired?

**A:** I have no idea _____.
                                      6.

**Q:** Is Marla going to be arrested?

**A:** Arrested? I have no idea _____!
                                            7.

**Q:** What about the stolen money? I am talking about . . .

**A:** Stolen money? I don't know _____ talking about!
                                                    8.

**84** UNIT 10

**Q:** What do you think we are talking about?

**A:** _____ is the fact that Marla comes to work late
9.

every day, isn't it?

---

## EXERCISE 6: Forming Noun Clauses

*This is one of* Aesop's Fables. Aesop's Fables *are stories that were written in ancient Greece.*
*They are about animals, but they always have a moral that applies to human behavior. Read*
*the fable about the Fox and the Stork. Write noun clauses to complete the sentences. Use*
*words from the questions in the box to form the noun clauses.*

> Had she liked the soup?
>
> Was she going to eat it?
>
> What did he deserve?
>
> What do you think?
>
> What was the Stork doing?
>
> Why did I (the stork) do this?
>
> ~~Would the Stork come to dinner?~~

Once upon a time, the Fox and the Stork seemed to be very good friends. One day the

Fox wanted to know if _____*the Stork would come to dinner*_____, so he invited her. She
1.

accepted, and she went to his home the following Friday. When they sat down to dinner, the

Stork noted that the whole dinner—a thick potato soup—was served in a shallow bowl. She saw

that the fox was eating his own soup, licking it up with his tongue, but she was wondering how

_____ her own soup. All she could do was wet the end of her
2.

long beak with it. Then Fox asked the Stork whether _____.
3.

"Did you like your soup?" he asked. The Stork didn't answer directly. She was overly polite. "Well,"

she said, "I hope you will return this visit, and come and have dinner with me soon."

So the next week, the Fox visited the Stork. When they sat down to dinner, the Fox saw a

beautiful meal of meat, vegetables, and potatoes—but it was all contained in a large glass jar that

had a very long neck with a narrow opening. The Fox was not able to put his mouth or even his paw

into the glass jar! He was frustrated. The only thing that he was able to do was to lick the inside of

the top of the jar, but all the delicious food was at the bottom of the jar, out of his reach. At the same

*(continued on next page)*

time, he saw _____: The Stork, with her unique long beak,

**4.**

was eating every piece of food in her jar, and obviously enjoying it.

The Stork laughed and said to the Fox, "Do you want to know why

_____? I did this because you were so mean to me when I

**5.**

had dinner at your house." Then she added, "I have one-upped you on your bad joke." And finally

the Stork asked, "Well, what do you think now? I'd like to know _____."

**6.**

The Fox was angry at first, but then he admitted that he deserved her one-upsmanship. He said

that he had gotten _____.

**7.**

## EXERCISE 7: Editing

*Read the online article about the healing power of laughter. There are seventeen mistakes in the noun clauses. The first mistake is already corrected. Find and correct sixteen more.*

                                              *laughter can*

Doctors have known for many centuries what ~~can laughter~~ do: Laughter can improve how

does a sick person feels; a sick person often *feels* much better when he or she laughs. However,

growing evidence has revealed the fact what laughter actually helps to *cure* the patient.

A famous and well-respected American editor, Norman Cousins, wrote about how did laughter

help cure him. It is a true story. This is what did happened:

In 1964, he was experiencing severe joint pain and fever. It was just after had he returned from a

strenuous trip abroad. The doctors diagnosed him with a serious illness that attacks the connective

tissues of the body, and they hospitalized him.

While he was in the hospital, he began to research what did the effects of stress do to the body.

It became clear if stress can be extremely damaging to the immune system. He read about the theory

that are harmful to the body negative emotions, so he wondered whether that the reverse was true:

If negative emotions are harmful to the body, could positive emotions improve health?

What did he do next was dramatic. He checked out of the hospital and checked into a hotel

suite in New York City. He supplanted his traditional medical treatment with an entirely different

approach. He hired a nurse who read humorous stories to him and played funny movies for him.

It was essential what he laughed a lot and laughed hard every day. In addition, he took huge doses of vitamin C, a supplement he strongly believed in. He kept a very positive attitude.

That turned out the treatment to be effective is well-known. It turned out to be so effective that in very little time Cousins didn't need any more painkillers or sleeping pills. He found what the frequent and intense laughter relieved the pain and helped him sleep.

He returned to work and to an active life. Because of who was he—a serious writer and editor—Cousins wrote about how had the experimental treatment worked in his book, *Anatomy of an Illness*. In 1989, the medical profession acknowledged that his focused self-treatment was indeed that had cured him. Cousins lived a healthy life for 16 years after the illness. He died in 1990 at age seventy-five of a heart attack.

## EXERCISE 8: Personal Writing

*Do you remember a humorous incident in your life, or a funny story? On a separate piece of paper, write two or three paragraphs about one of them. Use some of the phrases from the box.*

---

One day, something funny happened. What happened was . . .

At first, I thought that . . .

Then I realized that . . .

How this happened is something that . . .

What I heard was . . .

What I said was . . .

I wanted to know whether . . .

I didn't believe that . . .

Perhaps one day I will comprehend why . . .

I am convinced that . . .

---

# Direct and Indirect Speech

*Read the minutes from the Towers Condominium Association meeting. There are sixteen uses of indirect speech constructions. The first one is already underlined. Find and underline fifteen more.*

## MINUTES OF THE MAY MEETING

The monthly meeting of the Board of Directors of the Towers Condominium was held on May 22. The meeting began at 6:40 P.M. when Ms. Janet Jones, president, said, "The meeting is called to order. Welcome, Board members, unit owners, and our manager."

**Reports of Officers and Committees**

1. *East Side Homeowners Association.* Mr. Pantini informed the Board that the County Comission had rejected the proposal for a new high-rise office building on our street. The Commission was responding to the distressed residents, who don't want to see any more tall buildings in the area.

2. *The Towers Parking Committee.* Dr. Gardner reported that a new system is going into effect on June 1, and he said that all the residents would be receiving new parking chips for their cars. He told everyone to place the new chips on the front windows of their cars and said that the cars would sound a "beep" when they pass the sensors at the gate.

**Old Business**

1. "Four companies have submitted estimates for the costs to repair the elevators," reported Harry Green, chair of the Elevator Repair Committee. He stated that the Board would consider the proposals before the next meeting.

2. "We are still short-handed in the front office," the manager reported. "We haven't had a secretary for two months," he added. He asked if anybody knew of a good secretary. Ms. Sloane wondered whether the salary was too low. She said that she is the CEO of a small accounting firm, and she knows that salaries have to be competitive. She said that the association should place a new ad on the Internet with a higher salary.

**New Business**

John Allen from InterRes, a satellite company, presented a short proposal for a new wireless system for our building. Mr. Allen said that we could meet all our cable, telephone, and Internet needs by installing his system and said it would be much more economical than the systems we have. He asked the group who would be interested in the new system and asked where they could be contacted during the day.

**Closing**

Ms. Jones asked whether there was any further business, and the answer was negative. The meeting was adjourned at 8:05 P.M.

## EXERCISE 2: Forming Indirect Questions from Direct Questions

Mr. Benjamin Capa is eighty-seven years old. He doesn't hear well, and so he can't communicate very well. He has just registered at a clinic, where his nephew David has answered all the questions asked by the receptionist. Now David is telling Uncle Ben what the receptionist asked.

*Read the receptionist's questions in the first column. In the second column, write the indirect questions that David uses as he reports the conversation to his uncle.*

| **Receptionist asks David:** | **David tells Uncle Ben:** |
|---|---|
| 1. How does he spell his name? | She asked me ___*how you spell your name*___. |
| 2. What is his address? | She asked me _____. |
| 3. When was he born? | She asked me _____. |
| 4. Where was he born? | She asked me _____. |
| 5. Are you his closest living relative? | She asked me _____. |
| 6. What is his principal health complaint? | She asked me _____. |
| 7. How long has he had this problem? | She asked me _____. |
| 8. Is he in pain now? | She asked me _____. |
| 9. Does he have insurance? | She asked me _____. |
| 10. Will you ask your uncle to sign this form? | She asked me _____. |

## EXERCISE 3: Forming Indirect Statements and Questions

*The passage is another of* Aesop's Fables. *Read this fable. Then complete the passage about the fable by writing constructions of indirect speech.*

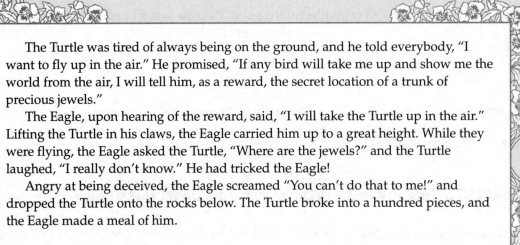

The Turtle was tired of always being on the ground, and he told everybody, "I want to fly up in the air." He promised, "If any bird will take me up and show me the world from the air, I will tell him, as a reward, the secret location of a trunk of precious jewels."

The Eagle, upon hearing of the reward, said, "I will take the Turtle up in the air." Lifting the Turtle in his claws, the Eagle carried him up to a great height. While they were flying, the Eagle asked the Turtle, "Where are the jewels?" and the Turtle laughed, "I really don't know." He had tricked the Eagle!

Angry at being deceived, the Eagle screamed "You can't do that to me!" and dropped the Turtle onto the rocks below. The Turtle broke into a hundred pieces, and the Eagle made a meal of him.

*The moral of the story is this:* You should not make a promise unless you know you can keep it.

The Turtle was not happy that he was always on the ground. He said

_____(that) he wanted to fly_____ up in the air. He promised _____
                        **1.**                                                        **2.**

any bird _____ him up and show him the world from the air, he
                        **3.**

_____ the location of a trunk of precious jewels.
                        **4.**

The Eagle said _____ up in the air. While they
                        **5.**

were flying, the Eagle asked the Turtle _____. The
                                                    **6.**

Turtle laughed and said _____. The Eagle screamed
                                    **7.**

_____. Then he dropped the Turtle on the rocks and
            **8.**

ate him up.

The moral of the story is _____ unless you know
                                        **9.**

you can keep it.

*Imagine that you are a reporter for a political journal. Your task is to report on a meeting that the governor of a small state has just had with some of the state's citizens. Change the direct quotations into indirect speech constructions for your article. Use a past form of the verb in the noun clause where appropriate, and change other words to keep the speaker's original meaning.*

1. Governor Jim Black said, "I am thrilled to be here."

   Governor Black said _____ *that he was thrilled to be there* _____.

2. He proclaimed, "I was elected last month to make great changes in the state."

   He proclaimed _____

   _____.

3. He stated, "I have been working hard to make these changes."

   He stated _____

   _____.

4. He added, "Just yesterday, I signed a law to raise teachers' salaries."

   He added _____

   _____.

5. He said, "In addition, tomorrow I'll be signing a law to bring more benefits to the elderly."

   He said _____

   _____.

6. He asked, "Does anyone have a question they'd like to ask me?"

   He asked _____

   _____.

7. A middle-aged woman stated, "I don't have children and I am not elderly."

   A middle-aged woman stated _____

   _____.

8. She wondered, "Why do I have to pay for these services?"

   She wondered _____

   _____.

*(continued on next page)*

9. The woman was becoming angry and glared at the governor. She shouted, "Can you tell me why?"

She shouted at him and asked _____

_____.

10. The governor replied with civility: "I understand how you feel."

The governor replied _____

_____.

11. Then he added, "But well-educated children will grow up to be better citizens, which will benefit everyone."

Then the governor added _____

_____.

12. He said, "And one day, you too are going to be elderly. Then you too can enjoy the increased benefits for older people."

He added _____

_____.

13. He said, "We have these problems and other serious problems in our state too, such as the economy. I won't sugar-coat the seriousness of these problems."

He said _____

_____.

14. He closed by telling the people, "But I will keep working hard with you to solve these problems."

He closed by telling the people _____

_____.

## EXERCISE 5: Changing from Indirect Speech to Direct Speech

*The column on the right has the actual words to a classic American jazz song, "The Darktown Strutters Ball." The column on the left tells the story of the song in indirect speech, as spoken by a young woman who is invited to a dance by a young man. Complete the song. Change the words from reported speech to direct speech.*

| Reported Speech | Words of the Song |
|---|---|
| 1. He said that he would be down to get me in a taxi. | "_____ *I'll be* _____ down to get you in a taxi, honey." |
| 2. He said that I'd better be ready about half-past eight. | "You _____ at half-past eight." |
| 3. He told me not to be late. | "Now, honey, _____ late." |
| 4. He said he wanted to be there when the band started playing. | "_____ to be there when the band _____ playing." |
| 5. He told me to remember that when we got there . . . | "_____ that when _____, honey . . ." |
| 6. The dances—he was going to dance them all. | "The dances—I _____ to dance them all." |
| 7. He said he was going to dance in both his shoes . . . | "I _____ in both _____ shoes . . ." |
| 8. . . . when they played the Jelly Roll Blues tomorrow night at the Darktown Strutters Ball! | "when _____ the Jelly Roll Blues tomorrow night at the Darktown Strutters Ball!" |

*Read the article about a public opinion poll. There are fifteen mistakes in indirect speech constructions. The first mistake is already corrected. Find and correct fourteen more.*

# SURVEY TELLS THE CONDITION OF THE COUNTRY

*Polls Today* conducted its annual survey about the condition of the country today. The poll asked
*what people thought*
~~did people think~~ about several issues and told them answer as honestly as possible. Here are some highlights

from the survey:

**Question 1. In general, do you approve or disapprove of the way the president is doing his job?**

When *Polls Today* asked if "Do you approve of the way the president is doing his job?" a little more than half

(51%) said that they approved. However, a large percentage (48%) stated not to agree with the president on

many issues, and 1% percent said that they didn't had any opinion.

**Question 2. Is the government doing enough to protect the environment?**

A large group (38%) stated what the government was not doing enough to protect the environment. They

wondered whether was the climate becoming too warm and whether would be lost too many trees within the

next 10 years. An equal number claimed that the environment was probably in good enough condition and that

they not to worry about it. The remaining 24 percent didn't say what did they think about this issue.

**Question 3. Do the citizens have access to good health care?**

About one-third (32%) said that they had adequate health care for now and the future. About one-quarter

(27%), though, wondered that would happen to them if they became ill or disabled. Of this group, several

expressed rancor and bitterness about the lack of health care available to them, compared with the universal

health care that exists in several other countries. The remaining 41 percent said that they weren't sure.

**Question 4. Are taxes too high?**

When asked that taxes were too high, 16 percent claimed that they were. This group is pushing hard to

minimize both taxes and government services. Astonishingly, 38 percent stated that taxes were not high

enough and that people would have to pay more for necessary services in the future. They said that they

didn't want to pay more taxes, but the bottom line is that more money is necessary to maintain the services

that exist now. The rest (46%) didn't said what they thought.

**Question 5. Is the quality of life better or worse now than it was 10 years ago?**

When asked how the quality of their lives was now, compared with what it had been 10 years ago, the population was again divided about 50–50. Forty-eight percent said Polls Today that the quality of their lives had improved over the last 10 years, and 46 percent said that it had declined. A small percentage of this group believes that the government is putting a positive spin on reports about conditions in the country and is not telling the truth about how bad really are things. About 5 percent reported that they didn't have an opinion.

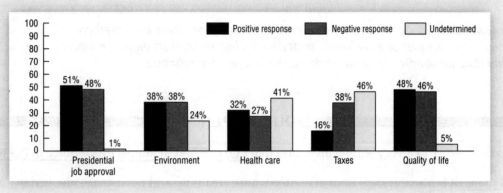

# EXERCISE 7: Personal Writing

*Have you ever had a problem due to miscommunication? Were you and another person unable to communicate your ideas and desires? On a separate piece of paper, write two or three paragraphs about the situation. Use some of the phrases from the box.*

---

I (he / she) asked whether . . .

I (he / she) replied that . . .

I (he / she) stated . . .

What I (he / she) really wanted was . . .

What I (he/she) really meant was . . .

I (he / she) was afraid to . . .

Neither of us understood . . .

Finally, I said . . .

At the end, (he / she) agreed . . .

We have / haven't been on good terms ever since . . .

---

# UNIT 12  Adjective Clauses: Review and Expansion

## EXERCISE 1: Recognizing Adjective Clauses

*Read the newspaper article about an invention and its inventor. There are nineteen adjective clauses. The first one is already underlined. Find and correct eighteen more. (Remember that some adjective clauses do not have a relative pronoun.)*

■ **LIQUID PAPER®** ■

This is the story of a very simple invention <u>that you can find in almost every office in the whole world today</u>. It is also the story of an inventor whose creativity and persistence resulted in a very useful product. What is the famous invention? It is Liquid Paper, the white liquid that covers up the mistakes you make when writing or typing. Bette Nesmith Graham—a secretary in Dallas, Texas, who had begun using white paint to cover up the typing errors in her work—invented it in the early 1950s.

At the time, Ms. Nesmith was a twenty-seven-year-old single mother. She was struggling to support herself and her young son by working as a secretary to the chairman of a big Dallas bank. When she began to work with her first electric typewriter, she found that the type marks she typed onto the paper didn't erase as cleanly as those from manual typewriters. So Ms. Nesmith, who was also an artist, quietly began painting out her mistakes with white paint that she had prepared at home. Soon she was supplying bottles of her homemade preparation, which she called "Mistake Out," to other secretaries in the building.

When she lost her job with the company, Ms. Nesmith turned to working full time to develop the Mistake Out as a business, expanding from her house into a small trailer she had bought for the backyard. In hopes of marketing her product, she approached IBM, which turned her down. She stepped up her own marketing and within a decade became a successful entrepreneur. The product, which came to be called "Liquid Paper," was manufactured in four countries and sold in nearly three dozen. In fiscal year 1979, which ended about six months before she sold the company, it had sales of $38 million. By the time Ms. Nesmith finally sold her business to Gillette in 1979, she had built her simple, practical idea into a $47.5 million business.

The story has a happy ending in more ways than one. Ms. Nesmith remarried and became Mrs. Graham. Her son, Michael, a musician of whom she was understandably proud, became very successful as one of the members of a music group called the *Monkees*, which appeared on an NBC television show for several years in the mid-1960s. Subsequently a country-rock musician, a songwriter, and a video producer, he then headed a production company in California, where he also directed some charities.

With some of her profits, Mrs. Graham established a foundation whose purpose is to provide leading intellectuals with the time, space, and compatible colleagues that they need to ponder and articulate the most important social problems of our era. Bette Nesmith Graham first developed a product that there was clearly a need for; then she used the substantial profits for charitable purposes, which is a fine thing to do.

The story of Liquid Paper and Bette Nesmith Graham is a story everyone can appreciate. It shows how an excellent product came to market because of the cleverness and perseverance of its inventor.

## EXERCISE 2: Using Relative Pronouns

*Read this essay from a university composition class. Complete the essay. Circle the correct relative pronouns, or — if no relative pronoun is needed.*

### THE TEACHER WHO INFLUENCED MY LIFE THE MOST

School was always very important to me. Therefore, it is not surprising that the person <u>which /</u>
**1.**
(who) influenced my life the most was a teacher. In my 12 years of school, I had many teachers
<u>whom / which</u> I have admired greatly, but Mrs. Thompson, <u>that / who</u> was my French teacher in the
**2.**                                                              **3.**
10th grade, is the teacher <u>— / which</u> I appreciate the most.
                                        **4.**

Mrs. Thompson was an excellent teacher, and I really liked the way she taught the class. It was
a class <u>where / which</u> I felt important. In this class, I was able to excel, <u>that / which</u> helped me feel
**5.**                                                            **6.**
better about myself. Before I took this class, I was not the kind of person <u>whom / who</u> spoke up in
                                                                     **7.**
groups. In fact, I was very quiet and did not socialize much. Because of the success <u>whose / —</u> I had
                                                                                             **8.**

*(continued on next page)*

in this class, though, I became more confident and at ease, something <u>when / which</u> also helped me
**9.**

to do better in my other classes. I became a better student and a better person.

My family did not have a lot of money, and it looked like I wasn't going to be able to attend the

university. However, Mrs. Thompson wrote strong letters recommending me for scholarships,

<u>whom / which</u> I submitted along with the applications. In the end, I was able to get a scholarship to
**10.**

attend the university. After my acceptance letter arrived, Mrs. Thompson gave me advice regarding the

classes I would take, as well as other academic matters. Those days at the beginning of my college

career were difficult for me. They were days <u>when / which</u> I really needed someone's advice, and
**11.**

Mrs. Thompson came through for me.

My final reason for choosing Mrs. Thompson is the subject <u>that / who</u> she taught me. This was
**12.**

my first class in French, a language <u>that / whose</u> I really liked to study. I enjoyed French so much
**13.**

that I then took another language—Spanish—the next year. I enjoyed studying both languages and

had excellent grades in all my language classes, an accomplishment <u>— / that</u> has given me the idea
**14.**

of becoming a language teacher myself. I can only hope that I will one day be able to teach as well as

Mrs. Thompson, <u>whom / whose</u> class had such a positive impact on my life.
**15.**

## EXERCISE 3: Using Relative Pronouns

*Read the job advertisements from the classified section of a newspaper. Complete the ads.
Circle the correct relative pronouns.*

———————————————— **SECRETARY** ————————————————

Computer Future is looking for a person (who) / which / whom has the right skills for a fast-paced,
**1.**

growing office. The current position, <u>that / which / whose</u> is being announced here for the first time,
**2.**

is for a front-office secretary. The ideal candidate for this position is someone <u>— / who / whom</u> is
**3.**

comfortable with advanced word-processing programs and all Internet functions. Our company

stresses excellent customer relations, so only those applicants <u>that / who / whose</u> people skills are
**4.**

excellent should apply; an outgoing personality is a requirement. We offer a competitive salary, full

health insurance, a generous retirement plan, and opportunities for professional growth, a

package <u>who / — / whom</u> other companies can only be envious of.
**5.**

## EXERCISE 4: Using Relative Pronouns

*Read the text from Dr. Jennifer Wise's call-in radio show. Complete the text, using the relative pronouns in the box. Write — if no relative pronoun is needed. Where more than one selection is possible, write all the possibilities.*

| that | when | where | which | who | whom | whose | — |
|------|------|-------|-------|-----|------|-------|---|

**CALLER:** Dr. Wise, I was wondering—who are the people _____*who, that*_____
                                                 **1.**

are most likely to catch colds or get the flu during the flu season? I

mean, it seems logical that extroverts, _____ gravitate
                                                **2.**

toward other people, toward crowds, while introverts don't, would be

the most susceptible. Is this true?

**DR. WISE:** Well, it's true because, statistically, the more people _____ you meet, the
                                                                               **3.**

more possibility you have of catching something. But, if you are basically healthy, and if

*(continued on next page)*

you are basically careful when you are in crowds, even though you are an extrovert, you

won't be at any more risk than introverts, _____ stay home more.
                                              **4.**

**CALLER:** What are the things _____ we can do to avoid catching a cold or the flu?
                                   **5.**

**DR. WISE:** Some people think there are certain things _____ make it easier for them
                                                           **6.**

to catch a cold. These may not be the same things _____ your mother
                                                      **7.**

warned you about, though. For example, a lot of people believe that you can get a cold

from sitting in places _____ there is a draft, or from wearing clothes
                          **8.**

_____ are not warm enough. These factors don't matter much, but there
   **9.**

are other factors _____ actually contribute to catching a cold easily. The
                     **10.**

things _____ are most important are these: 1) don't touch your face, and
          **11.**

2) wash your hands frequently.

**CALLER:** That's all?

**DR. WISE:** It's a lot. Most of us touch our faces one to three times every five minutes—200 to

600 times a day. This is a habit _____ is hard to break. The reason
                                    **12.**

_____ you should avoid touching your face is that thousands of germs
   **13.**

live on your hands. When you accidentally touch your eyes or your nose or your mouth,

those are the places _____ germs easily enter your body.
                        **14.**

　　Some cold viruses travel in the air from coughs and sneezes, but the common cold

usually spreads on objects or hands. So, if you have to shake hands with someone who's

obviously ill, or if you have to touch something the person _____ is ill
                                                               **15.**

has touched, you should wash your hands as soon as you can. If you cannot wash your

hands with soap and water, you can use an antibacterial gel, _____ is easy
                                                                **16.**

to obtain in tiny bottles _____ can fit into a pocket or purse.
                             **17.**

**CALLER:** So just two things?

**DR. WISE:** Well, those are two important factors. Another factor that lowers your resistance

to illness is not getting the rest _____ your body needs. People
                                      **18.**

_____ sleep patterns don't provide them with enough deep sleep will
   **19.**

more easily catch a cold than people _____ do get enough rest. Deep sleep
                                         **20.**

is especially important at times _____ people are under more stress than
21.

usual.

As for treating the common cold, nothing will cure it, but there are some steps

_____ you can take to lessen the symptoms. You may take aspirin or
22.

other medications _____ can make you feel better, stay in bed if you can,
23.

drink plenty of liquids, and take the home remedy _____ has been around
24.

for centuries: the chicken soup _____ your mother makes.
25.

**CALLER:** Thanks a lot, Dr. Wise.

## EXERCISE 5: Forming Adjective Clauses

*Read the passage about the Meyers-Briggs Personality Inventory. Complete the passage by
writing adjective clauses based on the sentences in parentheses. Sometimes more than one
relative pronoun is correct, and sometimes a relative pronoun may be omitted.*

Of all the personality measurement instruments that exist today, perhaps the Meyers-Briggs

Personality Inventory is the most well known. It is used extensively by human resources departments

in an effort to help them understand the people who work in their companies. The results of this test

show a strong correlation between personality type and job suitability.

What is the Meyers-Briggs Personality Inventory? Simply put, the Meyers-Briggs is a test

_____*which / that indicates an individual's personality type*_____. According to this test, there are four
**1. (The test indicates an individual's personality type.)**

main dimensions, or types, of personality. For each dimension, there are two categories.

The first dimension is a basic one: extrovert or introvert. An extrovert is a person

_____. These people
**2. (This person feels energized around others.)**

often have charismatic personalities and can become excellent leaders. An extrovert is

not very comfortable or productive being alone. In contrast, an introvert is a person

_____. An introvert feels most comfortable
**3. (This person's emergies are activated by being alone.)**

when he or she is not around other people, and in fact may embrace the idea of being alone.

The second dimension is connected to how a person notices and remembers

information. Some people in this category are referred to as sensors: those

_____. They rely on their past
**4. (These people pay attention to details in the world.)**

*(continued on next page)*

experiences and knowledge of how science works to make objective determinations. Sensors

have a lot of insight and are very practical people. In contrast, an intuitive is an individual

_____. Intuitives spotlight quickly what

**5. (The individual is more interested in relationships between people and things.)**

will probably be a successful move, mostly because they sense it is what people want. They are

sensitive to other people's feelings and act accordingly.

The third personality dimension _____ is

**6. (This test measures this dimension.)**

that of thinker or feeler. Have you ever had a boss _____?

**7. (Your boss made decisions objectively.)**

Maybe you thought some of his or her decisions were cold or impersonal. Perhaps they were.

Perhaps your boss was a person _____:

**8. (The person's primary way to reach a conclusion was this.)**

to determine what makes sense and what is logical. That boss was not a person

_____. Your boss was a thinker,

**9. (The person took other people's feelings into consideration.)**

not a feeler. He said exactly what he thought without mincing words. A feeler, unlike

that boss, makes decisions based on his or her own personal values and the feelings

_____ about the anticipated results of

**10. (He or she has feelings.)**

those decisions.

The final dimension deals with the type of place _____:

**11. (We prefer to live or work in this type of environment.)**

planned or unplanned. Judgers are people _____;

**12. (People prefer a planned and predictable environment.)**

they judge, or anticipate, what is going to happen and try to live their lives in accordance with

these plans.

In contrast, perceivers are more interested in keeping their options open. They want to be able to

respond to the needs of the situation at the moment _____.

**13. (Something happens at the moment.)**

Are you the kind of person _____, or do

**14. (The person's life must be planned in advance.)**

you prefer to take life one day at a time and have some room for spontaneity?

A test such as the Meyers-Briggs may help determine what type of personality an employee

has and the spot _____. At the same

**15. (He or she should be placed here to most enhance the company.)**

time, you as an employee might benefit from a test like this because you might find the place

_____.

**16. (You would be the happiest and most productive here.)**

*Read the facts about left-handed people. Each numbered sentence contains an identifying or non-identifying adjective clause. For each sentence, circle the letter of the sentence that means the same as the original. Pay special attention to punctuation.*

1. Left-handed people are people who are more comfortable when they use their left hand, not their right hand, for most tasks.

   **a.** People in general are more comfortable using their left hand for most tasks.

   **b.** Only some people are more comfortable using their left hand for most tasks.

2. Left-handed people, who are informally known as *lefties*, comprise about 12 percent of the world's population, and they are found all over the world.

   **a.** All left-handed people are informally known as *lefties*.

   **b.** Some left-handed people are informally known as *lefties*.

3. Because most tools are made for right-handed people, left-handed people, who are in the minority, often find it difficult to use these tools.

   **a.** Some left-handed people are in the minority.

   **b.** All left-handed people are in the minority.

4. Objects which are especially difficult for left-handed people to use include computer mouses, scissors, most stringed instruments, power tools, and light bulbs.

   **a.** Objects in general are very difficult for left-handed people to use.

   **b.** Some objects are very difficult for left-handed people to use.

5. For example, the original computer mouses, which were made for right-handed people, are difficult for left-handed people to use.

   **a.** All the original computer mouses were made for right-handed people.

   **b.** Some of the original computer mouses were made for right-handed people.

6. Fortunately for lefties, there are Internet sites that sell tools especially for left-handed people.

   **a.** All Internet sites sell tools made especially for left-handed people.

   **b.** Some Internet sites sell tools made especially for left-handed people.

7. On these sites, you can find computer mouses which are made for left-handers.

   **a.** These websites sell computer mouses for lefties.

   **b.** These websites may also sell computer mouses for everyone, lefties and righties.

*(continued on next page)*

**8.** Since left-handed people have to adapt to a right-handed world, some people believe that lefties, who have to work at fitting in, turn out to be more adaptable people.

   **a.** All lefties have to work at fitting in.

   **b.** Some lefties have to work at fitting in.

**9.** Some people believe that left-handed people often develop qualities that can lead them to be successful artists, scientists, or leaders.

   **a.** Some believe that left-handed people develop qualities that everyone has.

   **b.** Some believe that left-handed people develop special qualities.

**10.** Men who are left-handed outnumber women who are left-handed 2–1.

   **a.** There are more men than women in the world.

   **b.** There are more left-handed men than left-handed women in the world.

**11.** The list of lefties who are famous is long. It includes Aristotle, Simon Bolivar, Pablo Picasso, Albert Einstein, Fidel Castro, Paul McCartney, Rafael Nadal, Oprah Winfrey, Angelina Jolie, George H. W. Bush, and Barack Obama, among many others.

   **a.** Lefties in general are famous.

   **b.** Some lefties are famous.

## EXERCISE 7: Editing

*Read the passage about ways to categorize people. There are seventeen mistakes in the use of adjective clauses. The first mistake is already corrected. Find and correct sixteen more.*

       *that, which*
One of the ways ~~who~~ is used to describe people is to label them *extroverts* or *introverts*.

However, there are other methods whose people have used them to conveniently categorize members

of the human race.

For example, for people whose size is a little outside the normal range, there is the division into

*endomorphs*, who they tend to be fat, and *ectomorphs*, who are thin. The endomorph is stereotyped

as a relaxed person without obsessions, in contrast to the ectomorph, that is stereotyped as a person

whom is nervous and serious and who rarely smiles.

Another division defines people as Type A or Type B. Type A is the category which describes people they are very serious, ambitious, and driven. Type A originally described people, usually middle-aged males, whom were at risk of suffering a heart attack. Type B, on the other hand, labels a rather passive, ambitionless person which others frequently take advantage of and which is probably not a candidate for a heart attack.

Some people categorize human beings by their astrological signs. Astrology is the belief that stars and planets influence the Earth and human destinies. The date of a person's birth determines his or her astrological sign, which it is the name of one of the constellations of stars in the universe. This astrological sign that the person is born under determines their character and destiny. For example, a person whom was born between April 22 and May 21 is called a Taurus and is supposed to possess certain characteristics, such as friendliness and tact. A person that their birthday is between June 22 and July 21 is a Cancer and is supposed to be stubborn but effective.

Another theory used to categorize people is the theory of left-brained vs. right-brained people. According to this theory in its simplest meaning, right-brained people, that are intuitive and romantic, are the artists and creative people of the world. Left-brained people, who their thinking is very logical, often turn out to be mathematicians and scientists.

All of these theories—and many others what are too numerous to mention here—have provided attractive and sometimes amusing solutions to describe and understand people. Various theories for categorizing people, which it is always a difficult thing to do, will continue to come and go.

*What is your concept of the ideal teacher and the ideal student? In one paragraph, write a description of the kind of teacher you like best. In a second paragraph, imagine that you are a teacher. What kind of student would you prefer to have? Use some of the phrases from the box, appropriately finished with adjective clauses.*

---

**The Ideal Teacher**

I like a teacher who . . .

I would rather have a teacher that . . .

It's important to have a teacher whose . . .

The teacher uses instructional materials that . . .

There will be times when . . .

**The Ideal Student**

The ideal student is a person . . .

The ideal student is someone whose . . .

This is a person that . . .

The student will have free time that he or she . . .

As a teacher, I prefer to have students I . . .

---

## EXERCISE 1: Identifying Adjective Clauses and Adjective Phrases

*Read the wedding announcement from* The Sunday Times. *There are seven adjective clauses and five adjective phrases. Find and underline the adjective clauses. Find and circle the adjective phrases. The first of each is already marked.*

### The Sunday Times

## *Manning–Wolfe Marriage*

Carolina Manning, (daughter of Dr. and Mrs. John Manning of Hollywood,) California, was married on Sunday to Matthias Wolfe, the son of Dr. Maria and Mr. Douglas Wolfe of Boston. Reverend Harry Carter performed the ceremony at the All-Faiths Religious Center in Hollywood.

Ms. Manning will continue to use her name professionally. She is well known as the originator of the children's television show *Hot Ice Cream*, of which she is both the writer and producer. She has a degree in film studies from the University of Southern California and she also received a master's degree in cinematography from New York University. Her father, whose text on Shakespeare is required reading in many colleges, is a professor of English at Boston University. Her mother taught in the public school system for 30 years, the last 20 of which were at Grisham High School, where she was principal. She retired last June.

Mr. Wolfe is an independent producer. He previously produced movies for The Kallenbach Company, where he had worked for six years. He has a master's degree from the University of Southern California, from which he graduated magna cum laude, and subsequently taught film-writing there. Mr. Wolfe's father is an editor at Koala Publications, a children's book publisher. His mother, Dr. Maria Lopez Wolfe, is a pediatrician, currently serving as chief of pediatrics at Children's Hospital. The bride and bridegroom met at the University of Southern California as students. They soon discovered that they had common interests such as art and film, and both belong to Art Outreach, a program dedicated to encouraging children in the arts. Mr. Wolfe occasionally publishes his letters of opinion, some of which have drawn national attention, in well-known newspapers.

## EXERCISE 2: Forming Adjective Clauses with Quantifiers

*Read the article about the Moonrise Film Festival. Complete the explanations by writing adjective clauses using the words in parentheses plus **of**, and a relative pronoun (**whom, which, whose**).*

Serious film buffs, _____*all of whom appreciate*_____
**1. (all / appreciate)**
new, artistic films, gathered at the Third Annual Moonrise Film

Festival in Montana this week. There were 41 new films,

_____ highly engrossing
**2. (most / were)**
to the moviegoers. In general, the mood of the fans was upbeat,

in spite of the fact that the films— _____ about dark
**3. (were / several)**
subjects—were not particularly entertaining, but of a thoughtful nature. Since even these dark

films had been skillfully made, however, the moviegoing audience showed no objection.

   As always, the movies, _____ from abroad, covered a
**4. (came / a number)**
variety of subjects. There were movies from India, Peru, Iran, China, Japan, Canada, Brazil, Israel,

Sweden, and South Korea, _____ films in prestigious
**5. (all / have entered)**
festivals before and _____ recognition.
**6. (many / deserve / directors and producers)**
   A surprise came in the animation category. Six new animation films appeared on screen,

_____ with serious social topics. These two were produced
**7. (two / dealt)**
so beautifully that they are sure to be contenders for awards. The rest of the animation films,

_____ the hilarious *Absent-Minded Professor*, were comedies
**8. (was / one)**
and _____ fantasies for children.
**9. (were / the rest)**
   There were 10 documentaries, _____ to polarize the
**10. (a few / seemed)**
crowd. The political liberals, _____ wildly for the films they
**11. (some / applauded)**
liked, slightly outnumbered the conservatives, _____
**12. (most / didn't like)**
these same films, but appreciated others. Everyone was polite, and the appreciation for the film-

makers' talents transcended political views. Jacques Ma, who has previously produced only police

dramas, _____ the award-winning *Disorder in the Streets*,
**13. (an example / is)**
expertly constructed a compilation of stories of immigrants' lives and the difficulties they face.

   This relatively new film festival is definitely a winner. If such excellence in selection and

presentation continues, the Moonrise Film Festival will soon take its place among the great film

festivals of the world.

## EXERCISE 3: Reducing Adjective Clauses to Adjective Phrases

*Read the movie descriptions of late-night movies in a TV program guide. Complete the sentences by writing adjective phrases based on the adjective clauses in parentheses.*

1. **Planet of the Apes.** This remake of the 1960s classic is spectacular. After flying through a "worm hole" in space, an astronaut (Mark Wahlberg) crashes on a planet where apes rule over humans. He is aided by a sympathetic chimpanzee,

   _____*played by Helena Bonham Carter*_____, as he leads a small band
   **(who is played by Helena Bonham Carter)**
   of rebels against their captors.

2. **Finding Nemo.** Don't miss the adventures of Marlin, an overprotective clown fish

   _____. When he hooks up with a
   **(who is looking for his missing son)**
   funny tang fish in the search, the laughs don't stop. Brilliant animation with the voices

   of Albert Brooks and Ellen DeGeneres.

3. **Crazy Heart.** Jeff Bridges gives a fantastic performance as an aging country singer,

   _____with the help of a loving
   **(who is trying to change his destructive lifestyle)**
   woman. He tries to re-establish a relationship with his estranged son.

4. **The Last Samurai.** With gorgeous visuals of Japan in the 1870s, this is the story of Capt.

   Nathan Algren, an American military officer hired by the emperor of Japan. Algren,

   _____, undergoes a spiritual
   **(who is brilliantly portrayed by Tom Cruise)**
   rebirth during his encounters with the Samurai.

5. **The X-Files.** FBI agents Mulder and Scully seek the truth about conspiracies,

   extraterrestrials, and mysterious black liquid in this thriller mystery,

   _____.
   **(which was adapted from the TV series)**

6. **Deliverance.** Four men on a canoe trip struggle for survival. In a thrilling adventure

   _____, each of the men
   **(which has turned into a nightmare)**
   undergoes a change of character. Burt Reynolds stars.

*(continued on next page)*

**7. Diamonds Are Forever.** This is Sean Connery's sixth appearance as James Bond in a thriller

_____ on the trail of stolen gems.

    **(that zips him from Amsterdam to Las Vegas)**

**8. Titanic.** The Oscar-winning blockbuster, _____

    **(which stars Leonardo DiCaprio and Kate Winslet)**

as star-crossed lovers aboard the doomed ship, provides a moving story and

amazing visual effects.

**9. Star Wars Episode II: Attack of the Clones.** The saga about a faraway galaxy continues.

Anakin Skywalker (Hayden Christensen) makes progress in his Jedi training, falls in love

with the beautiful Queen Amidala (Natalie Portman), and grows into a young man

_____ .

    **(who is capable of a power that may destroy him)**

**10. The Godfather.** This movie, _____

    **(which is Francis Ford Coppola's Oscar-winning version)**

of a story about a power struggle among organized-crime factions in the 1940s, stars

Marlon Brando, Al Pacino, and James Caan. It is incumbent on the men to defend

themselves and exhibit their power in the most extreme ways possible.

## EXERCISE 4: Forming Sentences with Adjective Clauses and Adjective Phrases

*Combine the pairs of sentences to make single sentences. Use adjective phrases, adjective clauses, or adjective clauses with quantifiers.*

### Cinema Pubs: A New Experience in Moviegoing

**1.** Cinema pubs are small. Being small gives you a more intimate relationship with the film.

    *Cinema pubs are small, giving you a more intimate relationship with the film.*

_____

**2.** Cinema pubs offer independent sections of tables and comfortable swivel chairs. This allows

you to feel like you are in your own living room.

_____

_____

3. Servers come to each table before the movie begins and take orders for food and beverages. Most of the servers are local college students.

_____

_____

4. The ambience in the theater is similar to that in a cabaret. In a cabaret, there is an intimate feeling.

_____

_____

5. In accordance with the cozy atmosphere, the cinema pubs show small films. Many of the small films are foreign.

_____

_____

6. Although you have come to the theater to see a movie, you will also find that the cinema pub is a gathering place. People like to socialize here.

_____

_____

7. The idea of the cinema pub is beginning to catch on in the United States. The idea of a cinema pub is already popular in the United Kingdom.

_____

_____

8. Cinema pubs show recent films in a relaxed atmosphere. This makes them a welcome alternative to huge and impersonal movie multiplexes.

_____

_____

9. For a change of pace, see your next film at a cinema pub. See the film at the cinema pub that is nearest to you.

_____

_____

*Read the passage about filmmaking. There are seventeen mistakes in the use of adjective clauses and phrases. The first mistake is already corrected. Find and correct sixteen more. Delete, fix, or replace words, but do not change punctuation or add words.*

After World War II, Europe was the center of important developments in filmmaking, ~~they~~ *which* strongly influenced motion pictures worldwide. In Italy, well-known movies, two of them were Rossellini's *Open City*, made in 1945, and De Sica's *The BicycleThief,* made in 1948, started a trend toward realism in film. These directors, most of them preferred not to use artificial stories to spice up plots for entertainment, took their cameras into the streets. They wanted to make films who showed the real difficulties of life in the years after the war.

In the next decades, Federico Fellini—whose was an outstanding director—combined realistic plots with philosophical ideas. His films, the most famous of them is *La strada*, are now classics. *La strada* is a movie that it seems to be about circus people in the streets but really is about the meaning of life.

In France, a group of young filmmakers, calling the "New Wave," appeared during the 1950s. This group, who their focus was people, developed a new kind of film which stressed psychology instead of plot. It featured new camera and acting techniques, many of that we can see in movies such as Truffaut's *400 Blows*.

In England, another group of filmmakers, was known as the "Angry Young Man" movement, developed a new kind of realism. In Sweden, Ingmar Bergman used simple stories and fables to look at complex philosophical and social topics, some of whom are expertly explored in *The Seventh Seal*. The Spaniard Luis Bunuel, impressive film *Viridiana* made him famous, portrayed social injustices.

Postwar developments in filmmaking did not take place only in Western Europe. There was significant influence from Asian filmmakers, the first which was Akira Kurosawa of Japan, who made *Rashomon* in 1950. Indian filmmakers, like Satyajit Ray, who his movie *Pather Panchali* showed us life on the subcontinent of Asia, became well known. Even in Russia, where filmmaking was under state control, it was possible to make movies like *The Cranes Are Flying*, showing the problems whom individuals suffered.

In summary, after World War II, there were new types of movies on the scene telling different kinds of stories, making by new filmmakers from around the world.

## EXERCISE 6: Personal Writing

*What was the best movie that you have ever seen? What can you remember about it? Write two or three paragraphs about the movie. Begin with the sentence, "One of my favorite movies is . . ." Use some of the phrases from the box.*

> I liked the movie for a number of reasons, some of which are . . .
>
> The movie had some good actors, including . . .
>
> The movie had some really exciting (funny) scenes, examples of which are . . .
>
> I remember the scene taking place . . .
>
> There was an exciting (funny / romantic) plot involving . . .
>
> The movie had an interesting ending, resulting in . . .
>
> The director was _____, also known for directing . . .
>
> I like his (her) movies, all of which . . .
>
> The movie won some awards, including . . .
>
> I would have no trouble recommending this movie, one of the . . .
>
> Perhaps this movie will be shown again soon, in which case, . . .

# UNIT 14 The Passive: Review and Expansion

## EXERCISE 1: Recognizing Passive Constructions

*Read the police report in the* Daily News. *There are twenty passive constructions in addition to the headlines. The first one is already underlined. Find and underline nineteen more.*

### Storyville School Vandalized

STORYVILLE — Storyville's Country Day School <u>was vandalized</u> last weekend. Seven computers, three plasma TVs, and several pieces of expensive sports gear were stolen. The total value of the stolen items is approximately $14,000. The police believe that the theft was committed by an employee and an accomplice, but as of this morning, information as to their identity was still being sought. School officials could not be contacted for comment.

### Restaurant Burglarized After Hours

SPRINGFIELD — The Springfield Café was burglarized just before dawn on Sunday morning. Police found that the lock on the back door had been altered prior to the burglary. This is the third time since November that restaurants in the 3400 block of Aspen Avenue have been broken into. The restaurant owners are demanding more security in the area and are furious that crimes are being committed repeatedly and that the criminals are getting away with it.

Police Chief Bill Griffin stated that a full investigation is being made and that the thieves will probably be arrested shortly. The owner of the Springfield Café intends to have a better alarm system installed immediately.

### Hopeful Hijackers Arrested

MIDTOWN — Police have arrested two couples in an apartment in southwest Midtown. The couples were planning to hijack a plane and fly it to Hawaii for a vacation. They said they did not have enough money for plane tickets. The plan was not well developed at all and probably would never have been carried out. Police will not divulge the identity of the four people at this time. All four were using aliases, so their real identity has not been established.

### Cash Register Damaged, Waiter Is Fired

NORTHSIDE — An upset waiter at Pop's Place smashed the computer screen of a restaurant cash register after midnight on Wednesday. The waiter, twenty-two, was fired but not arrested. His manager wanted to have the incident documented by police and to have the alleged offender barred from the premises in the future. The damage is estimated at $1,100.

## EXERCISE 2: Using Active and Passive Constructions

*Read the travel brochure. Complete the brochure by forming either active or passive constructions, using the verbs in parentheses. Use a form of* **be** *in the passive constructions.*

TRAVEL, INC.

Here in Cancun, amid the ruins of the ancient Mayans, you __*will find*__ the
                                                         **1. (will / find)**
world's most beautiful beaches and clear blue waters. You _____ by the
                                                          **2. (will / caress)**
gentle breezes as you _____ around on the white sand. At night, as you
                       **3. (lie)**
_____ the sensuous Yucatán cuisine, you _____ by the
**4. (savor)**                                       **5. (will / thrill)**
strolling Mariachi musicians.

It wasn't always like this. A magnificent civilization stood on these shores centuries ago. It

flourished for 900 years. Then, around the year 900, it just _____. It had
                                                              **6. (disappear)**
apparently collapsed.

What was here more than a thousand years ago? There were vast cities that

_____ and laid out by architects, elaborate temples and palaces, huge
**7. (plan)**
pyramids, and carefully made ball parks. These amazing buildings _____ by
                                                                  **8. (constructed)**
the Mayans, here and in the nearby areas of today's Mexico, Guatemala, and Belize. The remains

of many of these constructions _____ today. At its peak, around 900 C.E., the
                                **9. (can / see)**
population _____ 500 people per square mile in rural areas and more than
          **10. (number)**
2000 per square mile in the cities, a density which is comparable to that of modern Los Angeles

County. The Mayan civilization thrived for centuries. Then, it _____. What
                                                               **11. (collapse)**
_____ to it?
**12. (happen)**

For many years, historians and archaeologists _____ by the mysterious
                                               **13. (have / fascinated)**
disappearance of the Mayans, who had enjoyed an advanced civilization. What kind of civilization

did they have? They had plenty of food because a large variety of vegetable crops

_____ by knowledgeable farmers. Cotton _____ and
**14. (grow)**                                       **15. (cultivate)**
_____ into beautiful clothing. Dogs and turkeys _____,
**16. (make)**                                               **17. (domesticate)**
although large animals were apparently not known.

*(continued on next page)*

The Mayans had a sophisticated system of writing. It _____ mostly on
                                                                **18. (appear)**
stone and wood. The words _____ on the inside or outside of their
                          **19. (often / write)**
architecture. Although much Mayan art _____ by artisans for the people,
                                       **20. (do)**
most of it _____ into large art projects. These large displays
           **21. (put)**
_____ by the kings, who wanted to have beautiful art objects of their own
**22. (order)**
images _____.
       **23. (make)**
   Fine pottery and small sculptures were _____. Gold, jade, shells, and
                                           **24. (produce)**
colorful feathers _____ to make jewelry and other ornamentation. Copper
                  **25. (cut)**
pieces and cacao beans _____ as money.
                       **26. (use)**
   The Mayans were especially knowledgeable astronomers and mathematicians. They

_____ a remarkably accurate calendar. Their civilization had been the most
**27. (produce)**
advanced in the Western Hemisphere until its end. What _____ by?
                                                       **28. (it / destroy)**
   The collapse _____ a sudden catastrophe, such as a terrific earthquake or
                **29. (could / have / cause)**
hurricane, or by disease or by war. Perhaps the collapse _____ by
                                                         **30. (cause)**
environmental disaster, such as a loss of trees (deforestation) leading to soil exhaustion and loss

of water, then ultimately to lack of food. Today researchers _____ that the
                                                             **31. (think)**
most likely explanation is an environmental one, and studies are continuing to find the definitive

cause. Until then, the collapse of the Mayan civilization _____ one of the most
                                                          **32. (remain)**
intriguing unsolved mysteries of the world.

## EXERCISE 3: Using Passive Constructions

*Read the text of an email in which a young scientist writes to her parents from Mars in the
year 2040. Complete the email by writing passive constructions using a form of* **be** *plus the
words in parentheses. Sometimes more than one answer is correct.*

Dear Mom and Dad,

   This is a pretty good place to be on my first job. Just think, a year ago I was still writing papers

and worrying about my dissertation, and now, here I am using my *cooking* skills on Mars, along

with my exobiology degree. I'll bet you never thought I __*would actually be paid*__ for doing
                                                        **1. (would / actually / pay)**
things most people think of as hobbies—gardening and cooking—and that what I studied in college

_____ in such a productive and useful manner.
**2. (would / actually / employ)**

Life _____ quite well here using the original plants that
                3. (sustain)

_____ up with us. The plants _____ here in growth
        4. (send)                                              5. (maintain)

chambers where lighting, nutrients, temperature, and humidity _____ by
                                                                        6. (must control)

computer. Crops _____ using sunlight, as here on Mars, sunlight is available
                      7. (cannot grow)

for only half of each rotation period. In addition, sometimes the Sun _____
                                                                              8. (obscure)

for months at a time by the giant dust storms we have here.

    Everything _____ efficiently here. There is no waste,
                      9. (has to do)

as all the waste that _____ by plants and humans
                            10. (produce)

_____ to nourish new growth. There are no rotting plants, because if any
        11. (recycle)

begin to rot, they _____ immediately and recycled as mulch. Nothing
                          12. (pick up)

_____ inadvertently. Everything _____ very
        13. (do)                                        14. (has to / plan)

carefully. It's so interesting to see how the power resources _____ and how
                                                                      15. (use)

every inch of space _____.
                          16. (have / utilize)

    You would be very proud of my creativity in using the vegetables. I'm particularly glad to have

tomatoes, which _____ to be like those famous New Jersey tomatoes. I
                      17. (develop)

_____ for my delicious salads, which _____ with
        18. (know)                                          19. (make)

the tomatoes, along with potatoes, black-eyed peas, and other packaged food that we brought with

us. As you know, no meat or fish of any kind _____ here, only the foods
                                                    20. (can / find)

that we grow in our labs. Even the water comes from plants. We put in our orders for water one

day ahead of time, and we _____ by a special water-collecting crew every
                                21. (have / it / collect)

morning. The water _____ through plant materials too, and believe it or
                          22. (filter)

not, it is excellent!

    Life here is pretty good, and the only problem is that I miss you and my friends a lot. I hope you'll

be able to visit me before the end of the year. A beautiful new hotel _____
                                                                              23. (build)

now and _____ in July.
              24. (will / complete)

    Text me before Sunday, when we'll talk online.


Your loving daughter,

Eliza

**A.** *Read "Action Line," a newspaper column that helps readers with problems. There are seven passive causatives in the readers' letters to "Action Line." The first one is already underlined. Find and underline six more.*

**B.** *Complete the Solutions by writing passive causatives using the words in parentheses.*

# *Action Line*

1. My grandparents have lived in their apartment building for nearly 30 years. Now they have termites, and the landlord is refusing to <u>have the building treated</u> by professional exterminators. He says that he can't afford it, so he's just having their apartment sprayed. I know that's not enough. What can be done?

   **Solution:** Action Line did it. We called the Department of Business Regulations, which handles complaints like yours, and they ___*have already had the landlord investigated*___.
   (have / already / have / investigate the landlord)
   If the landlord doesn't properly get rid of the termites by the 15th of next month, he will be fined $1,000.

2. I had some furniture sent to my house from Modella Furniture Company in North Carolina. The furniture arrived, but a leg on the table had broken off. I wrote to the company and spoke to a secretary there on the phone, but it has been two months now and nothing has been done. What can you do, Action Line?

   **Solution:** Action Line was able to get through to the president of the company. We arranged to
   _____, and Modella has
   (have / look at your table / by an insurance adjuster)
   agreed to pay for a replacement table if necessary.

3. I took my new, very expensive formal gown to Alfie's Alterations to have it shortened. It was shortened, all right! When I got it back, the skirt was five inches above my knees! Alfie's apologized and gave me credit to have future alterations done there, but this doesn't compensate me for the hundreds of dollars I spent on the dress, which is now ruined. Action Line, can something be done?

   **Solution:** Yes, it already has been done. Action Line sent a representative to Alfie's. Alfie Brown, the owner, said to replace the dress and to _____.
   (have / send the bill to him)

4. My car—an Admira—is eleven years old and has been running smoothly all this time. Then last month it began stalling. I have had it checked by my mechanic, and he wasn't able to fix it. I am at my wit's end, because I love this car. Any suggestions, Action Line?

   **Solution:** Action Line has contacted the manufacturer. They tell us that an eleven-year-old car is, of course, under no warranty, but since they want their customers to be happy, they said to take it to the nearest dealer, where you _____
   **(can / get / fix the problem)**
   if it's at all possible.

5. Our thirteen-year-old son volunteers at a shelter for homeless people. This work is very important to him. The trouble is that both my wife and I work full time and we live in a rural area with inadequate public transportation. The shelter used to have a car sent for him each day but can no longer do so. Any suggestions, Action Line?

   **Solution:** Action Line called the volunteer group Side-by-Side Rides. They pick up deserving people like your son and take them where they need to go. You can call the group at 555–0965 and arrange to _____.
   **(have / pick up your son)**

## EXERCISE 5: Using Passive Constructions with *Get*

*Read the text of an email from Marco to Ricardo. Complete the email by writing passive constructions, using a form of* **get** *plus the words in parentheses.*

Dear Ricardo,

I'm sorry to hear that you _____*got hit*_____ with money problems, although it
1. (hit)
sounds like some of them are your own fault. I'm also sorry that I won't be able to help you.

I've got some problems of my own. Like last week, when I had to _____.
2. (my car / fix)
It suddenly refused to go—right in the middle of rush-hour traffic! After two hours, it finally

_____ by a tow truck to a repair shop. The next day my car was running fine
3. (tow)
again. But I _____ $450 for the repair.
4. (charge)

This week has been even worse. On Monday, someone broke into my apartment. All my good

things _____: my TV, my sound system, and even my new bike. In the middle
5. (steal)
of all this, I also _____ by Lisa, the girl I wrote you about. "Get dumped" is an
6. (dump)

*(continued on next page)*

expression that means she doesn't want to go out with me anymore. About your situation: I think

you should get a night job. You really need the money, and working will keep you out of trouble. If

you can _____ by a hotel chain, for example, you might have the beginnings of
　　　　　　　　　7. (hire)

a really good managerial job later. I hear that they like to hire young people to work at night. If the

person does well, he often _____ to stay on for a better job. I think you would be
　　　　　　　　　　　　　　8. (ask)

great at it. All you have to do is behave yourself and make sure you don't _____
　　　　　　　　　　　　　　　　　　　　　　　　　　　　　　　　　9. (fire)

for doing something stupid. Hopefully, things will be better for both of us soon.

—Marco

## EXERCISE 6: Changing Active Constructions to Passive Constructions

On a cooking show on TV, the chef is cooking some Mexican food. He is also writing a book
about Mexican cuisine, *Menu Mexicana*, in which he describes some typical ingredients. The
chef uses recipes developed from foods grown by the ancient Mayans and other people who were
living in the area. On TV, the chef uses the active voice frequently. In his book, he will be using
more passive-voice sentences.

*Read the descriptions of the ingredients. Turn the underlined active constructions into
passive constructions. For each construction where there is a change, write the full subject
and verb, but not the rest of the sentence. Use a* **by** *phrase only if the agent is necessary.
(Do not include unnecessary words that refer to the agent, e.g.,* **people, somebody,** *or* **you.***)*

1.  **Sesame seeds**  People use sesame seeds in Mexican sauces. You can toast them easily.
　　　　　　　　　　　　　　　　　a.　　　　　　　　　　　　　　　b.

    The Spanish introduced them to Mexico. And before that, the Moors had brought them to Spain.
    　　　　　　　　　　c.　　　　　　　　　　　　　　　　　　　　　　d.

    a. _Sesame seeds are used_ _____

    b. _They can be toasted_ _____

    c. _They were introduced by the Spanish_ _____

    d. _They were brought to Spain by the Moors_ _____

2.  **Chorizo**  Chorizo is similar in appearance to a sausage. In Mexico, people make it of
    　　　　　　　　　　　　　　　　　　　　　　　　　　　　　　　　a.

    unsmoked meat and spices. In Spain, people smoke the meat.
    　　　　　　　　　　　　　　　　　b.

    a. _____

    b. _____

3. **Jicama**   Jicama is a brown-skinned root vegetable with a white, crisp flesh similar to that of

a radish. In Mexico, <u>street vendors sell jicama</u>. It is eaten in thick slices <u>that somebody has</u>
                       **a.**                                                    **b.**

<u>sprinkled</u> with salt, lime juice, and chili powder.

   **a.** _____

   **b.** _____

4. **Avocados**   <u>People consider avocados</u> a true delicacy. If they are hard, <u>somebody should</u>
                   **a.**                                                 **b.**

<u>allow them</u> to ripen. <u>People make a green salsa, guacamole</u>, from avocados. <u>People also use</u>
                              **c.**                                      **d.**

<u>avocados</u> in salads and as a decoration.

   **a.** _____

   **b.** _____

   **c.** _____

   **d.** _____

5. **Banana leaves**   <u>People steam meat</u> in little packets of banana leaves. First, <u>you must soften</u>
                       **a.**                                             **b.**

<u>the leaves</u> over a flame. Then, <u>you wrap the meat and other ingredients</u> in them.
                                           **c.**

   **a.** _____

   **b.** _____

   **c.** _____

6. **Tortillas**   These are round and look like pancakes. <u>People can eat them</u> with any meal. <u>People</u>
                                                                      **a.**

<u>make them</u> from corn or wheat flour. <u>People can now find tortillas</u> in supermarkets in many
     **b.**                                                 **c.**

other places in the world.

   **a.** _____

   **b.** _____

   **c.** _____

7. **Chilies**   <u>People use chilies</u> to season many different dishes. There are various kinds of
            **a.**

chilies. In degree of spiciness, they range from very mild to very hot. <u>Humans have consumed</u>
                                                                      **b.**

<u>chili-seasoned foods</u> for more than 8,000 years.

   **a.** _____

   **b.** _____

*(continued on next page)*

**8. Corn**

<u>People use corn</u> widely in Mexico. In Mexican cooking, <u>people waste no part of the corn</u>.
**a.**                                                   **b.**

<u>People use the ears, husks, silk, and kernels in different ways</u>. <u>Archaeologists found evidence</u>
                          **c.**                                       **d.**

that corn was being cultivated more than 5000 years ago.

**a.** _____

**b.** _____

**c.** _____

**d.** _____

## EXERCISE 7: Editing

*Read the speech by Marie Curie, made at Vassar College in 1921. There are sixteen mistakes in the use of the passive. The first mistake is already corrected. Find and correct fifteen more.*

    I could tell you many things about radium and radioactivity and how they were
       *discovered*
~~discovering~~, but it would take a long time. Since we have only a short time, I'll give you a

short account of my early work with radium. The conditions of the discovery were peculiar, and I am

always pleasing to remember them and to explain them.

    In the year 1897, my husband, Professor Curie, and I were worked in the laboratory of the School

of Physics and Chemistry, where he held his lectures. I was engage in work on uranium rays, which

had discovered two years before by Professor Becquerel.

    In my research, I found out that uranium and thorium compounds were active in proportion to

the amount of uranium or thorium that they got contained; in other words, the more uranium or

thorium that contained in the compound, the greater the activity.

    Then I thought that some unknown element must be existed among those minerals, one with

a much greater radioactivity than uranium or thorium. And I thought that it should be found. I

wanted to find and to separate that element, so I went to work on that with Professor Curie. We

thought we would have the project doing in several weeks or months, but it was not so. It took many

years of hard work to finish that task. There was not only one new element that we found—there

were several. But the most important was radium.

Now, if we take a practical point of view, then the most important property of the rays is the way they influence the cells of the human organism. These effects may use for the cure of several diseases. Good results have be obtained in many cases. What is considered particularly important is the treatment of cancer.

But we must not forget that when radium discovered, no one knew that it would prove useful in hospitals. The work was one of pure science. And this is proof that scientific work must be not considered from the point of view of its direct usefulness. It must be doing for itself, for the beauty of science.

There is always a vast field which is left to experimentation, and I hope that we may have some beautiful progress in the coming years. It is my earnest desire that this scientific work should carried on, hopefully by some of you, and that it will be appreciating by all of you, who understand the beauty of science.

## EXERCISE 8: Personal Writing

*On a separate piece of paper, summarize the plot of a mystery that you know from a book, a movie, a TV show or a radio program. On a separate piece of paper, write two or three paragraphs about it. If you can't think of one, invent a mystery of your own. Use some of the phrases from the box.*

```
. . . was / were stolen
. . . was / were valued at . . .
. . . was / were stopped
. . . was / were seen
. . . was / were hijacked
. . . was / were injured
. . . was / were arrested
. . . was / were discovered
. . . was / were found
. . . was / were never solved
```

# The Passive to Describe Situations and to Report Opinions

## EXERCISE 1: Recognizing Passive Constructions that Describe Situations and Report Opinions

*Read the transcript of a TV newscast. There are fifteen uses of the passive: nine that report ideas, beliefs, or opinions, and six that are stative passive. The first of each kind is marked. Find and underline the eight other passive reporting constructions, and find and circle the five other stative passives.*

(Good) evening, ladies and gentlemen! It <u>is being reported</u> at this moment that smoke signals have been coming from Pirates' Island, (which is) located very near the place where the sailboat *Belle* was known to be cruising yesterday. It is believed that the *Belle* must have sunk during a severe sudden storm. The sailboat is owned by the Crane family, and it is thought that the whole family of four were aboard, along with another family who is related to them—cousins from Canada, it was said. Navy helicopters are speeding out to the island at this moment.

Pirate's Island is a small island about two miles from shore. It is not connected by bridge to the mainland. It is surrounded by rocks and it is considered dangerous to sail near there. The Cranes are known to be excellent sailors and under normal circumstances could have avoided the dangerous rocks. But the squall that came up was said to have near-hurricane-force winds.

Oh, this just in! One Navy helicopter is landing. The pilot is reporting that he sees a group of people—the group is composed of seven or eight people, he says—waving at the plane. So, this is good news, viewers. The survivors are assumed to be all right. Stay tuned to this channel for more news after this message . . .

## EXERCISE 2: Using the Passive to Describe Situations and Report Opinions

*Read the article from a folklore website. Complete the article. Circle the correct verbs.*

There are many funny stories about the American legend Paul Bunyan. According to these stories, Paul was an enormous man and very strong. It <u>is saying</u> /(is said) that when he was born, he
1.
was the biggest baby in the whole world.

When Paul grew up, he became a lumberjack. He owned / was owned a
2.

Paul Bunyan and Babe

huge ox called Babe. Paul and Babe traveled west together. It is claimed /
3.
claiming that they cut and cleared hundreds of forests that they found /
4.
were found. Paul cut down the trees with his ax, and then Babe hauled the

logs away.

Paul Bunyan and the ox Babe liked to eat a lot. They both loved pancakes, and when they were

really hungry for breakfast, they said / were said to eat a breakfast that composed of / was composed of
5.                                                                          6.
a whole ton of pancakes and 40 barrels of milk!

Paul and Babe also thought / are also thought to have been very clever. They were so clever that
7.
they designed and built many of the most amazing places in the United States by themselves. They

alleging / are alleged to have built the Grand Canyon and the Great Lakes, places which located / are
8.                                                                                              9.
located in the middle of the North American continent. People said / are said these natural wonders
10.
appeared on Earth because Paul and Babe built them!

The legends of Paul Bunyan know / are known as "tall tales" because the exaggerations of the
11.
story are so "tall," or enormous. *Tale* is another word for *story*.

## EXERCISE 3: Using Passives to Report Ideas

*Read the article from* Hobbies *magazine. Complete the article by writing passive
constructions, using the correct forms of the words in parentheses.*

# BACKGAMMON: A HOBBY THROUGH THE AGES

Until recently, backgammon _____*was regarded*_____ in America as an exotic, unfamiliar
                                1. (regard)
game. Today, backgammon _____ to be the fastest-growing game in
                                2. (believe)
popularity, and it _____ to have millions of dedicated players, hundreds of
                        3. (say)
clubs, and an international circuit of major tournaments.

How old is backgammon? Historians are not sure. It _____ exactly when
                                                        4. (not / know)
the game originated, but when archaeologists excavated the ancient Sumerian city of Ur, they

found in the royal cemetery five game boards that closely resembled early backgammon boards.

From this, it _____ that the game existed 5,000 years ago. Similar to the
                5. (now / assume)

*(continued on next page)*

game boards unearthed at Ur was a board discovered among the treasures in the tomb of the

Egyptian king Tutankhamen, from around 1500 B.C.E. Backgammon _____
                                                                          6. (also / think)
to have been popular among the common Egyptians, because ancient Egyptian wall paintings

show people playing a table game.

   The ancient Greeks and Romans too _____ to have played a game like
                                              7. (now / believe)
backgammon. Plato commented on its popularity, and it _____ by those
                                                                 8. (claim)
who study ancient Greece that he might have played it himself. It _____
                                                                            9. (know)
that *tabulae*, a Roman version of the game, was popular in Pompeii, because a tabulae board

was found in the courtyard of almost every villa in the ruins there.

   When the Spanish explorer Francisco Pizarro arrived in Mexico in the early 16th century, he

described a game played by the native Aztec people which was remarkably like the Egyptians'

game. After this similarity had been established, it _____ that the early
                                                            10. (conjecture)
people of the Americas might have migrated to the Western Hemisphere from areas near Egypt,

bringing their game with them.

   We know quite a bit about backgammon in the 18th century. For example, backgammon

_____ to have been popular among clergymen and physicians in Europe
        11. (know)
and in America. Thomas Jefferson _____ by some scholars to have played
                                           12. (think)
it for relaxation during the time when he was writing the Declaration of Independence.

   Backgammon's popularity has risen and fallen through the ages. It _____
                                                                            13. (can / safely / assume)
that its popularity will fall and rise again.

## EXERCISE 4: Using Passives to Report Ideas

*Read the excerpt from the TV talk show "Raising the Modern Child." Margaret Gray (**A**), a grandparent, is asking Dr. Carl Clark (**B**), the host, for advice. Complete the conversation by writing passive constructions, using the correct forms of the words in parentheses.*

Old sayings:

*Children should be seen and not heard.* = It's all right if children are in view of adults, but they must always be quiet.

*Spare the rod and spoil the child.* = If you don't use a rod (a stick) to control children's behavior, they will grow up to be very unpleasant and spoiled.

**A:** I used to hear the saying that "children should be seen and not heard." I was brought up that way and tried to bring up my children that way. Now I see my daughter permitting her children to do almost anything they want. Isn't this kind of permissiveness bad?

**B:** The idea that children should be seen and not heard _used to be considered_ one of the
1. (used to / consider)
basic principles for raising children. However, it is a myth. In the modern world, this idea

_____ to have made a lot of trouble by causing neuroses in children.
2. (believe)

It _____ that if children always behaved properly, never did repulsive
3. (previously / think)
things, controlled all their feelings, and were just pretty to look at, they would grow up to

be polite, law-abiding citizens. But children are not just a font of enjoyment for parents. It

_____ that imposing too many restrictions and rituals can inhibit the child
4. (understand)
too much and can cause serious psychological problems.

**A:** But, Dr. Clark, doesn't letting a child always have his or her own way spoil the child?

**B:** Of course, if you don't set limits on a child's behavior, that is not good training. But it

_____ now that if you constantly frustrate children, and don't let them
5. (well / know)
express their feelings, that can lead to serious problems. The trick is to lead children firmly and

correct them gently.

**A:** I really can't agree with you, Doctor. I believe that if you spare the rod, you spoil the child.

Children need punishment.

**B:** That's not correct. Using the rod could not only lacerate the skin; it could lacerate the child's

personality too.

You _____ by many as being correct, Ms. Gray. But let me warn you: It
6. (might / perceive)
_____ by child-rearing experts these days that you MUST spare the rod. At
7. (widely / confirm)
the same time, you should not spoil the child. It _____ for quite some time
8. (has / well / establish)
now that children must be able to express themselves, but they must be taught to do so in a

socially acceptable way.

**A:** Well, Dr. Clark, you _____ all over the world to be the big expert, but I am
9. (know)
sorry, I just disagree with what you're telling me.

*(continued on next page)*

**B:** Well, Ms. Gray, for many years now my kind of thinking _____ correct.

10. (has / consider)

You are entitled to have your opinion. But don't worry about your grandchildren. What your

daughter is doing _____ to be the right thing.

11. (can / assume)

## EXERCISE 5: Editing

*Read the article from the* Planetarium News *about full-moon myths. There are thirteen mistakes in the use of the passive voice to describe situations and to report opinions. The first mistake is already corrected. Find and correct twelve more.*

FULL-MOON MYTHS

*is*

It often said that a full moon causes many bad things to happen. More crimes, disasters, and accidents are alleging to occur during the times when the moon is full, so many people take extra care during these times. People have been known to plan their lives around the phases of the moon; for example, is believed by some that certain phases of the moon are relate to the best times for certain activities, such as getting married, making important financial decisions, or praying at a shrine.

These beliefs about a full moon, however, are not true, according to many scientists. Numerous studies have been conducted, and no relationship between a full moon and higher rates of anything has been proven. A full moon is not connect in any way to increases in the rates of murders, traffic accidents, crisis calls to police or fire stations, births of babies, major disasters, assassinations, aggression by professional hockey players, psychiatric admissions, emergency room admissions, sleepwalking, or any other events that are often believe to be affected by the moon.

If the appearance of a full moon is really not relating to these kinds of occurrences, why are these moon myths assuming to be true by so many people? Sociologists say that the basis of many moon myths found in old folk tales. For example, it has claimed since ancient times that more births occur during a full moon and more crimes are committed during a full moon, even though reliable statistics have never confirmed these ideas. Beliefs like these are advanced by the effect of today's media; movies and books often depict strange happenings during a full moon. It makes a strikingly good story when events are seen as being controlled by the moon.

There are also some misconceptions that a full moon has a powerful effect on the human body. For instance, some people claim that, because both the Earth and the human body have composed of 80 percent water, the moon influences the body just as it does the Earth's tides. But this is not entirely true. Eighty percent of the *surface* of the Earth is water. The moon influences only *unbounded* bodies of water, such as oceans and seas. Unbounded bodies of water are those that have no boundaries; they don't surrounded by anything. But the water in the human body is bounded by the limits of the skin surrounding the entire body.

Even though the powers of the moon have been discredited by some scientific research, the moon is still considering a strong symbol of romance and mystery all over the world.

## EXERCISE 6: Personal Writing

*On a separate piece of paper, write two or three paragraphs describing a legend or a myth or a superstition that you know about. After your description, give your opinion about the topic. Use some of the phrases from the box.*

It is said that . . .

It is thought that . . .

It is believed that . . .

It is claimed that . . .

It is alleged that . . .

They are believed to . . .

They are thought to . . .

. . . are said to . . .

. . . are claimed to . . .

. . . is alleged to . . .

# UNIT 16  Gerunds

---

## EXERCISE 1: Recognizing Gerunds

*Read this letter from a university to a prospective student. There are twenty-seven gerunds. The first one is already underlined. Find and underline twenty-six more.*

### ZENITH UNIVERSITY

Dear Applicant:

Thank you for <u>writing</u> to Zenith University. You have asked what qualities are necessary for gaining admittance to the freshman class.

Zenith University seeks to attract academically talented students who will have the greatest possibility of succeeding and thriving here, and who will also participate in contributing to the growth of the university community. The most important factors are:

- Completing high school with a grade point average (GPA) of 3.5 or higher
- Achieving a score of 1875 or higher on the standardized Scholastic Aptitude Test (SAT)
- Being recommended by high school teachers and counselors
- Demonstrating evidence of being involved in the world

In addition, the Board considers the overall level of achievement, enrollment in honors courses, individual academic strengths, and class rank. For example, you must be in the top quarter of your high school class, and the higher your rank, the greater your chance of becoming part of our student body. Of course, receiving good recommendations from teachers and counselors also tells us that you will be able to succeed in your academic work here.

Taking interest in the world is shown by your having participated in extracurricular activities in high school, such as playing sports, writing for the school newspaper, and taking part in student government. Involvement is also evidenced by your showing concern for your community, in the context of activities like volunteering in hospitals and being active in political campaigns. Displaying an interest in other cultures coincides with an active curiosity, and the university looks favorably upon candidates who have spent time studying or traveling abroad.

Along with your application, you will send a personal essay. Writing this essay carefully is important, because it demonstrates your skills in thinking and in expressing yourself. The Board of Admissions carefully reviews every application for undergraduate admission in deciding whom to admit.

We wish you good luck in your application process.

Sincerely yours,

*Jeffrey V. Smith*

Jeffrey V. Smith
Director of Admissions

## EXERCISE 2: Using Gerunds in Sentences

*Complete the descriptions on the left with the sports on the right. Write the letters in the correct blanks.*

1. This is a sport in which the object is to pin your opponent to the ground. One of the oldest sports, ___*f*___ is practiced in several forms today, two of which are sumo and jujitsu.

2. This is a sport similar to canoeing. However, the boat is completely covered except for the opening in which the paddler sits. Although _____ is a recognized sport, the small, highly maneuverable boat it involves is also used in everyday life in the Arctic.

3. This sport is a contest of swords. The swords do not have sharp tips, and the participants wear protective clothing and wire-mesh face masks. You see a lot of _____ in movies about 17th-century Europe.

4. The triathlon consists of three sports: swimming, running, and _____. Each of these sports also appears individually at the Olympic Games.

5. This sport is a test of strength and is also used to build up strength for other sports. The participant lifts a bar which has heavy weights at each end, so it is called _____.

6. This sport—_____—is like a ballet in water. A swimmer or a group of swimmers performs dance-like movements, often in time with music.

7. _____ is performed in the water by one person who stands on a small board with a sail on it and uses the wind to move across the water. It is also called *boardsailing* or *sailboarding*.

8. This is a winter sport in which a partially enclosed sled with two or four persons races down an ice course on a hill or a mountain. In a non-competitive form, people have fun _____ down hills in the snow.

**a.** cycling

**b.** windsurfing

**c.** weight lifting

**d.** synchronized swimming

**e.** bobsledding

**f.** wrestling

**g.** fencing

**h.** kayaking

**132** UNIT 16

## EXERCISE 3: Forming Gerunds

*Read the text of an email from Diana to her fiancé, John. Complete the email. Use the gerund forms of the verbs from the box.*

| ~~bake~~ | carve | collect | keep | knit | play | read | ride | take | tell | travel |

John,

I'm so glad you're finally going to meet my family at our annual holiday get-together. I'm looking forward to being with them and to catching up on all their news. Before you actually meet them in person, let me introduce them to you right here, right now.

First there's Grandma. Grandma loves to make delicious breads, cakes, and pies. In fact, one year her cake won first place in a national competition. She will surely bring some tasty treats to the party. She's a star at _____baking_____ and I know you'll love her.
**1.**

Then, Grandpa. Grandpa loves to makes things out of wood. He exhibits and sells them at art shows every year, and he will have made some small articles for each of the grandchildren. He has been interested in _____ wood ever since he was a boy.
**2.**

Next, Uncle Sam. Uncle Sam wanted to be a concert pianist, but he became a dentist instead. He still loves the piano, though. _____ the piano with his whole family singing around
**3.**
him is his greatest pleasure.

Now, Aunt Millie. Aunt Millie will no doubt have made sweaters for all her nieces and nephews, as she does every year. _____ is her favorite activity.
**4.**

You'll be overwhelmed by cousin Lola. Lola has been to 47 countries. She's always going someplace. _____ is obviously her favorite activity, and _____ us about
**5.** **6.**
her latest adventures is her second favorite activity.

Cousin Ted is interesting. Ted works with a design firm and is an amateur photographer. He loves _____ pictures and will surely snap many photographs of all of us at the party.
**7.**

Now for Ted's wife, Elizabeth. She has an antique shop and she is very fond of old pieces of silverware. _____ antique forks, knives, and spoons is her hobby. She is small and
**8.**
sweet, and appears naïve and vulnerable, but she is really a smart and accomplished woman.

*(continued on next page)*

Ted and Elizabeth have three darling children: David, Monica, and Harvey. My cousin David is twelve years old, and he's adorable. David likes sports, but he doesn't like to study, and in fact, is having a hard time _____ up with his studies.

9.

Monica is ten years old. She loves horses. She goes horseback _____ every

10.

Saturday.

My little cousin Harvey is eight years old, and he is quieter than his older brother and sister. They say he is a "bookworm" because he likes books so much. In fact, _____ is the only

11.

thing he does.

These people are my family, and they are like my best friends. You already know me, and you've met my parents. I know that you and my family will get along really well and that you will fit right in.

Love,

Diana

## EXERCISE 4: Forming Past Gerunds

*Read this police report on a witness who was questioned about a robbery. Complete the report by writing the past gerunds of the words in parentheses.*

Officers Brody and Méndez investigated a robbery that occurred on the night of June

23 at 10 Seacoast Terrace, the home of John and Jane Butler. They questioned Mark Abbott, a

family friend and possible suspect. Abbott denied _____*having visited*_____ the Butler house

1. (visit)

on the night of the robbery. In fact, he regretted _____ there, saying that if

2. (not / be)

he had been, the robbery would never have happened. He admitted _____

3. (stop by)

there earlier that day. He couldn't recall _____ anything suspicious at the

4. (see)

house. Nor could he remember _____ anyone near the house. He mentioned

5. (meet)

_____ the house that evening, but he said that nobody had answered. Abbott

6. (telephone)

acknowledged _____ suspicious at that point, since the Butlers had said they

7. (become)

would definitely be at home. However, he explained that his _____ by to check

8. (not / stop)

the house was because of the lateness of the hour. Officers Brody and Méndez then excused him,

believing that he did not commit the robbery.

Read the advice column "Etta's Etiquette." Complete the column by writing passive gerunds using a form of **be** plus the words in parentheses.

---

## ETTA'S ETIQUETTE: How to Respond to Telephone Solicitations

**QUESTION:** Is there a polite way to respond to telephone solicitations? I hate

_____*being called*_____ by
　　　　　　　**1. (call)**

marketers, but I don't want to be rude to the

working person at the other end of the phone.

I remember _____
　　　　　　　　**2. (employ)**

as a telephone sales rep years ago, and I

didn't like _____ at
　　　　　　　　**3. (hang up on)**

all. But I'm really growing very tired of

_____ in the middle
　　　　**4. (interrupt)**

of dinner with my family and

_____ all evening
　　　　**5. (bother)**

long with offers of opportunities to win

a vacation, subscribe to a new telephone

plan, or contribute to a charity. My husband

and I work hard all day and would truly

appreciate _____ at
　　　　　　　　**6. (leave alone)**

night to have some peace and quiet!

**ANSWER:** In spite of people's

_____ these days
　　　　**7. (bombard)**

with hundreds of online ads per day,

soliciting business and money by telephone is

still a common practice. This is one of the

reasons that people use caller ID: to avoid

_____ in a
　　　　**8. (trap)**

conversation with a telemarketer.

　One way to deal with the annoyance of

telephone solicitation quickly and effectively

is this: Just say "I would really appreciate

_____ at home, but
　　　　**9. (not / disturb)**

I'll think about your offer if you'll just send

it to me in writing." Only a real, or genuine,

offer would actually be sent in writing; a

caller who is committing a fraud would

probably hang up quickly after hearing the

words "Send it to me in writing."

　No matter how much you try, you

probably can't escape _____
　　　　　　　　　　　　**10. (solicit)**

by businesses and charities.

_____ to respond
　　　　**11. (require)**

politely to this kind of intrusion is too

difficult for many people. They resent

_____ so many
　　　　**12. (interrupted)**

times in the past and end up shouting rudely

or slamming down the telephone. In

contrast, your _____
　　　　　　　　　　**13. (concern)**

---

*(continued on next page)*

about the feelings of the person at the other end of the line, your wanting to spare their feelings, indicates that you are truly a nice person, in spite of _____ 14. (annoy) so frequently in the past.

My advice to you is this: Turn off the phone during dinner. People can't help _____ by the ring of 15. (distract) the telephone. If the phone doesn't ring, you will avoid _____ by 16. (upset) these calls, and you can enjoy dinner with your family.

## EXERCISE 6: Using Possessives with Gerunds

*Read the text of two memorandums from a company's director of human resources. Complete the memos by writing the gerund and possessive forms of the words in parentheses.*

MEMORANDUM

To:      Fred Green, President

From:    Sally Evans, Director, Human Resources

Subject: Nominees for Employee of the Year

This year it is extremely difficult to choose the Employee of the Year because there are several outstanding team members. As you know, the award is based on the contributions a person has made to improve customer relations, sales concepts, and future market possibilities.

Here are five nominees:

- Bill Marvin, Assistant Advertising Director: Bill is a true leader.

  _____*His taking over*_____ during the newspaper strike and getting our ads on
  1. (take over / he)
  television greatly strengthened our market position.

- Julia Jones, his counterpart in Finance, as Assistant Finance Director: Julia is a genius at analyzing budgets. _____ new ways to cut costs has reduced our
  2. (find / she)
  expenditures by 19 percent this year.

- Mary Salisbury: _____ late every night has been productive.
  **3. (work / Mary)**
  Sales in her department are up more than in anyone else's.

- George Bloom: _____ to our firm as Director of Public
  **4. (come / George)**
  Relations two years ago was lucky for us. During this time, he has substantially

  enhanced the image of our company both locally and nationally.

- Henry Fan: Everybody knows that _____ of our website has
  **5. (constant / upgrade / Henry)**
  had excellent results. Our website has won three awards this year, and the number of

  hits has quadrupled since last year.

  Please contact me at your earliest convenience with your vote for the award recipient.

MEMORANDUM

To:     Fred Green, President

From:   Sally Evans, Director, Human Resources

Subject: Employees with Bad Reviews

   After the yearly review by their directors, I am calling to your attention three employees

whose performances must improve considerably within the next three months if the

company is going to keep them. These employees are:

- Nicole Anderson: Nicole can't stay anywhere near her sales quota. Sales are being lost

  all over the state because of _____ on the job.
  **6. (fall down / Nicole)**

- Barbara Green: Barbara's work is acceptable, but _____ is
  **7. (constant / complain / she)**
  demoralizing to her co-workers. Nobody wants to work with her.

- Jim Haley: _____ early on Fridays and
  **8. (leave / Jim)**
  _____ in at noon on Mondays is unprofessional. In spite of
  **9. (meander/ he)**
  his supervisor's warnings, Jim doesn't seem able to modify this behavior.

  Appropriate action is being taken by the supervisors.

*Read the passage about Keizo Miura. There are twenty-two mistakes in the use of gerunds. The first mistake is already corrected. Find and correct twenty-one more. Delete or fix words, but do not add or replace words.*

### Keizo Miura, a Japanese Skiing Legend
### 1904–2006

On February 28, 2004, Keizo Miura celebrated his birthday by ~~ski~~ *skiing* down a 2-mile run at a Rocky Mountain ski resort. A man's skiing 2 miles down a mountain run is not usually worthy of being noticed, but in this case it was—this birthday was his 100th birthday.

Miura celebrated his 100th year by descend the mountain together with more than 120 friends and family members from Japan, all regular and robust skiers. After the descent, Miura said, "There is no better way to celebrate my 100th birthday than being able to wholeheartedly enjoy ski with my family and friends."

Him succeeding in this descent was just one more of his many accomplishments. The year before, for his 99th birthday, Miura skied down Mont Blanc in the French Alps together with his eldest son, Yuchiro, and his grandson Yuta. Yuchiro is a champion skier too, no doubt because of having been inspiring by his father. Another of Miura's activities is mountain climb. At age seventy-seven, he succeeded in climb Mount Kilimanjaro, the tallest mountain in Africa.

Miura was a skiing teacher and a photographer of mountain landscapes. He was known for his fitness and his participate in outdoor sports at an advanced age. Miura might not have embraced the sport without have worked at the Aomori Forestry Bureau as a young man; it was there that his strong interest in skiing developed. After retire at age fifty-one, he continued put his energies into the sport, not only by ski frequently, but also by to work on the technical committee for the Ski Association of Japan.

To what did Miura credit his having stayed in shape for all those years? One thing was eating well. He ate nutritious food, such as unpolished rice, fish, seaweed, and soybeans. Another thing was exercising regularly. Every morning he went through a routine of move his neck left and right 100 times, open his mouth wide, and stick out his tongue. He said that this prevented the area around his mouth from be wrinkling. He also did squats and other exercises for to strengthen the body, and he walked 3–4 kilometers each day.

Miura benefited enormously from having been eaten healthfully and having exercising religiously for a half-century. "I still feel good," he said, almost at the end of his life. "It's about diet, it's about exercise . . . It's about making the most out of a long life." He said, "Ski isn't really the reason for my long life. The reason for my long life is my passion for ski."

Keizo Miura's long life ended just a few weeks before his 102nd birthday.

## EXERCISE 8: Personal Writing

*Have you had an excellent friendship in your life, or do you know about one? On a separate piece of paper, write two or three paragraphs about this friendship. Use some of the phrases from the box, making sure they are followed by appropriate gerunds.*

> One of the best friends I have ever had / known about is . . .
>
> I have always appreciated . . .
>
> We enjoy / enjoyed . . .
>
> I remember . . .
>
> We always talked about . . .
>
> I couldn't understand his / her . . .
>
> I never resented his / her . . .
>
> He / She was very good at . . .
>
> We were interested in . . .
>
> We were terrible at . . .
>
> We never worried about . . .

## EXERCISE 1: Recognizing Infinitives

*Read this excerpt from a report by a sociology student. There are eighteen infinitives and infinitive phrases. Underline them. The first one is already underlined. Include **not** where it appears as part of the infinitive.*

Human beings need <u>to be loved and cared for</u>. When warm feelings exist between people, it is natural to give and to accept love. In fact, a common proverb is: "It is better to give than to receive."

Children who do well in school seem to be receiving strong and consistent love and support from their families. On the other hand, many antisocial adolescents appear not to have been given much tender, loving care during their childhood. In fact, their childhoods can be described as wretched. In their desire to be included in a group, some teenagers are easily seduced into gangs. Often they are disappointed not to receive from other gang members the love that they had been yearning for.

After spending years in a gang, it is common for these young people to become hardened; their hardened attitude is "a tough nut to crack," according to police officers and social workers. It becomes extremely difficult for them to re-enter society. Unfortunately, most are expected to continue through their lives in this sad and hopeless scenario. However, some who are fortunate enough to have been reached and touched by enlightened and caring social workers do reform and become productive members of society. With guidance and help, it is possible, even for those exhibiting antisocial behaviors, to be rehabilitated.

The purpose of this paper is to identify agencies and facilities in this state which have done significant work in rehabilitating troubled youngsters and to outline their programs of treatment. In the final section of the paper, I attempt to evaluate these programs.

## EXERCISE 2: Using Infinitives

*Complete the conversation with infinitive forms of the verbs from the box. Use each verb only once. Four infinitives are passive.*

| | | | | | | |
|---|---|---|---|---|---|---|
| celebrate | enjoy | give | include | ~~invite~~ | joke | know |
| remember | see | sing | spend | tease | tell | |

It's 7:00 on a Saturday night. Bob and Carol are arriving at the home of their friends, Ted and Alice. Carol thinks that the two couples are going out to dinner to celebrate her 30th birthday.

**TED:** Hi, guys. It's great to see you!

**BOB:** Hi, Ted. Hi, Alice. It's great of you _____to invite_____ us out to dinner!
1.

**TED:** Well, it's a special night. We don't get _____ Carol's 30th birthday
2.

very often!

**CAROL:** [*entering the home*] Well, you're the only ones I would want _____
3.

the time with!

**ALICE:** Only us? What about all your dear friends who would like _____
4.

"Happy Birthday" to you?

**CAROL:** Like at a party? Oh, no, I hate those parties where I have to try hard

_____ myself. I just never have a good time . . .
5.

**ALICE:** Well, Carol—Surprise!

**TEN GUESTS:** Surprise!

**CAROL:** Surprise? A surprise party! Oh, my goodness! Well . . . I'm speechless . . . but . . . well,

I'm really very surprised _____ you all here! And delighted!
6.

**GUEST:** And we're all delighted _____ in the festivities!
7.

**TED:** How about a little speech, Carol? Everyone here wants _____
8.

what it feels like to turn thirty.

**CAROL:** You're kidding, right? Most of you turned thirty years ago! Ted, I remember a couple

of years ago when you said that you didn't want _____ a party for
9.

any birthday, but after we all celebrated your 30th together, you said that you were so

glad _____ in that way by your friends. Does that ring a bell?
10.

**TED:** It sure does, Carol! I remember it well.

*(continued on next page)*

ALICE: You're right, Carol. Ted loves _____ with you. You know that!

**11.**

CAROL: I do know that, and _____ you the truth, it's fun

**12.**

_____ by Ted.

**13.**

EVERYBODY: Happy birthday, Carol!

## EXERCISE 3: Using Infinitives of Purpose

*Match the places on the left with the activities on the right. Then write sentences telling the activity that would be your reason for going to each place. Include infinitives of purpose. Use the example sentence as a model.*

| | | |
|---|---|---|
| _h_ | **1.** Antarctica | **a.** photograph large wild animals |
| _____ | **2.** The Caribbean | **b.** shop for original designer clothes |
| _____ | **3.** Switzerland or Colorado | **c.** dance the samba and bossa nova |
| _____ | **4.** Egypt | **d.** sail, swim, dive, and snorkel |
| _____ | **5.** Japan | **e.** visit the pyramids |
| _____ | **6.** Kenya | **f.** ski |
| _____ | **7.** Paris | **g.** meet Mickey Mouse and Donald Duck |
| _____ | **8.** Italy | **h.** observe penguins |
| _____ | **9.** Brazil | **i.** see Mount Fuji |
| _____ | **10.** Disneyland | **j.** walk around the ruins of ancient Rome |

**1.** *I would go to Antarctica (in order) to observe penguins.* _____

**2.** _____

**3.** _____

**4.** _____

**5.** _____

**6.** _____

**7.** _____

**8.** _____

**9.** _____

**10.** _____

## EXERCISE 4: Choosing Infinitives

*Read the article from the website of a support group for procrastinators. Complete the article by using the correct infinitive forms of the verbs from the boxes.*

**Leonardo da Vinci: A World-Class Procrastinator**

| be | change | complete | design | have | leave | think | ~~use~~ |
|----|--------|----------|--------|------|-------|-------|---------|

Leonardo da Vinci was a famous painter and inventor who lived in the 15th and 16th centuries. His most famous painting, the *Mona Lisa*, is in the Louvre Museum in Paris. He studied both art and science. He invented many mechanical devices

_____to be used_____ by soldiers in war and for
     **1.**

defense. He also designed bridges and cathedrals, and other buildings. He produced a huge amount of work, but it is said that, at the end of his life, he

said that he was sorry _____ so
     **2.**

many pieces of work unfinished.

As an inventor, much of Leonardo's work was

_____ of new and better ways
     **3.**

to do things. He was always full of original ideas, and many of these were drawn or described in his notebooks. Among them were ideas for the airplane and other flying machines, the parachute, the submarine, a car made with armor for protection, a water pump, contact lenses, and some musical instruments.

If someone in those days wanted _____ in his possession an advanced
     **4.**

new weapon, he would ask Leonardo to design it for him. If someone wanted a method

_____ the direction in which a river flowed, Leonardo was the person to figure
     **5.**

*(continued on next page)*

that out. If someone wanted a huge, custom-designed statue, it was Leonardo who could make it.

Leonardo was the go-to person of his time _____ 6. something new, something

that might turn out _____ 7. extremely useful or beautiful. Leonardo planned

_____ 8. all the big projects that he drew in his notebooks, but in fact, he often

failed to do that.

| avoid | be | finish | focus | go | make | possess | start |

What happened instead was that the projects remained unfinished. At the beginning of each

one, he was excited _____ 9. , but he seldom had enough time or enthusiasm

_____ 10. it. It was very difficult for him _____ 11. on one single

project for a long time unless he was forced _____ 12. back to it.

Moreover, he owed a lot of people artwork. People had paid Leonardo _____ 13.

paintings and sculptures, but, for some reason, he seemed _____ 14. finishing the

product, even though the patrons would extend the deadline for years.

Leonardo was clearly a genius. But he also seems _____ 15. a world-class

procrastinator. Even with all his procrastination, however, he is known _____ 16.

one of the most creative minds of his time and of all time. Maybe there is hope for all of us

procrastinators afterall!

*Read this entry from Beth's diary. Complete the entry by writing the infinitives of the verbs in parentheses. Use past and passive forms where they are needed.*

Dear Diary,

Today is the first anniversary of Grandpa Max's death, and I have been thinking about him all

day. How fortunate I am ____to have had____ a Grandpa like him. He was a very educated and
                           **1. (have)**

learned man, but more than that, he was warm and loving. It was easy for us _____
                                                                              **2. (love)**

him; he was always doing things that made us adore him. I thought about how when we were

little he sometimes used to pretend _____ a big, growling bear—we would be so
                                      **3. (be)**

delighted _____ and _____ one of his big bear hugs that we would
          **4. (pick up)**            **5. (give)**

squeal with pleasure. And I remember how he taught me _____ a bicycle when I was
                                                        **6. (ride)**

five. I had been yearning _____ by my older cousins to ride bicycles with them, but I
                          **7. (invite)**

wasn't able to until Grandpa taught me how.

I loved it when he would come _____ us. He always brought us little gifts that
                               **8. (visit)**

were guaranteed _____ us laugh, like a ring that squirted water and a cuckoo
                 **9. (make)**

clock with Mickey Mouse inside. And when we needed someone _____ to, Grandpa
                                                             **10. (talk)**

was such a good listener. He would encourage us _____ stories, _____
                                                 **11. (tell)**                **12. (imagine)**

big things, and _____ to reach bigger goals.
                **13. (try)**

Then, when I was about eight, I remember that I was afraid _____ far from home.
                                                            **14. (go)**

I was afraid of monsters, and I expected _____ by one at any moment. Grandpa
                                          **15. (attack)**

persuaded me _____ down the street with him, past one more house each time we
             **16. (walk)**

went out together, until we got to the end of the block. Then, with him, I managed

_____ two blocks away from home, then three, until finally I was able to go
**17. (go)**

everywhere, and I forgot about the monsters. Years later, on my 16th birthday, Grandpa

permitted me _____ him around the block in his car, and I felt so proud, even though
             **18. (drive)**

my cousin Johnny said that Grandpa must have been crazy _____ me do that.
                                                         **19. (let)**

I would like _____ able to tell him I loved him just one more time before he died.
             **20. (be)**

_____ a grandpa like Grandpa Max is very sad. But I think that never
**21. (lose)**

_____ my Grandpa Max would have been even sadder.
**22. (have)**

## EXERCISE 6: Using Infinitives

*Read the text of an email from Ricardo to Marco. Complete the email. Use the verbs from the box above each section to form infinitives. Use the past and passive forms where they are needed.*

| be | do | flunk | get | ~~give~~ | learn | work |
|----|----|-------|-----|----------|-------|------|

Dear Marco,

You sure handed out some strong advice. Well, it came to the right place. I took your suggestion and applied for a job at a hotel. The manager offered _____to give_____ me a job at the
**1.**
front desk, starting next Monday night. He wants me _____ all aspects of the
**2.**
job while working. I think I can manage _____ and study during the semester,
**3.**
although it will be difficult _____ both at the same time. I'm really trying not
**4.**
_____ this time.  I want _____ out of this mess, so I have no
**5.**                                    **6.**
choice. _____ heavily in debt is a terrible thing!
**7.**

| allow | give | leave | show up | take |
|-------|------|-------|---------|------|

I am expected _____ for work at 5:00 P.M. I'll work until 1:00 A.M., unless I
**8.**
decide not _____ a break. In that case, I'll be permitted _____
**9.**                                                                    **10.**
at midnight. The manager said some nights might be slow enough _____ some
**11.**
time for studying at the desk, but I am required _____ first priority to the details
**12.**
of the job.

| get | give | invest | take | tell | trick |
|-----|------|--------|------|------|-------|

I am really sorry _____ myself into such a mess. It sure was dumb.
**13.**
Sometimes I think that when brains were being given out, I was unlucky enough

_____ a very small one. I don't know what I was thinking when I allowed myself
**14.**
_____ advantage of in the way that I was. The guy on the phone sounded so
**15.**
smart when he was persuading me _____ money in his operation.
**16.**

I am really embarrassed _____ like that, especially since now, of course, the
**17.**
trick seems so obvious. I'm asking you not _____ anybody about this.
**18.**

| be | behave | forget | get | go out | pursue | talk | tell |

And, what about you and Lisa? If she is important to you, I hope you won't just decide

_____ about her. Instead, you have to continue _____
        **19.**                                                                        **20.**

her. The problem might be the way you sometimes talk to people. Try _____
                                                                                     **21.**

more diplomatic with Lisa than you are with me and with everyone else. Sometimes you are

so honest that girls are reluctant _____ to you about any delicate subject.
                                                                   **22.**

They don't want _____ about harsh realities; they want you to be sensitive.
                                                              **23.**

_____ Lisa back, Marco, you have to be prepared _____
          **24.**                                                                 **25.**

much better than you usually do. Call her and very nicely ask her _____ with
                                                                                 **26.**

you. Maybe she will. Let me know what happens.

Thanks for helping me out.

—Ricardo

## EXERCISE 7: Editing

*Read this personal essay from an applicant to Zenith University. There are sixteen mistakes in the use of infinitives. The first mistake is already corrected. Find and correct fifteen more.*

                                     *to*

"To be or not be"—this is a famous quotation from Shakespeare's *Hamlet*. The quotation is

relevant to me because for the past two years I have been thinking about what I am and what I

want being.

In spite of having quite an average upbringing, I was different from my friends because I

preferred to not watch TV, but to read. Not that I didn't participate in childhood games and high

school sports—I was involved like most young people, and my parents encouraged to take part in

several activities. But I also chose to reading for a few hours each day, or more likely, each night.

Sometimes I didn't even stop going to sleep. As a child, I read the usual children's books, but I soon

attempted to read newspaper articles and magazines about science, and a few years later, about

philosophy. Since I had learned to read without difficulty at age three, it was easy enough for me

stepping up to a higher level.

*(continued on next page)*

Because of my interests in science and philosophy, I have always tended to balance the one area with the other in my mind. The result of spending so much time reading and trying to integrate everything I was absorbing was that I became quite a reflective person. I didn't appear being an intellectual kid with its connotation of "geek." (I have always been a computer geek, though. I have almost never written in longhand.) I seemed acted like everybody else. And, in truth, I was like everyone else except that I also had a more introspective side than most kids.

This description of myself is meant to show that I have been thinking about myself and what I wish becoming. The truth is that I do not know yet; it is too soon know. This is why I hope to attend Zenith University—get a broad exposure to all the humanities and sciences and to finding the field where I will be able maximize my abilities and find fulfillment. At the moment, I think I would like be an archaeologist and do research about the beliefs and religious practices of ancient peoples. But I will seek to expose myself to many disciplines at Zenith, and to benefit from learning about all of them.

In Zenith's motto, the words "To learn is to grow" are meant for me. That is what I expect do and will endeavor to doing at Zenith University.

## EXERCISE 8: Personal Writing

*Have you ever procrastinated? Do you have a habit of procrastination? On a separate piece of paper, write two or three paragraphs about your habit of procrastination, or something that went wrong because you procrastinated. Use some of the phrases from the box, appropriately followed by infinitives or other verb forms.*

> I wanted to . . . , but . . .
> I had hoped to . . . , but . . .
> Now I can't afford . . .
> It has been difficult for me . . .
> I keep trying . . .
> I will be required . . .
> I am advised . . .
> I am lucky . . .
> In the future, I expect . . .
> I intend . . .

## UNIT 18  Adverbs: Sentence, Focus, and Negative

### EXERCISE 1: Recognizing Adverbs

*Read the article. Underline the adverbs. Describe the type of adverb by writing above it: write S for sentence adverb, F for focus adverb, and N for negative adverb.*

**WHAT IS CAUSING GLOBAL WARMING? IS IT HUMAN BEINGS?**

**Yes, humans are causing global warming.**

1. *S*
   Unfortunately, the Earth is getting warmer and warmer. The levels of carbon dioxide ($CO_2$) in the atmosphere are the highest they have been in the last 650,000 years. Never has the Earth been in such danger of severe climate change. Clearly, the levels of carbon dioxide are causing that change.

2. It is only human-produced $CO_2$ that is warming the Earth, not natural $CO_2$ released from the land and the oceans.

3. These greenhouse gas emissions produced by humans, not changes in the Sun's radiation, are what is causing global climate change, essentially.

4. It is not only emissions from cars and industry that cause the $CO_2$ levels to rise. Certainly other big causes are air conditioners, heaters and other heat sources, and large asphalt parking lots to name a few.

5. Nearly all climate-change studies show humans as the main cause. With effort, we can control our $CO_2$ levels, and hopefully, reverse global warming.

**No, humans are not causing global warming.**

1. The Earth has had warmer and colder periods throughout history. Actually, temperatures of the Earth in the 11th century (1000–1100 C.E.), before fossil fuels were used, were almost the same as they were in the 20th century from 1900 to 1990.

2. Rising $CO_2$ levels are just a result of global warming, not a cause of it.

3. Mainly, global warming and cooling are caused by natural fluctuations in the heat emitted from the Sun, and not by the small effect of gases, such as $CO_2$ and methane, that are produced by humans.

4. Rising temperatures are also caused, significantly, by water vapor, which is the most abundant greenhouse gas in the atmosphere, and not by $CO_2$. The concentrations of water vapor change because of natural storm systems and ocean currents. Even studies by reliable institutions show that this is true.

5. It is nature, basically, not human activity, that is responsible for climate change. Surely, this will become increasingly clear in the future.

*Read the text of an email from Marco to Ricardo. Complete the email. Circle the correct adverbs or adverbials.*

Hey, Ricardo,

I'm glad that you took the job as night clerk in the hotel. Things will work out for you. Almost /
**1.**
(Just) be serious about your work and your studies. By the time I come home, you will have saved up

almost / even enough money to get out of debt, about 90 percent of it, right?
**2.**

Well, there are you / you are at home, and not in as terrible a state as usual, and I am / am I
**3.**                                                                              **4.**
here in the U.S., giving you advice, when clearly I am in terrible shape myself. Unfortunately, my

relationship with Lisa has gone downhill. In fact, it has completely crashed. In fact, I hardly / neither
**5.**
*have* a relationship with her. I think about her always / almost every minute, although now I almost /
**6.**                                                          **7.**
scarcely ever see her. I don't never / ever see her downtown and I rarely / even run into her on
**8.**                                             **9.**
campus. Not only / Only does she refuse to go out with me, but she ever / never returns my phone calls.
**10.**                                                                 **11.**
Sometimes / Never in my whole life have I met anybody like Lisa, and occasionally / never have
**12.**                                                                        **13.**
I been so miserable. Neither / Obviously, she is not interested in me. Maybe she simply got bored
**14.**
with me. Maybe she thinks I'm just / even a student in transit and not worth an investment of her
**15.**
time. Luckily, as I told you, I have made some friends here, but rarely / only do they call me, because
**16.**
I seem so depressed all the time. Ricardo, I really am depressed. I know that there are other girls

besides Lisa. A few girls who know me even / only invited me for dinner, but clearly, I can't go out
**17.**
with them. I guess I'm hardly / just a prisoner of love—an unrequited love. No way / Little can I go
**18.**                                                                      **19.**
on like this!

Frankly, I don't care about anything at all these days. Little / Just does Lisa know how miserable I
**20.**
am. If she one day / ever finds out, I'm sure she won't call me. But, if she does call, even / ever just to
**21.**                                                                        **22.**
say hello, I'll be the happiest man in the world. Only / Never when that happens will I be able to live
**23.**
like a normal person again.


—Marco

*Rewrite this ad for a political candidate by inserting the adverbs in parentheses before the words or phrases they focus on. (In items that have two sentences, rewrite only the first sentence. The second sentence is intended to clarify the focus of the first.)*

# Voters!

Aren't you fed up with the incompetent and corrupt politicians in office?
The time has come to throw the rascals out! Ron Rong and all his friends have almost ruined our state. But Don Deare has come along just in time to save us!
Do you know some of the things Ron Rong has done?

1. Ron Rong said he wanted to do what was best for the state. **(only)** He didn't want to do anything else. *He said he wanted to do only what was best for the state.*

2. But he used up the state's money. **(really)**

   _____

3. He put his friends in the best jobs. **(only)** Nobody else got these jobs.

   _____

4. He paid for his friends' so-called business trips. **(even)** He did everything he could for his friends. _____

5. He did the minimal work. **(merely)** He never willingly did any more work than the minimum.
   *only / just (in this sentence it means only)*

   _____

6. He appeared in his office, dispensed favors, and went out to play golf. **(simply)** Isn't that the image of the stereotypical politician?

   _____

7. He didn't care about the people of this state. **(just)**

   _____

8. This state will be saved if you elect Don Deare. **(only)** It will not be saved in any other way.

   _____

This is another ad for the same political candidate. Rewrite each item by inserting the negative adverbs in parentheses at the beginning of the sentence and making any other changes in form that are needed. (If there are two sentences, rewrite only the second sentence.)

## ★ ★ ★ ★ *Vote for Don Deare!* ★ ★ ★ ★

1. Don Deare is great. He loves the people; he acts to help them. **(not only / but)**

   *Not only does Don Deare love the people, but he acts to help them.*

2. He works almost 365 days a year. He takes a vacation. **(seldom)**

   *seldom does he take a vacation,*

3. His wonderful and loving family would like to have him spend more time at home. He is able to spend much time with them, however. **(rarely)**

   *rarely is he able to spend much time with them, however.*

4. Although he is not able to spend enough time with his family, he is a loving and considerate husband and father. He neglects his family. **(never)**

   *never does he neglect his family.*

5. He is an honest man. He would accept a bribe. **(no way)**

   *No way would he accept a bribe.*

6. He makes informed decisions after looking at each problem carefully. He takes action. **(only then)**

   *only then does he take action,*

7. People realize how many hours he has volunteered at the shelter for the homeless. **(little)**

   *little do people realize ------*

8. He thinks of himself first. **(never)**

   *never does he think of himself first*

9. Don Deare has an excellent record. He has served the people very well as a civic volunteer; he will do even more for them as a senator. **(not only / but)**

   *not only has he seved the people very well as a civic volunteer; but he will do ---*

## EXERCISE 5: Using Adverbs of Place: *Here* and *There*

*Read the descriptions of six situations. Complete the descriptions by using the words in parentheses to make a phrase or sentence beginning with* **Here** *or* **There**. *Use contractions where appropriate.*

### Situation 1

On a popular late-night talk show, the host is introduced by a drum roll and a shout by the

announcer of these words: "_____Here's Jay_____!"
        (is / here / Jay)

### Situation 2

On a television talk show, the host might introduce a guest by saying this: "And

_Here he is_, ladies and gentlemen: the number one men's tennis player in
    (is / here / he)

the world . . . !"

### Situation 3

Dolly Parton, a country singer, composed and sang a song about a man she couldn't get out of her

mind. The title of the song is "_here you come_ again,"
        (You / Here / Again / Come)

### Situation 4

In a children's game called "Hide and Seek," all the children run and hide, except one,

who searches for the others. After counting to 10, the child cries out, "Ready or not,

_here I come_!"
    (I / here / come)

### Situation 5

Harry and Betty have been having some difficulty in their marriage. Everything between them

becomes a controversial issue, and they argue about it. They went to a counselor for help. After

they expressed their different perspectives, the counselor said, "Well, _there lies the problem_.
                                    (lies / there / the problem)

I can see that you are not communicating well enough. I think that if you can improve your

communication techniques, your marriage will be a lot happier."

### Situation 6

Two tourists are standing across from the White House. Suddenly three large black cars come

out, accompanied by several motorcycles. A familiar-looking man is sitting in the back seat of

the second car.

**Tourist A:** Wow, look! _there goes the president_!
                (president / there / the / goes)

**Tourist B:** Are you sure? Was that really the president?

*Read the transcript of the radio broadcast about a controversial issue. There are thirteen mistakes in the use of adverbs. The first mistake is already corrected. Find and correct twelve more.*

Have you seen the TV ads for different medications? A national physicians' group wants to prohibit the advertising of medicines on TV. Not only <u>do</u> the ads make people interested in those medicines, but they compel many of those people to ask their doctors to prescribe them. Consumers want a "quick fix" for their health problems, and may not fully understand the risks involved.

The physicians say this kind of advice from patients to their doctors is not a good idea. A doctor does not like to refuse patients' requests, but the medicine the patient asks for could be the wrong one. The doctor wants just the patient to improve and he or she knows which one is best. Requesting an advertised drug challenges the medical doctor's judgment.

Here a story is from a doctor. A patient came to the doctor, wanting a medication he had seen on TV. The medicine was a strong pain reliever, and the patient wanted it to relieve his headaches. He begged even the doctor for the medicine. Only he wanted the attractive pink pill he had seen on TV. But the doctor wanted to find out what was causing the headaches, not to find a temporary cure just. The doctor persuaded the patient to have a general physical examination. He took many blood tests and did even an electrocardiogram to examine the patient's heart. The doctor found that the patient was allergic to many environmental products and to all almost kinds of fish. Those allergies were causing the headaches. It's a good thing that the doctor didn't write just a prescription for the patient's headache relief. By persevering, not only the doctor found the correct diagnosis, but he was able to cure the patient.

On the other hand, a pharmacists' organization disagrees about TV advertising. The pharmacists think that advertising basically medications is a good thing. They say that advertising the medicines on TV sheds some light on what is available. They say that more knowledge about medicines only is good; it can't be bad.

The pharmacists say that the ads educate consumers about diseases and the options for treatment. They encourage TV viewers to visit their doctors and ask about the advertised medicine.

Some people believe that TV advertising should be uncensored and that companies should be able to advertise whatever product they want. Since it is not compulsory to buy the advertised product, consumers can make their own choices.

It is good to have obviously information, but when it comes to advertising medicines on TV, the issue remains controversial.

## EXERCISE 7: Personal Writing

*You and your friend disagree about some controversial issues, such as the best type of government, welfare payments to the poor, global economies, medical ethics, or capital punishment. Think about one of these issues, or one of your own, and describe your thoughts in two or three paragraphs on a separate piece of paper. Use some of the phrases from the box.*

> The issue is . . .
>
> You have a good point, but I just think . . .
>
> I only want to inform you that . . .
>
> Actually, the truth is that . . .
>
> Clearly, what I believe is . . .
>
> Unfortunately, . . .
>
> Never before has . . .
>
> We will not only . . .
>
> Rarely will . . .
>
> Only then will we . . .

## EXERCISE 1: Identifying Adverb Clauses

*Read the* World Review Magazine (**A**) *interview with Dr. Milton Scope (**B**), a professor of sociology and an expert in what makes happy families. There are twelve adverb clauses. The first one is already underlined. Underline eleven more. Then identify the clauses as one of the following:* **time, place, reason, condition,** *or* **contrast**.

---

**WORLD REVIEW**

## What Makes a Happy Family

**A:** Dr. Scope, just what *does* make a happy family?

*contrast*
**B:** There is a cliché that all happy families have some things in common. <u>While this may be trite</u>, it is also true.

**A:** Really? What are these things?

**B:** Well, in happy families, even though family members may argue, they have a basic concern for each other. Since every person needs to know that somebody really cares for and about him or her, this is perhaps the most prevalent factor.

**A:** Is this caring enough to keep young people on the road to productive lives and certainly away from nonsocial behavior?

**B:** No. Of course it's not so simple, but . . . a person who feels connected to others is more likely to act in socially acceptable ways, whereas a person who does not feel connected often acts in antisocial ways.

**A:** So, is being connected the principal factor?

**B:** It is very important.

**A:** Tell us what else is important.

**B:** When family members support each other's goals, the family feels united.

**A:** Give us an example.

**B:** Well, if a parent is hoping to be promoted at work, everybody is supportive and shows interest. If a youngster is trying to make the basketball team, the other family members show encouragement and warmth.

**A:** What happens in times of trouble?

**B:** When one family member is having trouble, the others should exhibit concern and try to help. Suppose, for example, that a family member has been fired from a job. This person may suddenly feel totally worthless in society, although, of course, this is not true. In fact, precisely because this person doesn't have a job, he or she needs to feel valued as a human being.

**A:** So, is that the key word, *valued*?

**B:** I think it is. People need to feel valued, appreciated. They also need to feel secure among the family members. They need to know that their families will always be there for them even if they are irritable, depressed, ill, unemployed—or whatever.

**A:** Does the economic status of the family matter?

**B:** Of course, economic stability is favorable. But happy families exist wherever you look, in all economic strata. And unhappy families as well.

**A:** Well, thank you very much doctor. We certainly feel a little more enlightened than we did before.

*Read the passage about a student who has a chronic problem. Complete the passage. Circle the subordinate conjunctions.*

Why can't Johnny make the team in any sport? (Although) / Since
**1.**
Johnny is in excellent physical shape, he has never been able to

get on a school team. Johnny has tried out for the football team,

the basketball team, the baseball team, and the hockey team. But

(whenever) / where he tries, he always gets eliminated. (Even if) / Only if
**2.**                                                                              **3.**
the coaches like him at first, not one of them has ever picked him to

be on the final team. He always ends up being an also-ran. Johnny

should be picked (because) / although he plays several sports very well.
**4.**
And he is strong. His problem? He is always late. He never arrives

at practice on time. Until / (By the time) he arrives at a practice, the
**5.**
players have already been on the field for 15 minutes. Unless / (As soon as) he arrives, he gives the
**6.**
coach an excuse. But the excuse is not enough.

For each sport, he has arrived late to the first two practices. (After) / Until he arrives late for the
**7.**
second time, the coach gives him the bad news: "You're off the team. Good-bye." In his mind, Johnny

thinks that the coaches are practicing partisanship; he says that the coaches favor players whom

they like more. The truth is that the coaches like players whom they can depend on, and Johnny is

not one of those players.

(Even though) / Now that he promises to arrive on time at future practices, nobody believes him
**8.**
anymore. Johnny is having a hard time in life. Even if / (Only if) he starts being punctual will he be
**9.**
successful in sports or, more importantly, be successful (wherever) / whereas he goes.
**10.**

*Read the descriptions from a catalog on the next page. Complete the descriptions. Use the adverb clauses from the box.*

| | |
|---|---|
| anywhere you shop | as soon as warm weather arrives |
| ~~because it is necessary~~ | even if it's raining outside |
| even though he may already have | if your loved one loves |
| when you want | wherever a busy person travels |

## GREAT GIFT IDEAS

**1.** _Because it is necessary_ for all her work, especially when she travels, you must get her this exceptional new laptop.

**2.** For the whole family, this deluxe cooler set will be ready for picnics and fun _____.

**3.** _____, this collapsible suitcase on wheels will be a big convenience.

**4.** You won't find a better, more efficient, or more affordable tablet than this one _____.

**5.** _____ to tell her that you love her very much and want to marry her, present her with a beautiful diamond like this.

**6.** _____ all the necessary equipment, any fisherman will be thrilled to receive our new lightweight aluminum fishing rod, almost guaranteed to catch the fish for him!

**7.** _____ preparing interesting dishes, delight him or her with this versatile food processor.

**8.** Our 1,000-piece set of interlocking plastic pieces will be so fascinating to your little ones that they will be kept occupied all day long, _____.

## EXERCISE 4: Using Adverb Clauses

*Read the transcript of the voicemail recording for Adventure Travel Tours. Complete the transcript. Use the correct words or phrases from the box above each section. There is one extra item in each box.*

| as soon as | ~~because~~ | unless | until | wherever |
|---|---|---|---|---|

Thank you for calling Adventure Travel Tours. ____Because____ the demand for our new,
**1.**

affordable adventure tours is so heavy, our agents are not available to assist you now. Please be

patient. _____ an agent is available, you will be connected. _____ you are
**2.**                                                              **3.**

connected to an agent, we will keep you entertained with music and will provide some information

of interest to you. _____ you want to go to experience an extraordinary adventure trip,
**4.**

Adventure Tours will get you there effortlessly.

*(continued on next page)*

| as soon as | even though | if | unless | while |
|---|---|---|---|---|

_____ scaling a mountain is what you want, we've got monthly trips to the Alps, as
5.

well as yearly sojourns to the Himalayas. For these trips, you'll need a lot of stamina! Perhaps you're

interested in going on a safari. Adventure Travel Tours will book you with reliable, knowledgeable

guides to keep you safe, _____ dangerous wild animals may be lurking nearby.
6.

_____ you have a guide who is intimately familiar with the area, you won't know where
7.

and how to see the animals up close. Make your reservations now _____ the supply of
8.

low-fare vacation packages lasts. An agent will be with you shortly. Please continue to hold.

## EXERCISE 5: Forming Complex Sentences with Adverb Clauses

_Combine the pairs of sentences to form single complex sentences using the subordinating conjunctions in parentheses. Place commas where they are needed, but do not change any words in the sentences. Sometimes more than one answer is correct._

1. There are so many new sports. Some people can't keep up with them. **(now that)**

   _Now that there are so many new sports, some people can't keep up with them._

   _____

2. We turn to certain sports channels on TV. We see athletes at various venues, jumping, diving,

   somersaulting over dangerous landscapes, and otherwise contorting themselves. **(when)**

   _____

   _____

3. These athletes push themselves to dangerous and extreme levels. This category of sports is

   called "extreme sports." **(because)**

   _____

   _____

4. Extreme sports are dangerous. They are becoming more and more popular among young

   people all over the world. **(although)**

   _____

   _____

5. It is inevitable that something will go awry at one time or another. **(as)** Many people think extreme sports should not be encouraged.

_____

_____

6. Extreme sports are not seen at the Olympic Games yet. There are twice-yearly competitive games showing extreme sports on some sports channels. **(even though)**

_____

_____

7. These games are called "The X-Games." "X" represents the word _extreme_. **(since)**

_____

_____

8. They have been increasingly popular. They first appeared on television in 1995. **(since)**

_____

_____

9. There will be more and more participants in extreme sports. There are young people who want to compete in "real adventure." **(wherever)**

_____

_____

## EXERCISE 6: Editing

_Read the transcript of two sportscasters broadcasting a football game. There are twelve mistakes in the use of adverb clauses. The first mistake is already corrected. Find and correct eleven more._

RAY: Hello, football fans! What a fantastic game this is! We're coming to you from Starz Stadium
now, ~~by the time~~ _while_ the two best football teams in the league are on their half-time break.

The score stands at 0–0. The Panthers and the Leopards have each been undefeated after

this season began. They've won wherever they've played, at home or away. This game will

decide the league championship. Arnold, what do you think? When the game will be over,

which team is going to have the higher score?

_(continued on next page)_

**ARNOLD:** That's impossible to say, Ray. Both teams are in great shape. They're just about equal. We don't know who will win. Unless the Panthers win, it will be because of their terrific offense. They've been perfecting their offense ever since the new coach arrived. On the other hand, if the Leopards win, will it be because of their superb defense, which is just about perfect this year.

**RAY:** I think that the Panthers have the edge with their offense. Unless they will make a big mistake, that offense is going to win the game for them.

**ARNOLD:** You may be right, Ray, but don't forget—the Leopards have won all their games although their defense has been so great. Only if the Panthers' offense is fantastic, they won't be able to score because the Leopards' super defense will stop them.

**RAY:** Could be. At the beginning of the game, it looked like the Panthers were going to score. But then, right after Lowell—the Panthers' top scorer—got possession of the ball, Brown—the Leopards' strongest player—blocked his shot and stopped the point.

**ARNOLD:** I think we agree. Since the Panthers have a terrific offense, they can't score easily against the Leopards' defense.

**RAY:** Right. I think the Panthers could score. But only if the Leopards make an unlikely error in defense the Panthers will score.

**ARNOLD:** Right! This sure is one exciting game!

**RAY:** You bet! Whereas the teams are equally good, the game is going to be really close until the last second of play. We won't know the winner until the game will be over.

## EXERCISE 7: Personal Writing

*Are sports important? Should sports be in a school's curriculum? Some people think they should be included, and some people think they should not be included. What do you think? Write two or three paragraphs about why sports should or should not be included in a school's curriculum.*

Sports should / should not be an important part of a school's curriculum because . . .

If sports are / are not included, . . .

Because sports are / are not important for . . .

Although studying is important, sports . . .

When young people take part in sports, . . .

Before a student joins a team, . . .

Since many people like to play _____, it . . .

I like to play _____, although . . .

Only if our team wins the next game,

## EXERCISE 1: Recognizing Adverb and Adverbial Phrases

*Read this flyer from the Parks Department, which was sent to the parents of schoolchildren. There are fourteen adverb and adverbial phrases. The first one is already underlined. Find and underline thirteen more.*

# Happy Summer Vacation, Parents!

We wish all of you an enjoyable and safe summer.
Here are some safety tips for your summer activities.

**Safety in the car**

- <u>Before starting on any car trip</u>, you should make sure that everybody's seat belt is fastened.
- While in the car, wear your seat belt at all times.

**Boating safety**

- When in a boat, children should always wear life jackets.
- Riding in a boat, neither children nor adults should engage in active physical games or horseplay.
- Remember that the sailor must always be on the lookout for other boats and obey the right-of-way rules of the sea. On seeing another boat, the sailor must make sure that the other boat sees him.
- Return to your dock carefully and slowly. Having docked, all the passengers must get off in an orderly manner.

**Safety for swimmers**

- The best thing to ensure safety is for every child to learn to swim correctly. Being able to swim, a child can enjoy the water.
- Children must never swim alone. While in the water, a child must have a responsible adult nearby.

**Riding a bicycle**

- Make sure that your children know all the rules about bicycling: where to ride, how to pass, how to signal, how to cross streets, etc. Having learned these rules, children are much more responsible bike riders.
- When riding bicycles, children should always wear helmets. This is not a petty concern; helmets have saved countless lives.

**Protection from the sun**

- Suffering from severe sunburn, thousands of people have to seek medical care in emergency rooms every year. This does not have to happen to you and your family.
- Before going out in the sun, children and adults alike should apply sunscreen. Get sunscreen with an SPF of 30 or more. Use just a little bit; the lotion shouldn't be oozing out of the tube.
- A bandana on your head will not protect your face from the sun. Wear a hat with a brim, or a visor, to protect your face. A child, not wanting to wear a hat, might object to this precaution, so in that case, be sure that the child is using sunscreen.
- Don't forget the importance of a good pair of sunglasses. When buying sunglasses for children, you should be sure that the lenses are made of polycarbonate and that they will not pop out.

We look forward to seeing you again at the beginning of the next school year.

*Read the report of a traffic accident, written by a man to his insurance company. Complete the report. Circle the correct words or phrases to form adverb or adverbial phrases.*

**ACME**
INSURANCE COMPANY

### TRAFFIC ACCIDENT REPORT

To be completed by the customer: In your own words, describe the accident. (Write or type clearly.)

Last Monday morning, I was driving to work. (Upon entering) / Entered Highway 17 at Entrance
1.
43, I immediately encountered very heavy traffic. (After having rained) / After rained all night,
2.
the weather was still bad, and road conditions were not good. (While driving) / While driven slowly at
3.
about 20 miles per hour because of the bad weather and low visibility, I kept several yards behind
the driver in front of me. Suddenly, the car in front of me stopped, and, (hit) / (hitting) the
4.
brakes immediately, I stopped, too, about two feet behind the car. But, about two seconds
later, I heard and felt a crash from behind me, and I was jolted forward, (crashing) / (crashed)
5.
into that car ahead of me. (Stunned) / Having stunned by the crash, at first I didn't realize
6.
what was happening. Being dazing / (Being dazed) from the impact, but not hurt, I saw the driver
7.
in the car ahead opening his door and getting out onto the highway. To my amazement, I then
saw several people walking next to the cars in front of me. (Being) / Having curious, and able to open
8.
the door of the car, I got out too. Then it dawned on me: I had been part of an "accordian
type" accident. (Before realizing) / Before being realized that, I had been wondering why these
9.
people were walking along the highway. I saw that about 16 or 17 cars were involved, each one
(having crashed) / having crashing into the car in front of it.
10.
After acknowledge / (After acknowledging) each other, we all got out of the rain and sat in our
11.
cars, (waiting) / after waiting for the police, whose sirens we already heard.
12.
(Having arrived) / Being arrived on the scene, the police quickly evaluated the situation, talked to
13.
each of us briefly, and gave us forms to fill out. Not been / (Not having been) accused of causing
14.
this accident, I was relieved. However, the damage to my car is extensive.
(Since notifying) / Since being notified your company of the accident as soon as it occurred, I am
15.
now awaiting payment.

## EXERCISE 3: Forming Sentences with Adverbial Phrases

*Combine the pairs of sentences into single sentences. Make the first sentence an adverbial phrase and the second sentence an independent clause. Use present participles, past participles, or **having** plus past participles. You may move the noun subject to the second clause to replace the subject pronoun, but do not add any words.*

1. Many people try to stay healthy. They quickly adopt the latest health recommendations.

   *Trying to stay healthy, many people quickly adopt the latest health recommendations.*

2. People hope to lower their cholesterol levels. They minimize their intake of animal fats.

   *hoping to lower their .... people minimize*

3. People know that fiber in the diet is excellent for digestion. They are consuming more fresh fruit, vegetables, and whole wheat products.

4. Heavy people know that they weigh too much. They diet to lose weight.

5. Senior citizens don't want to become decrepit. Many of them exercise regularly to avoid this.

   *not wanting to become ... . Many senior citizens ----*

6. People were told that vitamin C, vitamin E, and beta-carotene greatly reduce cancer risk. They began buying these nutrients in large quantities.

   *~~having~~ being told .... , people began buying*

7. People have known for a long time that too much salt and sugar is unhealthful. They buy a lot of salt-free and sugar-free products.

8. People learned that using good sunglasses will protect their corneas. Many have bought good sunglasses.

_____

_____

9. Some people believe that eating fish will raise their intelligence level. They eat a lot of fish.

_____

_____

10. People realize that they can contribute to their own good health. They eat much more knowledgeably than they used to.

_____

_____

## EXERCISE 4: Using Adverb and Adverbial Phrases

*Read the information about traveling in Europe. Circle the letter of the phrase that best completes each sentence.*

1. Last year, two friends and I visited two countries in Europe where we had never been before. As we had only two weeks and a rather limited supply of money, _____ and made careful plans for the trip.

   **a.** we did a great deal of research

   **b.** research was done about the best places to go

   **c.** researched the trip

2. After discussing the advantages and disadvantages of the various countries that we might visit, _____.

   **a.** France and Italy were the choices

   **b.** our top choices were France and Italy

   **c.** we chose France and Italy

*(continued on next page)*

**3.** We were very excited to arrive in Paris. It was very expensive! However, _____ the costs carefully, we were not floored by the high prices we found there.

    **a.** we had investigated

    **b.** having investigated

    **c.** before investigating

**4.** Then, _____ the real French countryside, we took a train south for a three-hour ride and rented bikes to cycle around in a small rural area. We stayed at a very nice inn in a small town.

    **a.** having experienced

    **b.** wanting to experience

    **c.** being experienced

**5.** _____ a wonderful week in France, we flew to Rome.

    **a.** Spending

    **b.** Though spending

    **c.** After spending

**6.** We traveled all over Rome, particularly _____ the ancient ruins. We were thrilled with their beauty, as well as the beauty and interest of the rest of the city.

    **a.** enjoying

    **b.** enjoy

    **c.** enjoyed

**7.** Next, we rented a car and drove south to Naples. _____ there early, we had a chance to stroll around the city before checking into a small hotel.

    **a.** Since arriving

    **b.** Because we arrived

    **c.** Arrived

**8.** The next day we drove south to Pompeii. _____ in the distance.

    **a.** We saw Mount Vesuvius driving along the road

    **b.** Driving along the road, we saw Mount Vesuvius

    **c.** Having driven along the road, we saw Mount Vesuvius

**9.** _____ the ancient site, we heard a fascinating talk from a local tour guide.

    **a.** Before we enter

    **b.** Before entered

    **c.** Before entering

**10.** _____ by the eruption of the volcano Mount Vesuvius in the year 79 C.E., Pompeii had been a prosperous ancient city.

(**a.**) Destroyed

  **b.** Having destroyed

  **c.** Destroying

**11.** In the year 79 C.E., the lava from the volcano came down so suddenly that the people in the city were covered in it _____ their ordinary activities. No one was able to elude it.

  **a.** even though going about

  **b.** because going about

  **c.** while going about

**12.** Leaving Pompeii, we returned to Rome. Then—too soon—_____ our two weeks in Europe, we flew back home . . .

(**a.**) upon completing = ( when we completed )

  **b.** being completed

  **c.** completed

**13.** . . . after _____ the best time of our lives.

  **a.** upon having

  **b.** having had

  **c.** had

## EXERCISE 5: Editing

*Read the passage about Shakira. There are sixteen mistakes in the use of adverbs and adverbial phrases. The first mistake is already corrected. Find and correct fifteen more. Delete or fix words, but do not add words.*

                             known

Shakira Isabel Mebarak Ripoli, ~~having~~ professionally as Shakira, is a singer, songwriter, dancer, and philanthropist. Born and raising in Barranquilla, Colombia, Shakira began performing in school, being shown her vocal ability with rock and roll, Latin, and Middle Eastern music at an early age.

She wrote her first poem at age four, and she recorded her first album at age thirteen. After have had a commercial failure with that album and with another, Shakira decided to produce her music

*(continued on next page)*

herself. In 1995, upon released *Pies descalzos* (translation in English: *Barefoot*), she became famous all over Latin America and in Spain. Since then, Shakira's music has been very well received, and she has been enormously successful.

There is another side to Shakira, besides that of being a performance star. She has a lot of compassion for poor people, especially children, who cannot obtain an education. As a young girl, Shakira had seen the suffering of street children slept in parks every night, and she made a promise to herself to help them someday. Having achieving career success, she used much of the money she had earned to improve the lives of children. She created a foundation having provided education and meals for poor children in her country. She said, "Because growing up in Colombia, I saw that education can be a child's way out of poverty and a way to fulfill his or her potential."

The name of the foundation, taking from her first successful album, is *Pies descalzos*. The first school was built in a small Colombian city. After that, Shakira's foundation built many more schools served disadvantaged children and their families through education, counseling, nutrition, and income-generating projects. Inspiring by the success of the Pies Descalzos Foundation in Colombia, Shakira founded the U.S.-based Barefoot Foundation in 2008. Having supported worldwide education today, it encourages governments to increase spending on educational programs.

Recognizing for her education advocacy, she is the Goodwill Ambassador for UNICEF, a United Nations agency, and she is also the Honorary Chair of the Global Campaign for Education, an organization having held governments responsible for their commitment to securing education for all.

Shakira's life shows that a person can have success and fame while work to make the world a better place. With Shakira's compassion, a blow has been struck against poverty.

## EXERCISE 6: Personal Writing

*How do you define "compassion"? Do you know a compassionate person? (Maybe it is you.) How would you describe this person? Write two or three paragraphs describing "compassion" and the compassionate person that you know. Use some of the adverb and adverbial phrases from the box.*

> "Compassion" is . . .
>
> When realizing . . .
>
> Upon learning about . . .
>
> By being available, . . .
>
> Having the opportunity, . . .
>
> While waiting . . .
>
> Wanting to help . . .
>
> Having found a good friend, . . .
>
> If called upon to do boring or unpleasant tasks, . . .

# Connectors

*Read the transcript from "Around the Stars," a television show about news and gossip from Hollywood. There are twenty-five uses of connectors. The first one is already underlined. Find and underline twenty-four more.*

Good evening, ladies and gentlemen. We are here to bring you the latest news from Hollywood.

First of all, a major new studio has been created. The three biggest motion picture producers have just joined forces to form the core of a new studio. As a result, Big Three Productions, as it is going to be named, will be the largest studio ever in Hollywood. Moreover, it has more money behind it than any studio in Hollywood has ever had. In addition, seven megastars have joined the group as junior partners; therefore, they will have a financial interest in the success of the company. Big Three Productions is expected to produce excellent financial results from the start.

There are, however, several lawsuits pending against the three partners, because of the complicated business dealings they had with their previous studios. For instance, the ex-wife of one of the partners has brought a lawsuit against him; she claims that he and their previous studio owe her $7 million for her starring role in *Turner Towers*. She left the movie set because she couldn't get along with the director; nevertheless, she says that she vividly recollects being fired by the director, so she was prevented from making a living.

Next, we have reports that movie queen Rosalinda Rock has finally found happiness. She and actor Fox Craft were married secretly last month in a small town in Nevada. There had been reports that Fox was involved with an Italian starlet, but these reports have turned out to be false. Rosalinda and Fox are on their honeymoon now; afterwards, they'll be in residence at their home in Sun Valley, or they'll be at their beach house in Santa Monica. Fox gave Rosalinda a diamond-and-emerald necklace as a wedding present; he had already given her a 10-carat diamond ring several weeks earlier. Rosalinda says she wants to stay home, at one of her homes, to have children while enjoying domestic life. She's going off to Tahiti right after the honeymoon, nonetheless, for several months on location.

Finally, nobody can predict who this year's winners of the Academy Awards are going to be. First, the pictures this year seem better than ever before. For example, the adventure story *Running in Space* has stunned everyone with its special effects, and it has impressed the critics with its incredible plot. It's a definite contender for the best picture award. Likewise, *I Remember When*—a beautiful film that taps into everyone's nostalgia—moved even the most macho of men to tears. On the other hand, the award could go to any one of several fine comedies, or the brilliant horror movie *Drackenstein* might be the first of its genre to win.

The suspense over the Academy Awards is tremendous, and everybody is eagerly awaiting the big night. Meanwhile, join us again every night at 9:00 to learn more of what's really going on Around the Stars.

## EXERCISE 2: Using Connectors

*Complete the sentences on the left with the correct clauses or phrases on the right. Write the letters in the correct blanks.*

1. Hurricanes and earthquakes are similar because ___f___.

2. However, an earthquake is even more terrifying just because _____.

3. An earthquake gives no warning; on the other hand, _____.

4. Weather satellites, in fact, send signals, so _____.

5. Consequently, people can prepare for hurricanes by _____.

6. Additionally, they can _____.

7. If you don't live in a coastal area, you can stay in your home; otherwise, _____.

8. Many people in places like Florida are experienced in making preparations for hurricanes, since _____.

9. An area may be prepared; nevertheless, _____.

a. there is plenty of warning before a hurricane

b. putting up shutters to protect their homes

c. you are advised to move inland to a higher area

d. a lot of hurricanes occur there

e. it can still suffer extensive damage

f. they can both cause extensive damage

g. the weather bureau can issue warnings several days in advance

h. make sure that they have enough food and flashlight batteries

i. it strikes so suddenly

*Read the text of an email from Ricardo to Marco. Cross out the connectors that are NOT*
*appropriate in the sentences. Cross out either one or two items in each underlined set. Pay*
*attention to the punctuation.*

Dear Marco,

Now I'm really worried about you. I'm the one who's always asking for advice, ~~and~~ / but / yet this
**1.**
time, I'm the one who's giving it. I'm the one who is always in a mess; <u>however / besides / instead</u>,
**2.**
this time you're the one in trouble.

<u>First / Next / Finally</u>, no matter what, you have to get a hold of yourself. <u>Yet / Therefore /</u>
**3.**                                                                                                                    **4.**
<u>Otherwise</u>, you are going to spiral downward and feel worse and worse. <u>Furthermore / In contrast /</u>
**5.**
<u>In addition</u>, you won't be able to do anything well—studying, <u>for instance / for example /</u>
**6.**
<u>nevertheless</u>, or even winning at cards—in this depressed mood that you're in. <u>And / But / Plus</u> Lisa
**7.**
or any other young woman you may meet is going to find you very boring, <u>moreover / however / so</u>
**8.**
you'll definitely find yourself without a girlfriend. <u>Therefore / Otherwise / Nor</u>, even though you feel
**9.**
terrible, you've got to get out in the world again. <u>However / For instance / Nevertheless</u>, you
**10.**
mentioned that other girls had asked you to dinner—you should accept their invitations. Who
knows? You might have a wonderful dinner. <u>Plus / Besides / Instead</u>, you might even find a really
**11.**
pleasant relationship.

Now, enough about you. Let's get back to me. I got fired. I was doing everything right, <u>finally / but / so</u>
**12.**
I still got fired. It was a terrible experience. <u>Thus / Furthermore / Nor</u>, it couldn't have happened at a
**13.**
worse time: I'd just found out my landlord is raising the rent.

I'll hang in there, <u>and / though / therefore</u> I'll let you know when I find a new job. <u>In the meantime /</u>
**14.**                                                                                                                     **15.**
<u>Therefore / So</u>, I hope to have some better news from you soon.

—Ricardo

*Read the passage from an education journal. Circle the letter of the phrase that most logically completes each sentence.*

Though all the students in a single classroom have the same textbook, the same teacher, and essentially the same learning situation, it is generally accepted that individual students learn in different ways. Since every student has a different learning style, every student develops a unique set of learning strategies.

1. In addition to _____ , there are also differences in testing styles.

   **a.** differences in learning styles

   **b.** the types of questions

   **c.** all of the students working together

2. Consequently, the type of question that the student is being asked _____ .

   **a.** is not the single most important area to be considered here

   **b.** can have a strong impact on how well a student does on a particular exam

   **c.** is pegged to a large standardized test

3. Some students, for example, perform well with objective questions, such as multiple-choice items. This category also _____ .

   **a.** is the main part of many university examinations, at both the undergraduate and graduate levels

   **b.** includes true–false, matching, and completion or fill-in-the-blank questions

   **c.** emphasizes multiple choice because it is easier for the teacher to score many papers quickly

4. In contrast, other students prefer discussion questions because _____ .

   **a.** they do not like to talk to others very much

   **b.** their English comprehension is at a surprisingly low level of development

   **c.** they are good at organizing their ideas in an essay format

5. Students in this latter group may not be good at multiple-choice questions, nor _____ .

   **a.** are they able to do highly complex problems in mathematics and science

   **b.** are they likely to do well with essay questions

   **c.** are they skilled at true–false or other objective types of questions

*(continued on next page)*

**6.** In an ideal classroom situation, students would have exams that matched their preferred

   testing styles. However, _____.

   **a.** this is not practical

   **b.** this would consume too much paper

   **c.** this idea merits further attention from educators

**7.** It is simply not possible for a teacher to write 30 distinct exams for 30 individual students.

   The only thing that students can do, therefore, is to _____.

   **a.** concentrate on the kind of question that they do best with

   **b.** encourage other students to study as much as possible

   **c.** develop strategies for dealing with all kinds of exam questions

**8.** In fact, this is exactly what good learners do. Because good learners _____, they are

   successful on all kinds of exams and have therefore been labeled "good learners."

   **a.** concentrate on the kind of question that they do best with

   **b.** encourage their peers to study as much as possible

   **c.** develop strategies for dealing with all kinds of exam questions

## EXERCISE 5: Maintaining a Good Flow of Ideas with Connectors

*Read the online chat between Marco and Ricardo. Complete the sentences with the correct connector from the words and phrases in each box.*

| |
|---|
| **MARCO:** Hey, Ricardo. I see you're on chat. |

| |
|---|
| **RICARDO:** Hey, Marco. What's up? |

| furthermore | however | in contrast | otherwise |
|---|---|---|---|

| |
|---|
| **MARCO:** I got your email. You are really direct, and ____furthermore____ you are right. I have to shape<br>                                                                            **1.**<br>up. I have to forget about Lisa; _____, this is very hard to do.<br>                                              **2.** |

| |
|---|
| **RICARDO:** Right. How are you gonna do that? |

| afterwards | although | meanwhile | though |
|---|---|---|---|

**MARCO:** The problem is that I can't forget about her. She will be in my memory forever. We had been

spending so much time together. I am trying to forget her, _____.

                                                  **3.**

**RICARDO:** You have to meet someone else.

**MARCO:** Yes, I am doing other things and, _____, I am trying to meet another great gal.

                                                 **4.**

**RICARDO:** Lots of luck!

| because | besides | in spite of | otherwise |
|---|---|---|---|

**MARCO:** And you? So you lost another job.

**RICARDO:** Yeah.

**MARCO:** You have to keep the next job, when you actually get one. You have to get a better attitude.

_____ you'll keep losing job after job!

          **5.**

**RICARDO:** I know you're right, friend, but please don't lecture me.

**MARCO:** OK, OK! Well, here's what I hope. I hope that you find a good job, and _____

                                                                         **6.**

that, that you keep it.

| because | however | in spite of | plus |
|---|---|---|---|

**RICARDO:** And I hope that you find a nice girl. _____ you pass all your courses.

                                                 **7.**

**MARCO:** _____ the bad luck we've had, I think that there is hope for us!

             **8.**

*Correct the composition for a college English class. There are twelve errors in the use of connectors. The first one is already corrected. Find and correct eleven more. Do not change word order or punctuation. Sometimes more than one answer is correct.*

**WHY I PLAY BASKETBALL**

I'm the center on my basketball team. I like to play basketball for a lot of reasons:

~~Next~~ *First*, I like the teamwork. It really feels good to be part of a group whose members depend on each other. In contrast, when I throw the ball to one of my teammates, I know that he will almost certainly catch it. We have practiced hundreds of times but have perfected our skills pretty well. Thus, a win is due not only to a teammate's scoring, but in part to my passing, and in part to each member of the team.

Second, I like the competition. I like the feeling of playing to win, nor the adrenaline rush when you know that you have to fight hard; otherwise, your heart beats faster, you breathe more rapidly, and you sweat a lot.

Third, I like the physical exercise. I think pushing myself to my physical limit is good for my body. It regulates the glucose level, among other things. I am not afraid of overdoing the exercise, nor do I have fears of being hurt during a game.

Finally, I like the glory. I love it when the crowd roars to encourage us, and I love it when I hear the cheerleaders shouting my name. However, it sure makes a guy feel important to be recognized around town as a big hero.

Are there any drawbacks? Yes. It's terrific to play basketball, because there are some negative aspects. Being part of a team is great; furthermore, you have to practice all the time and you don't have much of a private life. Playing in competition is exciting, moreover you don't get much chance to relax. Getting all that physical exercise feels wonderful; therefore, you might get seriously hurt. (A guy I know was temporarily paralyzed because the left lobe of his brain had been injured.) In fact, there's a negative aspect to each of the things I like about basketball, and these drawbacks are relatively unimportant.

In conclusion, I totally enjoy being a basketball player although I love the teamwork, the competition, the physical exercise, and the glory.

## EXERCISE 7: Personal Writing

*Do you sometimes forget things like people's names or where you left your keys? Possibly your parents or grandparents do. Are there any actions you can take (or someone else could take) to improve memory? Write two or three paragraphs about being forgetful and about steps that can improve a person's memory. Use appropriate connectors. Use some of the phrases from the box.*

**EXAMPLE:**   1. I am / _____ is always forgetting things.

OR

2. I think that I / _____ could improve (my / his / her) memory by . . .

---

_____ is / am always forgetting something. Consequently, . . .

_____ is / am very absent-minded. Therefore, . . .

It's sometimes easier to remember things if you peg the idea to . . .

A football player I've heard of had a serious head injury, so . . .

You can hurt yourself if you play football without a helmet. Moreover, . . .

If you ride a bicycle, wear a helmet. Furthermore, . . .

Because I / _____ forgot to lock the door, . . .

Although I / _____ locked the door, . . .

---

## UNIT 22 Conditionals; Other Ways to Express Unreality

### EXERCISE 1: Recognizing Unreal Conditionals

*Read the article from the website of a chocolate manufacturer. There are nine unreal conditional sentences. The first one is underlined. Find and underline eight more.*

# CHARLOTTE'S CHOCOLATES

| Home | Order Online | Factory Tour | **History of Chocolate** | Contact Us |

Dictionaries define *chocoholic* as a person who has an obsession for chocolate. The world is full of chocoholics. Yet, if an unusual sequence of events had not occurred, these people would probably never have tasted chocolate.

Chocolate was unknown outside of the Americas until the early 1500s. That's when it was discovered that the Aztec Indians there drank a delicious, dark, foamy beverage called *chocolatl*, made from the beans of the native cacao plant. These cacao beans were so highly valued in the area that they were used by the natives as money in the marketplaces; a pumpkin could be bought for 4 cacao beans, for example, and a rabbit could be bought for 10. The Aztecs evidently had chocoholics as well as chocolate. Their king, Montezuma, normally drank 50 pitchers of *chocolatl* a day; it is said that if he didn't, he felt a very strong physical need for it.

When the Europeans first tasted chocolate, it was too bitter for their tastes, so they added sugar to it, If they hadn't added sugar, they wouldn't have been able to consume it. With the added sugar, they liked the drink very much and brought it back to Spain. Chocolate first appeared in Europe as a thick, sugared, chilled beverage. Soon chocolate houses, like coffee houses, sprang up; however, only the rich people could enjoy the drink because of its high cost. The common people could have enjoyed chocolate much sooner if it hadn't been so expensive. It remained largely a privilege of the rich until the invention of the steam engine, which made mass production possible in the late 1700s. If the steam engine had not been invented, mass production of chocolate would not have been possible at the time.

Doctors of the era reported that chocolate was an effective medicine which gave people energy. When people wanted to feel stronger quickly, they could take some chocolate. Chocolate contains theobromine, a substance similar to caffeine; it is actually the theobromine which causes people to feel energized after drinking chocolate. If chocolate didn't contain theobromine, it wouldn't have the stimulating effect that it has.

Chocolate was primarily a beverage until the 1800s, when a Swiss chocolatier discovered that chocolate combined well with milk solids. If that chocolate maker had not made the discovery, chocolate would not have evolved into the solid milk chocolate that we know. Of course, someone else would probably have invented the solid milk chocolate if the chocolatier hadn't already invented it. Since solid chocolate was invented, we have had chocolate candy, chocolate cakes, chocolate cookies, and chocolate ice cream, and many people all over the world enjoy chocolate.

While too much chocolate is not good for you, recent medical reports have brought good news to chocoholics. Dark chocolate is healthful! Dark chocolate contains a large number of antioxidants, which help destroy bad things in the body. A small bar of it every day can help keep your heart and cardiovascular system in good condition. Says one chocoholic who has chocolate every day, "Quite frankly, if I had a day without chocolate, it would be like a day without sunshine."

## EXERCISE 2: Relating Unreal Conditions to Real Conditions

*Read these sentences expressing unreal conditions. After each one, write new sentences that express the real condition.*

1. If chocolate weren't so delicious, people wouldn't crave it.

   Chocolate *is* _____ *delicious* _____.

   People _____ *crave it* _____.

2. If chocolate hadn't been brought back to Europe by explorers, it might not be popular today.

   Chocolate _____.

   It _____.

3. If air-conditioning hadn't been developed in the 20th century, beastly hot places like Florida would not have become popular locations to live.

   Air-conditioning _____.

   Places like Florida _____.

*(continued on next page)*

**4.** If sweltering tropical areas didn't have air-conditioning, people couldn't live there comfortably.

Sweltering tropical areas _____.

People _____.

**5.** If dinosaurs still roamed the Earth, humans wouldn't be living today.

Dinosaurs _____.

Humans _____.

**6.** If butterflies didn't have wings, they couldn't flutter over flowers.

Butterflies _____.

They _____.

**7.** If it weren't raining, we could hail a taxi. But since the weather is so bad, there aren't enough

taxis for all the people who want one.

It's _____.

We _____.

**8.** If I had a larger bureau, there would be enough room in it for all my socks, T-shirts,

and underwear.

I _____.

There _____.

**9.** If Sam didn't love Sue, he wouldn't have given her that nice engagement ring as a token of his

love and commitment.

Sam _____.

He _____.

**10.** If I knew how to speak Russian, I wouldn't mutilate the language the way I do. My Russian

is terrible!

I _____.

I _____.

## EXERCISE 3: Matching Real and Unreal Conditional Clauses in the Present and Future

*Complete the **if** clauses on the left with the result clauses on the right. Write the letters in the correct blanks.*

1. If the temperature goes down to 0° C (32° F), ___k___.
2. If the temperature were 0° C (32° F) right now, _____.
3. If a plant doesn't have water and light, _____.
4. If this plant had some water and light, _____.
5. If this water in this pot were at 100° C (212° F), _____.
6. If water reaches a temperature of 100° C (212° F), _____.
7. If it snowed in Costa Rica, _____.
8. If it snows in Alaska, _____.
9. If a rock is thrown into the water, _____.
10. If this boat developed a leak, _____.
11. If a dog senses danger, _____.
12. If that dog sensed danger, _____.
13. If an egg falls on the floor, _____.
14. If that egg fell on the floor, _____.

a. it barks
b. it won't live
c. it's not unusual
d. water would freeze
e. it would bark
f. it sinks
g. it boils
h. it breaks
i. it would grow
j. it would sink
k. water freezes
l. it would break
m. it would be unusual
n. it would be boiling

## EXERCISE 4: Forming Unreal Conditionals

*Read the facts about geography. Complete the unreal conditional sentences by writing **if** clauses and result clauses. Base the clauses on the information in the preceding sentences.*

### FACTS FROM AROUND THE WORLD

1. The Panama Canal connects the Atlantic and Pacific oceans in the middle of the Americas.

   Ships don't have to travel around the tip of South America to go from New York to California.

   *If the Panama Canal didn't connect the Atlantic and Pacific oceans* _____,

   ships would have to travel around the tip of South America to go from New York to California.

2. Saudi Arabia is an oil-rich country. It is a major exporter of oil.

   _____,

   it would not be a major exporter of oil.

3. Oranges don't grow in Canada. As a result, Canada imports oranges.

   If oranges grew in Canada, _____.

*(continued on next page)*

**4.** Thailand has a tropical climate. As a result, rubber trees grow there.

_____,

rubber trees wouldn't grow there.

**5.** Coffee was brought from Africa and planted in Brazil. Brazil became a large producer

of coffee.

If coffee hadn't been brought from Africa and planted in Brazil, _____

_____.

**6.** Russia is such a large country that it has 11 time zones.

If Russia were not such a large country, _____.

**7.** The Chinese government has made huge efforts to save the panda. Because of this, the panda

population has not declined in recent years.

_____,

the panda population would have declined in recent years.

## EXERCISE 5: Forming Real and Unreal Conditionals in the Present and Future

**A.** *Read Divya's blog, or online journal. Complete the blog by writing the present unreal conditional forms of the verbs. Use the words in parentheses, changing the verb forms where necessary and adding **did** or **would** as necessary. Use contractions where appropriate.*

| DIVYA'S BLOG | Home | Blog | CV | Life |

**NOVEMBER 24:**

I have just come from yet another family dinner where I had to endure all the questions

from family members about why I am not married. This really upsets me! They don't have

an inkling about how I feel. I'm not married because I choose not to be.

_____ *If I chose to be married, I would be married* _____.

　　　　　**1. (I / choose / be married / I / be married)**

Actually, part of the reason is that I never meet anyone I really like. In fact, I meet a lot of

weirdos, so it's better to go out with my friends, and better not to get involved with anyone.

Perhaps, if _____.

　　　**2. (I / meet / the right man / I / have a different feeling about it)**

As usual, everyone was worried about me, thinking that I'm lonely, and giving me too much

advice! If _____. But I have a
   **3. (I / not have / a lot of friends / I / be lonely)**

lot of friends, so I'm fine. Maybe if _____.
                                   **4. (I / not like / my job / I / be unhappy)**

But I like my job a lot. I'm tired of being nagged about the subject of marriage all the time.

I really wish _____.
            **5. (people / won't leave / me alone)**

   Actually, though, I wouldn't mind having a partner in life. If only

_____! Not to sound greedy,
   **6. (I / can / meet / the perfect man tomorrow)**

but sometimes I wish _____
                 **7. (I / have / it all)**

—a successful career, travel, an active social life, and a husband and children. I think I could

manage it. In fact, my intuition tells me that Mr. Right will be coming along very soon.

Hey, gals—are you having the same problems with your family? Post your comments on

this blog.

**B.** *Read the comments posted to Divya's blog. Complete the sentences by writing present or future real conditional forms, using the words in parentheses. Add* **do, does,** *or* **will** *where necessary. Use contractions where appropriate.*

**DIVYA'S BLOG**                    Home    Blog    CV    Life

COMMENTS:

Hey, Divya! You gotta put up with your family! They really do mean the best for you, you

know. Here's what to do: If _____ nagging, just smile and
                        **1. (they / start)**

say nothing. Every time. Eventually they'll stop.                    *Posted by: Betsy*

*(continued on next page)*

I find that's often a good idea: to say nothing. As the saying goes, "It's better to keep silent

and be thought a fool than to speak and remove all doubt." If I have something to say,

_____ because I prefer to at least keep the illusion of
        **2. (I / often / not / say it)**

being intelligent!                                                          *Posted by: Tania*

---

I think you need assertiveness training, Tania. This is not about intelligence. If you don't state

your opinions or feelings, _____, and you are going to
                            **3. (nobody / understand / you)**

feel hurt. Your opinions and feelings are as valuable as anybody else's.      *Posted by: Ruth*

---

Well, I often keep myself from speaking too, but for a different reason. If

_____, I will be able to listen. I like to think about what
        **4. (I / not / speak)**

people are saying before I speak. And I hope they listen to me too.           *Posted by: Sandy*

---

Mr. Right may or may not come along. You are having a good life with or without him. Tell

that to your family. Tell them that you are having a good life even if

_____.                                        *Posted by: Ted*
        **5. (Mr. Right / not come along)**

Divya, I think your intuition is right. The right guy is going to come along soon. If

_____, you will know it right away.      *Posted by: Maria*
        **6. (Mr. Right / come / along)**

## EXERCISE 6: Forming Unreal Conditionals in the Past Time

*Read the text of an email from Marco to Ricardo. Complete the email by writing past unreal conditional forms, using the words in parentheses. Use contractions where appropriate.*

Dear Ricardo,

All's well that ends well, as Shakespeare said. Even though a lot of bad things happened to me,

my year here in the United States has actually been pretty good. First, and most important, I met

Suzie. It's a good thing, because if I _____ *hadn't met* _____ Suzie, I would have been
                                        **1. (meet / not)**

suffering over Lisa for a really long time. Suzie has taken over my life, and everything is better

since I met her, including the food. Yes, Suzie is a wonderful cook. If I had known Suzie earlier, I

__wouldn't have had to eat / wouldn't have eaten__ all those terrible meals at the beginning of the semester. If I had
**2. (not / have to / eat)**

known Suzie earlier, I __wouldn't have been__ so lonesome and homesick then, and I
**3. (not / be)**

__would never have suffered / never would have suffered__ over Lisa like a stupid, lovesick puppy the way that I did. If only I
**4. (never / suffer)**

__had met__ Suzie when I first came here!
**5. (meet)**

 Enough about me! You're doing fine, Ricardo, even though things didn't work out at the hotel. It's

great that you got a new job, and it sounds very glamorous to be the assistant to a movie director!

As my mother always says, "Things work out for the best," and for you it's true! Who knows? Maybe

you'll even become a movie star yourself. Of course, you might become very snobbish as a movie star

and wish that you __had never met__ me or anybody else from our childhood. But I
**6. (never / meet)**

don't think that will happen.

 Actually, I wish that the bad stuff this year __hadn't happened__, but as I said,
**7. (not / happen)**

everything's turning out OK. You have a great and glamorous new job, you're paying off your

debts, and you have a future. I will finish school here, and I have a wonderful new girlfriend.

If we __hadn't made__ some of the mistakes we did, these good things
**8. (not / make)**

__would've passed__ us by. What you should do is visit me here in the United States
**9. (pass)**

when you are between movies, or maybe when you come to the United States "on location."


See you soon, I hope.

—Marco


## EXERCISE 7: Editing

*Read about a situation in a law office. There are seventeen mistakes in the use of
conditionals and other ways to express unreality. The first mistake is already corrected.
Find and correct sixteen more.*

### What is the situation?

Robert and Cynthia are good friends and are both lawyers at the Marks and Hobbs law firm.

 *is*
They both hope to be selected as partners at the end of the year. If a person ~~will be~~ selected to be a

 *will have*
partner, he or she will become a part-owner of the law firm and therefore, ~~would had~~ a secure

*(continued on next page)*

future there. Robert and Cynthia's supervisor, Henry Marks, has told Robert that he is likely to get a partnership at the end of the year but that Cynthia isn't. *Should Robert tell Cynthia this?*

## What should Robert do?

*He should tell her. (And he might tell her.)* If Cynthia had not become a partner, she will have no future in the firm. Robert and Cynthia are good friends, and they should be honest with each other. If Cynthia will find out the truth now, she can get another job. Furthermore, if Robert would not tell her, he will have to lie to Cynthia for the rest of the year. In addition, Robert should think, "If the situation is reversed, would I want to know the truth?" The answer is "Yes."

*He shouldn't tell her, and in fact, he has decided not to tell her. He thinks:* If he has told her, it would destroy the confidence that his boss has in him. In fact, if Robert would broke the confidence, he himself might not be promoted; Henry would lost confidence in him.

## What happened?

Robert told Cynthia, who confronted Henry. Henry, of course, was angry at Robert for breaking a trust, and he told Robert that he was no longer a candidate for the promotion.

## What does everyone think now?

*Robert*: What a mistake! I wish I don't tell Cynthia! She could have worked happily for the remainder of the year if I haven't told her. My intuition told me that I shouldn't tell her in order to spare her feelings; however, my desire to be honest with her was more important to me. But it ended badly for both of us. If I hadn't told her, I will be in line for a promotion now. Now neither of us will be promoted.

*Cynthia*: I appreciate Robert's friendship, but I'm really sorry he has lost his own opportunity. If I am Robert and the situation be reversed—would I have told him? Maybe not.

*Henry*: I never should have told Robert anything. If I had kept the information to myself, none of this would had happened. Now I have lost the trust and confidence of two good colleagues. I wish I have their confidence again, but that's not possible. If only it is easy to be the boss of this law firm!

## EXERCISE 8: Personal Writing

*Have you ever had an intuition about something that turned out to be correct? Perhaps you felt a warning about something bad about to happen. Or maybe you had a feeling that if you did a certain thing, you would have good luck. Write two or three paragraphs about an intuition that you have had. Use some of the phrases from the box.*

```
If I hadn't . . .
If I didn't . . .
If I were . . .
If my friend had . . .
If my friend hadn't . . .
If my friend were . . .
If I had . . .
If I am . . .
I wish that . . .
If I . . .
I hope that . . .
```

## EXERCISE 1: Recognizing Implied and Inverted Conditions and Subjunctives in Noun Clauses

*Read this passage. If the underlined material is an implied condition, write **IMP** above it. If it is an inverted condition, write **INV**. Then find and circle the three clauses with subjunctive verbs.*

### THE CAN OPENER: Where Would We Be Without It?

It is difficult to imagine life today *INV* <u>had the can opener not been invented</u>. <u>Without the simple little tool</u> that we take for granted, how would we open cans? It is essential that we have the can opener to gain the enormous convenience that the use of canned goods gives us. <u>Were there no can openers</u>, we wouldn't be able to so easily consume all the foods that we do. <u>Were there no can openers</u>, we would not be eating the canned meats, the prepared sauces, the familiar soups, or the out-of-season fruits and vegetables that are so much a part of our daily lives. <u>But for canned tuna</u>, the tuna sandwich most likely wouldn't have become popular.

First developed in England in 1810, the first "tin canisters" were actually made of iron and were sometimes heavier than the food they contained. British soldiers in the War of 1812 opened cans of food with bayonets or knives, or when those methods failed, they would shoot their rifles at the cans to open them. <u>A better way to open cans had to be found; if not</u>, the soldiers would continue with their unreliable and sometimes dangerous methods of opening the heavy containers.

Within a few years, the cans began to be made of a lighter metal. Then in 1858, a "can opener" was devised. This opener looked like a curved bayonet, and <u>it had to be used correctly. If not</u>, it could be lethal. It was used during the U.S. Civil War in the early 1860s, although it was far from perfect. <u>Had the U.S. military not discovered this primitive can opener</u> during that period, it would soon have become extinct. Clearly, though, a better can opener was needed. Necessity demanded there be a tool that safely and easily opened tin cans, and in 1870 that device was finally invented: William J. Lyman patented the prototype of the modern can opener. With this new device, people could now open tin cans easily, and the demand for canned goods grew. By 1895, canned goods were a familiar sight on grocery store shelves. <u>Without canned goods</u>, no grocery store would last long.

How fortunate we are that lightweight cans and easy-to-use <u>can openers were invented</u>; <u>otherwise</u>, we would not have the convenience and variety in foods that we do today. More than convenience, a can opener is one of the necessities of life; <u>should there be an emergency</u>, such as a long power outage, canned foods—and thus, a can opener—would be of top importance. It is absolutely necessary that every family have a can opener, right along with flashlights and batteries.

## EXERCISE 2: Choosing Phrases in Inverted and Implied Conditions and Subjunctives

*Read the direct mail ad from National Neatniks, an organization that organizes the rooms in your house. Circle the correct words or phrases to complete the sentences.*

 # National Neatniks, Inc.
We will make your home organized, beautiful, and happy.

Do you think you are a slob? You are not! (Were you)/ Are you really a slob, you <u>would not be / be will not</u>
1.                          2.
looking for help to organize your home.

Our company, National Neatniks, will get you organized quickly. We organize your kitchen, family room, bedroom, home office, or garage and show you how to stay organized. With your cooperation, we <u>will have/ would have had</u> a basic reorganization plan for your home within half a day. From the
3.
doormat everyone steps on in front of your front door, through the well-ordered rooms, to the inviting patio and backyard, your whole house and whole life will be in good order and serene.

*(continued on next page)*

No place for all your pots and pans and dishes? We can help! We will maximize every inch of kitchen space that you have. With a plan, we <u>had arranged / can arrange</u> all your things neatly. We will
**4.**
recommend that each item <u>would be put / be put</u> in a certain place, that others <u>be given / were given</u>
**5.** **6.**
away, and that others <u>be thrown / would otherwise be thrown</u> into the trash.
**7.**

Teenager's bedroom a pigsty? Lighten up! We'll clean up his room and organize everything. Teenagers are not usually cooperative and flexible, but we have experience with intransigent teenagers. You don't have to be the overbearing parent who demands <u>for the room to be neat / that</u>
**8.**
<u>the room be neat</u>; we will do that job for you. Is your home office a mess? No problem! We will organize your files, streamline all your paperwork, and get more than a semblance of order into your office in less than a day.

Let us assess your mess. We will give you a written estimate of the time that will be involved in the reorganization. We will propose that the rooms <u>be organized / organize</u> according to an overall plan,
**9.**
and we will follow this plan through to completion. <u>Without / With</u> a good plan, we would not get the
**10.**
beautiful results that we are accustomed to getting. So, you may be feeling that you are at the end of your rope, but you are not! With our help, you will right your ship very quickly.

Here's what some of our clients say about us:

• National Neatniks are the best! Without them, I <u>don't get / would never have gotten</u> the smooth-
**11.**
running routine that I now have in my kitchen. Everything is perfect.

*from Harriet*

• My husband and I heartily love National Neatniks. They cleaned up our home office so beautifully. They insisted <u>that my husband get rid of / for my husband to get rid of</u> boxes of old papers, and it
**12.**
has made room for a new printer/fax/scanner/copier machine, a new chair, a new bookshelf, and even a mini-refrigerator.

*from Olga*

• I couldn't believe it! National Neatniks actually got my teenager to straighten up his room. They put in shelves and drawers, and there was a place for everything besides on the floor or on the bed. <u>Did I not see / Had I not seen</u> it with my own eyes, I <u>would never have believed / don't believe</u> it!
**13.** **14.**

*from Marzo315*

- National Neatniks lives up to its name. They told us it was advisable <u>that we put up / that we</u>

  **15.**

  <u>will put up</u> shelves in the garage, and now we are so proud of having the neatest, most beautiful

  garage in town, thanks to the neatness obsession of the Neatniks.

*from Kim*

## EXERCISE 3: Using Inverted and Implied Conditional Forms in the Past Time

*Complete the following answers to questions on an American history examination. Fill in the blanks with the appropriate conditional forms of the verbs in parentheses. Use* **would** *in the result clauses unless another auxiliary is indicated.*

1. The American colonists formally gained their independence from England in 1783. Had

   the Americans _____*not gained*_____ their independence from England, America
   
   **(not / gain)**

   _____*would have remained*_____ a British colony.
   
   **(remain)**

2. George Washington was known in all the American colonies because he was a general who

   fought in the Revolutionary War. Had George Washington _____ in
   
   **(not / fight)**

   the Revolutionary War, he _____ in all the American colonies.
   
   **(not / know)**

3. In the American Civil War, fought from 1861 to 1865, the North had greater resources and

   finally won the war. Without these resources, the North _____ the
   
   **(might / not / win)**

   Civil War.

4. The railroads were very important to the development of the American West and

   directly contributed to the growth of California. Without the railroads, California

   _____ as quickly as it did.
   
   **(not / grow)**

5. In 1903, the Wright brothers flew the first successful airplane, and thus began the era of

   aviation. It was the first and most notable flight, but others had been close to flying successes

   too. Had the Wright brothers _____ in their flight, it is likely that
   
   **(not / succeed)**

   someone else _____ shortly thereafter.
   
   **(succeed)**

6. By the mid-20th century, life in America had changed because of the automobile. For one

   thing, many people moved from the city to the suburbs. But for the automobile, the suburbs

   _____ so quickly.
   
   **(not developed)**

*(continued on next page)*

7. By the 1970s, the bald eagle—the national symbol of the United States—had become an endangered species. However, due to strong efforts by environmentalists, the eagle is no longer endangered. It's a good thing that environmentalists made their efforts; otherwise, the bald eagle _____ extinct.
**(already / become)**

## EXERCISE 4: Using Inverted and Implied Conditional Forms in the Past Time

*Read the statements about modern inventions. Complete the corresponding conditional sentences that express the opposite situations. Use* **would** *or* **wouldn't.**

How do major inventions change our lives? Think of how life over the centuries has been changed by various inventions.

1. We have can openers, with which we are able to open cans.

   Without can openers, *we wouldn't be able to open cans* .

2. By using forks and chopsticks, we don't have to use our fingers to eat.

   Without forks and chopsticks, _____.

3. Because electricity was discovered, we have electric lights, movies, television, and computers.

   Had electricity _____.

4. Jet planes did not exist 100 years ago; people did not travel extensively then.

   Had jet planes _____.

5. Television is available throughout the world; as a result, fashion, music, and basic values are very similar in many places.

   Were television _____.

6. Because computers were developed, businesses are able to obtain the data they need to function in today's world.

   Had computers _____.

7. With computers, the general public has easy access to extensive information.

   Without computers, _____.

8. A person who has a cellular phone is able to communicate from remote places.

   Should a person not _____.

## EXERCISE 5: Forming Implied and Inverted Conditions

*Read the statements of common facts. Complete the conditional sentences that follow.*
*Describe different outcomes in the past or present, or possible outcomes for the future.*

1. The original Olympic Games were played in ancient Greece and inspired the modern Olympic Games of today.

   Had *the original Olympic Games not been played in ancient Greece, they would not have*

   *inspired the modern Olympic Games of today* .

2. The Roman general Julius Caesar conquered several areas of the world; as a result, people in those areas speak "Romance" languages.

   Had _____

   _____ .

3. The English settled North America, while the Spanish and Portuguese settled South America. As a result, people in North America speak English, not Spanish or Portuguese.

   Had _____

   _____ .

4. Blue jeans were invented in 1849. Everyone all over the world today is wearing blue jeans.

   Had _____

   _____ .

5. Penicillin was discovered in 1928, and because of it, hundreds of millions of lives have been saved.

   Had _____

   _____ .

6. Dolly the sheep was cloned in 1997. This has raised amazing scientific possibilities and troubling ethical questions.

   Had _____

   _____ .

*(continued on next page)*

**7.** There is no gravity in a spaceship. Objects float in the air there.

Were _____

_____ .

**8.** It's possible that the polar ice caps will melt somewhat. In that case, certain coastal areas

might be flooded.

Should _____

_____ .

## EXERCISE 6: Using the Subjunctive in Noun Clauses

*Read the page of advice from a travel guide. Complete the sentences with noun clauses based on the information in parentheses. Use subjunctive verbs.*

### TRAVEL TIPS • When in Rome, Do as the Romans Do

**1.** (A driver must keep to the right-hand side of the road.)

In the United States and many European countries, it is essential *that a driver keep to the*

*right-hand side of the road* .

**2.** (Drivers have to stay on the left side of the road.)

In Japan and England, however, it is mandatory _____

_____ .

**3.** (People should remove their shoes before going inside a house.)

In some places, such as Japan and Saudi Arabia, it is important _____

_____ .

**4.** (People should keep their shoes on.)

In other places, it is expected _____

_____ .

**5.** (People must not eat pork products.)

In some places, religious laws demand _____

_____ .

**6.** (A sick person should be treated with modern medicine.)

In some places, doctors recommend _____

_____ .

**7.** (A sick person should use herbal remedies.)

In other places, they advise _____

_____ .

**8.** (A waiter should be summoned by whistling.)

In some places, it is suggested _____ .

**9.** (A waiter must not be summoned by whistling.)

In other places, it is important _____ ,

_____ ,

because this would be considered exceedingly rude.

**10.** (A traveler ought to learn about customs in various places.)

Logic suggests _____ .

## EXERCISE 7: Editing

*Read this essay. There are seventeen mistakes in the use of implied conditions, inverted conditions, and subjunctives. The first mistake is already corrected. Find and correct sixteen more.*

### What Is Necessary to Have a Perfect World

I have often fantasized about the perfect world. It would be perfect not only for my family and

me, but for everyone.

*were we* OR *if we were*

First of all, ~~we were~~ living in a perfect world, there would be food for everyone. No one would

be starving or without regular sources of food. Second, in this perfect world, everything would been

clean and free of pollution. With clean air and toxin-free water, humans, animals, and plants would

stayed healthy. Third, all diseases would be conquered; we will be free of cancer, AIDS, and heart

disease. Without those diseases, people could lived longer and be free from terrible suffering.

Scientists had already discovered a cure for these diseases, we could now be anticipating a much

longer lifespan. Fourth, were the world in perfect condition, there will be no crime. Societal and

psychological factors would not breed the violence that they do. And last, there would be no wars.

All countries and all peoples would live together, harmoniously, as one.

*(continued on next page)*

While these goals may appear unrealistic, it would be wise not to abandon them. Had diplomats abandoned the idea of one world, we don't have the United Nations today, or other organizations to help global populations. Had scientists given up their search for cures, we will not have found the means to conquer polio, tuberculosis, some types of pneumonia, and many bacteria-caused diseases. Had civic-minded individuals been less tenacious, we did not have cleaned up the cities and water and air as much as we have. Had not we learned and taught better methods of agriculture and food distribution, many more people would be starving today.

What if there are a universal law like this: All the *haves*—those people who *have* a decent life and more than enough material things—must make concrete contributions to a perfect world? Local governments would require that citizens gave a specified amount of time or money each year to a recognized community project. What if it were required by law that young people studying the histories of all major cultures? Knowing about other cultures would have expand people's minds and help them to understand each other better. Would such compulsory programs work? They might. They would, hopefully, help the citizens of the world to think of others who live in different situations. It is absolutely essential that hope are expressed not only in words, but also in actions; otherwise, the world would not be a better place tomorrow than it is today.

*What was a serious problem you faced in the past, and how did you deal with it? How would you advise a dear friend or relative to solve a similar problem today? Write two or three paragraphs about the topic. Use some of the phrases from the box.*

One of the most serious problems I have ever faced was . . .

Had I known at the time that . . .

It was essential that . . .

Without a lot of luck at that time, I . . .

But for . . . , I would have . . .

It's indeed fortunate that this happened. What if . . .

Now, if you are facing a similar problem, . . .

It is advisable that you . . .

In fact, it is urgent that you . . .

I recommend that you get a good lawyer / doctor / counselor / accountant, etc.

Without a good professional, you . . .

You need good professional advice. Otherwise, . . .

You have to solve this problem soon. Furthermore, . . .

# WORKBOOK ANSWER KEY

In this answer key, where the contracted form is given, the full form is often also correct, and where the full form is given, the contracted form is often also correct.

## UNIT 1 (pages 1–8)

### EXERCISE 1

2. begins
3. see
4. are not necessarily reading
5. read
6. have become
7. like
8. are
9. don't need
10. don't weigh
11. always have
12. are traveling
13. prefer
14. feel
15. smell
16. enjoy
17. have been contemplating
18. have decided
19. love

### EXERCISE 2

2. is looking for
3. answers
4. solves
5. have
6. communicate
7. like
8. train
9. pay
10. are trying

### EXERCISE 3

We <u>need</u> higher taxes in this town. Probably nobody <u>believes</u> me, but this is true. Nobody <u>wants</u> to pay more money, but everybody <u>desires</u> more services and a better quality of life. I <u>know</u> that these things are true:

1. We <u>don't have</u> enough police officers. More police officers <u>mean</u> safer streets and safer neighborhoods.
2. We <u>love</u> our children, and we <u>want</u> a good education for them. However, it <u>doesn't appear</u> that we are going to get the smaller classes, pre-kindergarten classes, and proper student advising that our young people <u>deserve</u> until we find more money.
3. We drive on some roads that are in bad condition and are badly lit. We need to fix the roads and put up more and better lighting.

We <u>owe</u> it to ourselves and our children to maintain and improve our community. When our citizens <u>understand</u> the value of their tax contributions, they will <u>not mind</u> paying a little more now toward a better future.

### EXERCISE 4

2. need
3. talk
4. don't use
5. text
6. send
7. 's ringing
8. is happening
9. love
10. travel
11. drive
12. get
13. tells
14. knows
15. directs
16. change
17. want
18. finds
19. am asking
20. is giving
21. download
22. get
23. write
24. record
25. weighs
26. doesn't do
27. does not take
28. is not

### EXERCISE 5

2. (fit) exactly
3. (looks) beautiful
4. (seems) hard
5. (answered) correctly
6. (tastes) delicious
7. (tasted) quickly
8. (sound) good
9. (look) sad
10. (sings) well
11. (am feeling) tired
12. (are) impatient
13. (answered) patiently; (feel) good
14. (seem) clear; (punctuate) clearly

### EXERCISE 6

2. have been waiting
3. is bothering
4. have you been
5. have you had
6. know
7. have taken
8. realize
9. am not
10. is not looking
11. am sitting
12. is sitting
13. have entered
14. input
15. ask
16. do
17. don't / do not leave
18. don't / do not need
19. have
20. are using
21. am sending
22. like
23. saves
24. likes

## EXERCISE 7

*am writing*
I ~~write~~ to you in English today so we can both
*haven't written*
get more practice. Sorry that I ~~don't write~~ sooner, but
I have been really busy. Classes in my intensive
*have been going on*
English program in Chicago ~~are going on~~ for about
*have*
six weeks. The instructors ~~has~~ given homework
*study / have been studying*
every day, and I ~~have been study~~ every night in order
to stay on top of the assignments. In fact, I
*am studying*
~~study~~ right now because I have a big test tomorrow.
Besides that, we have an assignment to write a two-
*have not written*
page essay. It's due tomorrow, but I ~~have not been~~
~~writing~~ it yet. You may remember that I tend to
put difficult things off until the last minute—I am a
procrastinator.

I am complaining about all the homework, but
the truth is that my English is improving rapidly.
*have learned*
Besides in my classes, I ~~have learn~~ a lot of English
in the past six weeks by talking with people around me
in the city. In my apartment building, most people
*speak*      *need*
~~are speaking~~ English, and when I ~~am needing~~
something, I speak to the manager in English. For
example, the plumbing in my apartment often
*have explained*
doesn't work, and I'~~m explaining~~ the problem to the
*know*
manager several times already. Now, I ~~am knowing~~
the plumber pretty well because the same plumber
*comes*
~~is coming~~ every week!

*been*
On the negative side, the weather has ~~being~~
*It's rained / It rains*
terrible this month. ~~It's raining~~ almost every day. In
*miss*
addition, I don't like the food here. I ~~am missing~~ real
home cooking. Of course, I don't do without meals.
*getting*     *'ve lost*
I just don't enjoy them. In fact, I'm ~~get~~ thinner. I ~~lose~~
*talk*
about five kilos so far. And I feel lonely. I'~~m talking~~
*haven't made*
to many people every day, but I ~~don't make~~ any new
*'s happening*
friends yet. What's new with you? What ~~happens~~ at
home? Send me an email soon.

## EXERCISE 8

*Answers will vary.*

## EXERCISE 1

2. had lost
3. died
4. missed
5. would often go
6. fell
7. had had
8. would be
9. was going to see
10. had been dating
11. had accepted
12. used to be
13. broke
14. has recently bought

## EXERCISE 2

| | | |
|---|---|---|
| 2. 1, 2 | 7. S, S | 12. 2, 1 |
| 3. 1, 2 | 8. S, S | 13. 2, 1 |
| 4. 2, 1 | 9. S, S | 14. 1, 2 |
| 5. S, S | 10. 1, 2 | 15. 2, 1 |
| 6. 1, 2 | 11. 1, 2 | |

## EXERCISE 3

2. lived
3. were living
4. would
5. used to be
6. was
7. had risen
8. had been growing
9. continued
10. were benefiting
11. would reach
12. reached
13. have lived

## EXERCISE 4

2. learned
3. was
4. came
5. hadn't passed
6. was studying
7. worked
8. passed
9. established
10. retired
11. had been practicing
12. would treat
13. has been
14. got
15. had been taking
16. got
17. would take
18. have had
19. got
20. have been working
21. used to work
22. got
23. has become
24. arrived
25. hadn't expected
26. would succeed

## EXERCISE 5

| | | |
|---|---|---|
| 2. fix | 6. promises | 10. has |
| 3. is | 7. buy | 11. came |
| 4. call | 8. didn't | 12. going to |
| 5. hasn't | 9. would | 13. will |

## EXERCISE 6

| | | |
|---|---|---|
| 2. b | 6. c | 10. b |
| 3. d | 7. b | 11. b |
| 4. d | 8. a | 12. d |
| 5. a | 9. c | |

## EXERCISE 7

I am writing this blog now, during my last week
*have been*
in this country. I ~~am~~ here as an exchange student
since January 1st of this year, and I'm leaving on
*came*
Friday. When I first ~~have come~~ to this country last
*would*
January, I knew that I ~~will~~ find things very different
than they were at home. And that's good, because the
reason I had decided to come here was to experience
*had*
a completely different culture. I ~~have~~ been studying
English for six years when I left home, and wanted
to know first-hand about life in an English-speaking
culture.
*met*
On January 1st, my host family ~~was meeting~~ me
*liked*
at the airport. I ~~like~~ them immediately and they
*liked*
~~were liking~~ me too. Two days later, I started going
to school with my host sister. I made a lot of new
friends. All year, I studied hard for my classes, played
on the soccer team, and went to parties, just like
American students. Many of my American friends
*had*
~~were having~~ boyfriends or girlfriends. I would always
be interested in them and the people they were
*date*
dating, but I didn't ~~dated~~ anyone. I never wanted to
have a boyfriend myself partly because of all the
drama and heartache and anxiety, but mostly
*going*
because I knew that I was ~~go~~ to have an arranged
marriage. In my country, we don't have the custom
of dating like here. There, parents arrange marriages
for their children.

Of course, everyone in school knew about the
arranged marriages in my country, and they had
a lot of questions for me. They felt sorry for me
because they couldn't imagine marrying anyone they
*love* *force*
didn't ~~loved~~, or that their parents would ~~forced~~ them
to marry. But it isn't like that at home! There, the
parents introduce their children to each other, and
if the couple like each other enough, they marry. If
not, if either of the couple doesn't want the marriage,
their parents look for someone else. By the time I left
*had*
home, my parents ~~have~~ not yet found anyone for me,
but I knew that they were looking, and I knew that
they were going to continue to look until they found
the right husband for me.
*used*
Before I came here, I ~~was used~~ to wonder about
the system of choosing your own spouse. The divorce
rate here is very high. At home, most marriages last,
partly because experienced and loving family play an

important part at the beginning when they choose
the spouse. I see, though, that it is possible—very
possible—to have a happy marriage, arranged or not.
*have*
My host family is an example. The parents ~~had~~ been
married for 25 years, and they have a wonderful life
and a great family. I have learned a lot during my
time here: that there is more than one way to live,
and more than one way to find a good spouse.

## EXERCISE 8

*Answers will vary.*

## UNIT 3 (pages 19–29)

### EXERCISE 1

| | | |
|---|---|---|
| **2.** 1, 2 | **6.** S, S | **10.** 2, 1 |
| **3.** 2, 1 | **7.** 2, 1 | **11.** 1, 2 |
| **4.** 1, 2 | **8.** 2, 1 | **12.** 2, 1 |
| **5.** S, S | **9.** 1, 2 | |

### EXERCISE 2

| | |
|---|---|
| I don't think **P** | I hear **F** |
| I'm sending **P** | I'll be sitting **F** |
| you will improve **F** | waiting **F** |
| I haven't finished it **P**✓ | I'll be going **F** |
| I've written **P**✓ | I will have received **F**✓ |
| I'm also thinking **P** | |
| do you think **P** | |
| are hiring **P** | |
| If I post **F** | |
| I'll get **F** | |
| I probably will have heard **F**✓ | |
| I'll redo **F** | |

### EXERCISE 3

| | |
|---|---|
| **2.** is just starting | **9.** is |
| **3.** 're traveling | **10.** have |
| **4.** will win | **11.** play |
| **5.** will see | **12.** are going to win |
| **6.** will take | **13.** will be traveling |
| **7.** will be playing | **14.** is |
| **8.** will train | |

### EXERCISE 4

| | | | |
|---|---|---|---|
| **2.** b, c, d | **4.** a, b, c | **6.** a, b, c | **8.** a, b, d |
| **3.** a, d | **5.** a, c, d | **7.** b, c | **9.** all correct |

### EXERCISE 5

| | |
|---|---|
| **2.** start | **9.** stop |
| **3.** arrive | **10.** permits |
| **4.** introduce | **11.** return |
| **5.** will board | **12.** will feel |
| **6.** sail | **13.** are going to |
| **7.** are going to see / will be seeing | remember |
| **8.** will describe | **14.** look |

## EXERCISE 6

2. award
3. graduates
4. will have heard
5. will succeed / is going to succeed
6. is going to take / is taking / will take
7. will have been operating
8. will become / is going to become
9. will get / is going to get
10. will we be following
11. will have been working
12. will have traveled / will have been traveling
13. will have seen
14. will have become
15. will have / are going to have

## EXERCISE 7

In 2000, the most populous urban area in the world was Tokyo, and in 2025 it will still ~~is~~ *be* Tokyo.

By that time, the population of Tokyo will ~~gain~~ *have gained* 4 million people, but the population of two cities in India—Bombay and Delhi—~~have~~ *will have* grown a lot more, by more than 10 million people each. In 2025, Bombay will ~~has~~ *have* more than 26 million people.

In 2000, the second most populous urban area was Mexico City. In 2025, Mexico City ~~has~~ *will have* more people than it did in 2000, but it ~~not~~ *will not* be in second place any longer; it will be in sixth place.

The same ~~going~~ *is going* to happen in regard to New York City. In 2000, 18 million people ~~are~~ *were* living there; in 2025 about 2 million more people ~~are~~ *will be* living there.

However, New York will ~~drops~~ *drop* down from third place to seventh place.

The newest big city in 2025 will ~~have been~~ *be* in Bangladesh. Its capital, Dhaka, ^*will* have 22 million people at that time, and it will ~~has~~ *have* become one of the largest urban areas in the world.

Cities that were once among the largest cities of the world—Shanghai and Calcutta—are going ^*to* remain on the list, but they ~~don't will~~ *won't* be at the top of the list anymore. Buenos Aires and Los Angeles will have ~~dropping~~ *dropped* from the list entirely. When 2025

arrives
~~will arrive~~, there ^*will* be more people in large cities in Asia than on any other continent.

## EXERCISE 8

*Answers will vary.*

## UNIT 4 (pages 30–38)

### EXERCISE 1

| | | |
|---|---|---|
| 3. b | 8. b | 13. a |
| 4. a | 9. b | 14. b |
| 5. b | 10. a | 15. b |
| 6. a | 11. a | 16. a |
| 7. a | 12. b | 17. a |

### EXERCISE 2

| | |
|---|---|
| 2. had to | 8. must |
| 3. have to | 9. doesn't have to |
| 4. must | 10. has to |
| 5. 'd better | 11. should have |
| 6. 'd better not | 12. didn't have to |
| 7. are supposed to | 13. have got to |

### EXERCISE 3

| | | | |
|---|---|---|---|
| 2. b | 5. b | 8. b | 11. b |
| 3. c | 6. a | 9. a | |
| 4. c | 7. b | 10. c | |

### EXERCISE 4

2. ~~should~~ / will have to / ~~might~~; had better / should / ~~could~~
3. ~~should not~~ / ~~must not~~ / don't have to; can't / ~~should not~~ / aren't allowed to
4. should / ~~has got to~~ / ought to; shouldn't / ~~is not allowed to~~ / ~~might not~~
5. are not supposed to / shouldn't / ~~must not~~; ~~are not supposed to~~ / are not allowed to / can't
6. ~~must not have to~~ / won't have to / ~~were not supposed to~~; ~~might have~~ / ~~must have~~ / should have

### EXERCISE 5

| | |
|---|---|
| 2. should I buy | 8. was supposed to do |
| 3. have to pay | 9. are supposed to say |
| 4. Should I have bought | 10. will have to come |
| 5. shouldn't have bought | 11. might have turned out |
| 6. had better be | 12. could have brought |
| 7. didn't have to bring | 13. could have gotten |
| | 14. could have been |

## EXERCISE 6

This is a true story about one of my students, Ana. I remember the first day she came to my class:

She couldn't to speak [*couldn't speak*] any English at all. She spoke only Spanish. All the students were supposed to [*C*] speak only English in class, but Ana was able to say only a few words. She felt uncomfortable, but she shouldn't have felt [*C*] that way. The situation was not unusual, and several students were in the same situation.

One time during the holidays between school terms, the dorms were closed, so the students have to find [*had to find*] a place to live during the break. Ana stayed with an American host family, and after the vacation, she asked me what she might to do [*might do*] to thank her new friends for their hospitality.

"Well, you could send [*C*] them a gift," I told her.

"Or you must just send [*could just send*] them a nice card." Ana decided that she will send [*would send*] [*C*] a card. She asked, "Am I supposed to get [*C*] a separate card for each member of the family?"

"No, you haven't to do [*don't have to do*] that. What you ought to do [*C*] is get a nice card for the family and write a thoughtful message inside."

"But my English is not so good," she protested.

"OK, bring me the card, and I'll help you write your message," I offered.

Ana was extremely busy and easily could had forgotten [*could have forgotten*] her good intentions, but she didn't. The next day after class, she showed me a beautiful card. On the front of it were the words "In sympathy." On the inside were the words "You have my deepest sympathy. You are in my thoughts at this time."

This was a big mistake! The card that Ana had bought was a sympathy card, a card that you send when someone has died. Ana had confused the Spanish word *simpatico*, which translates to "nice" in English, with the English word *sympathy*, which expresses the emotions of feeling sorry about someone's death.

When Ana realized her mistake, she had a good, long laugh, and I chuckled too. She said that she must have asked [*should have asked*] someone to help her pick out the right card. Now Ana's English is excellent, and she must not need [*does not need*] any help any more.

## EXERCISE 7

*Answers will vary.*

### EXERCISE 1

2. have won a big victory
3. be very effective
4. be operating well
5. have taken the objects
6. speak Japanese
7. be very brave
8. want to anger the voters
9. have been a meteor shower
10. have snowed recently; like skiing

### EXERCISE 2

2. can't
3. might, could
4. must
5. could, could
6. should
7. might, might
8. must

### EXERCISE 3

2. must
3. might
4. must
5. could
6. must
7. may
8. could
9. must
10. must
11. must
12. might
13. may not
14. can't
15. must not
16. should

### EXERCISE 4

2. a
3. a
4. a
5. c
6. b
7. c
8. a

### EXERCISE 5

2. could be
3. might have put
4. could have eaten
5. shouldn't have put
6. should become
7. might have
8. shouldn't eat
9. must have
10. has to be

### EXERCISE 6

*Answers will vary. Possible answers:*

2. False  Georgia is only six months old. A baby couldn't have committed a murder.
3. True  It's possible. We have no information about how Mr. Nelson was killed. The murderer could have used poison.
4. True  It's possible. She was envious of the money, so she had a motive.
5. False  We have no reason to make this conclusion. She was asleep at the time.
6. True  He loved his brother, so it is very unlikely that he killed him.

**7. False**  We have no information about the murder weapon. It might not have been a gun.

**8. True**  This is a logical conclusion. Because she was envious of the Nelsons' money, it means that they had more money than she did.

## EXERCISE 7

I guess you must not ~~be~~ be entirely happy over
 *may / might / could*
there. Are you lonely? It ~~should~~ be that you're not trying hard enough to make friends. Go out and
 *may / might*
socialize with people! At first, they ~~must~~ not be so friendly, but after people get to know you, they
 *like*
should ~~liked~~ you. You're a cool guy, even though you are a little shy.
 *not be*
I think that you may ~~be not~~ going out enough. It can't be good for you to stay home all the time. If you study at the library, for example, you may
 *meet*
~~have met~~ some nice people there. It's possible. And how about going off-campus to meet people? It could
 *happen*
~~happened~~ that you will meet another Ms. Right at an international movie group or a tango group.

But enough about you. Let's talk about me now. You think you've got problems? Last week Emilia left me, right after I got fired. That's right. I lost my
 *have*
job. Emilia must ~~had~~ decided I wasn't going to be a
 *should*
good provider. I admit I ~~must~~ have shown up on time every day, and I didn't, so that's probably why they fired me: because I was late to work a lot. I must have been crazy to be so lazy on that job at the
 *have*
software company. I could ˄ had a nice future at that company, but I blew it.

Anyway, here I am—no job, no girlfriend. I'm feeling pretty down myself. Let me hear from you, friend.

—R

## EXERCISE 8

*Answers will vary.*

## EXERCISE 1

| | |
|---|---|
| flexibility NC | evidence NC |
| muscles C | activity NC |
| heart C | brain C |
| lungs C | condition NC |
| joints C | people C |
| inactivity NC | skin NC |
| health NC | posture NC |
| cigarettes C | exercise NC |
| research NC | stress NC |
| exercise NC | moods C |
| BMI C | sleep NC |
| risk C | regularity NC |
| heart disease NC | quality C |
| cancer NC | life NC |
| blood pressure NC | gym C |
| diseases C | fun NC |
| | results C |

## EXERCISE 2

Circle: culture, lodging, shopping, weather, air, scenery, snow, water, wilderness, recreation, hiking, camping, skiing, tourism, music, art, dance, entertainment, transportation, commerce, forestry, mining, software, biotechnology, livability, pride, beauty, hospitality

## EXERCISE 3

| | | |
|---|---|---|
| **2.** a | **5.** f | **8.** g |
| **3.** i | **6.** h | **9.** b |
| **4.** d | **7.** c | **10.** e |

## EXERCISE 4

| | |
|---|---|
| **2.** a game of | **7.** a glass of |
| **3.** a piece of / a slice of / a serving of | **8.** a piece of |
| **4.** a serving of | **9.** a clap of |
| **5.** a piece of / a slice of | **10.** a flash of |
| **6.** a piece of / a slice of / a serving of | **11.** a drop of |
| | **12.** a piece of |
| | **13.** a period of |

## EXERCISE 5

| | |
|---|---|
| **2.** A devoted partner | **8.** a compatible companion |
| **3.** integrity | **9.** warmth |
| **4.** work | **10.** work |
| **5.** great fun | **11.** a job |
| **6.** love | **12.** A good salary |
| **7.** practicality | **13.** respect |

## EXERCISE 6

2. strawberries
3. beans
4. rice
5. peanuts
6. tomatoes
7. potatoes
8. cookies
9. cheese
10. chocolate
11. salmon
12. a pumpkin, pumpkin
13. a turkey, turkey

## EXERCISE 7

The brain is a complex organ. It weighs only
   *pounds*
about 3 ~~pound~~, but it controls all our behavior, our
     *senses  sight*
motor functions, and the five ~~sense: sights~~, hearing,
taste, smell, and touch. Doctors have estimated that
the brain has 100 billion nerve cells, called *neurons*.
*A piece*       *a*  *sand*
~~Piece~~ of brain tissue the size of ^grain of ~~sands~~
contains 100,000 neurons.

              *cells*
  As we get older, we tend to lose some brain ~~cell~~.
However, if you take care of your brain, you may
reverse that process. You can do several things to
increase your mental agility even when you are
young.
  How do we take care of our brains? Recent
studies have found that the same things that keep
your heart in good condition will also keep your
brain in good condition. Here's what you can do:

- Even in your 40s, take care to keep your
 *cholesterol*
 ~~cholesterols~~ down.
      *fat*
- Get rid of fat, belly ~~fats~~ in particular.
- Eat antioxidants, especially ~~a~~ berries and red
    *Research*
 grapes. ~~A research~~ shows that both protect
 against aging signs and can improve your
 learning and motor skills as well.
           *beans*
- Eat foods with a lot of fiber, such as ~~bean~~,
 *nuts*
 ~~nut~~, and cereal but don't eat ~~a~~ sugar. (Too
  *sugar*   *blood*
 much ~~sugars~~ in the ~~bloods~~ actually can
 damage the memory center of the brain.)
- Get plenty of physical exercise.
- Get plenty of mental exercise: do puzzles,
    *a*
 learn ^new language, practice brushing your
 *teeth*     *hand*
 ~~tooth~~ with your other ~~hands~~.
    *sleep*
- For the best ~~sleeps~~, sleep in a cool room.
        *hour*
- Take a midday nap of at least one ~~hours~~.
 Midday REM sleep is good for problem-
 solving skills.

## EXERCISE 8

*Answers will vary.*

## UNIT 7 (pages 57–64)

## EXERCISE 1

| | | | |
|---|---|---|---|
| 2. a | 7. the | 12. a | 17. — |
| 3. the | 8. — | 13. a | 18. — |
| 4. a | 9. the | 14. — | 19. an |
| 5. a | 10. a | 15. — | 20. the |
| 6. a | 11. the | 16. — | |

## EXERCISE 2

| | | | |
|---|---|---|---|
| 2. a | 9. an | 16. a | 23. — |
| 3. — | 10. a | 17. a | 24. an |
| 4. the | 11. — | 18. a | 25. — |
| 5. — | 12. a | 19. the | 26. — |
| 6. — | 13. the | 20. The | 27. The |
| 7. The | 14. The | 21. — | |
| 8. a | 15. — | 22. the | |

## EXERCISE 3

| | | | |
|---|---|---|---|
| 2. a | 9. A | 16. the | 23. — |
| 3. a | 10. the | 17. a | 24. The |
| 4. The | 11. a | 18. the | 25. — |
| 5. the | 12. the | 19. — | 26. the |
| 6. the | 13. the | 20. — | |
| 7. an | 14. — | 21. the | |
| 8. a | 15. the | 22. — | |

## EXERCISE 4

| | | | |
|---|---|---|---|
| 2. an | 9. — | 16. a | 23. — |
| 3. the | 10. — | 17. the | 24. — |
| 4. the | 11. The | 18. the | 25. — |
| 5. an | 12. — | 19. a | 26. the |
| 6. a | 13. The | 20. the | 27. the |
| 7. The | 14. — | 21. a | 28. — |
| 8. a | 15. the | 22. — | |

## EXERCISE 5

| | | | |
|---|---|---|---|
| 2. the | 10. the | 18. — | 26. the |
| 3. the | 11. — | 19. — | 27. — |
| 4. — | 12. — | 20. — | 28. — |
| 5. — | 13. — | 21. — | 29. the |
| 6. the | 14. — | 22. the | 30. the |
| 7. — | 15. the | 23. the | 31. the |
| 8. the | 16. The | 24. — | |
| 9. the | 17. the | 25. the | |

## EXERCISE 6

| | | | |
|---|---|---|---|
| 2. — | 9. the | 16. the | 23. a |
| 3. the | 10. The | 17. the | 24. — |
| 4. an | 11. the | 18. — | 25. — |
| 5. the | 12. the | 19. — | 26. — |
| 6. the | 13. — | 20. — | 27. — |
| 7. — | 14. — | 21. — | 28. — |
| 8. — | 15. — | 22. — | 29. — |

## EXERCISE 7

Your Metropolitan Zoo needs you! Would you like to "adopt" *an* animal? You can "adopt" one by contributing ~~a~~ money, which will be spent for its care. With your adoption, you will have ~~a~~ *the* satisfaction of knowing that your support is keeping "your" *The* animal alive and well. ~~A~~ money pays for food that your animal needs, ~~a~~ special equipment, and ~~an~~ extra time and ~~a~~ specialized attention from *a* designated zoo employee.

In need of adoption right now are two tigers, one lion, two camels, *a* family of four chimpanzees, and one gorilla. Which animal would you like to adopt?

Both our tigers are females; we are hoping to obtain *a* male from Pakistan or China next year. ~~A~~ *The* lion, recently named Mufasa by a group of ~~the~~ schoolchildren, is three years old. Both camels are *the* Arabian kind, with one hump, not *the* Bactrian kind, with two humps. ~~The~~ *The* chimpanzees in our zoo act just like *a* human family. They take care of each other, play, and sometimes even have ~~a~~ little fights. Sometimes, the two little ones push each other until one of them topples over. Our gorilla is *the* most polular animal at *the* zoo and also *the* most expensive to maintain. He needs several sponsors. He puts on a show every afternoon by interacting with ~~a~~ *the / Ø* visitors. He loves ~~an~~ *the* applause that he gets.

As a sponsor, you will receive free admission to ~~a~~ *the* zoo and receive ~~a~~ news and updates about your adopted animal regularly. In addition, your name and *the* name of your animal will appear on the program at our annual banquet. Please find it in your heart to contribute to *the* well-being of our animals. Become *a* sponsor today!

## EXERCISE 8

*Answers will vary.*

UNIT 8 (pages 65–72)

## EXERCISE 1

What do **all** executives need to understand today's business world? They need the kind of cutting-edge education that Global University provides: an overview of the international business **environment**, analyses and **strategies** for **a great many** markets, and **plenty of** personal **interaction** with experienced business people from **many** countries throughout the world. Global University offers this education.

- Earn **enough** credits to get your **MBA** degree in **one year** (full-time), or in **two years** (part-time). **Both** courses cover the same material, and **each** course confers the same prestigious degree.
- Students will intern for **one month with a** local international company. **Some** students **work abroad** for this internship.
- **All our** students must be proficient **in two** languages: English plus **one** other.

If you want to know how to function effectively in **the business** world, and to be able to make **a lot of** money while doing it, apply to Global University now.

Comments from **a few** graduates:

"I gained **a lot of** confidence. I know that I have **a great deal** of the **knowledge** I need to succeed in business." *JS from Shanghai*

"I had **little** real knowledge of how the business world works **before** I came to Global. Now I can identify **most** problems and approach solutions in a systematic way." *JLB from Paris*

"There are **few** graduate business **programs** that can match Global's. There's not **much** information that they don't offer about business, **every** aspect of it." *RL from Kuala Lumpur*

"After graduating, I joined a financial firm at a good salary. I am gaining the **expertise** needed to solve **most** problems. In **a few** years, I expect to become a partner. *BB from New York*

"At first, I had **a little** anxiety about competing in the business world. But I've become confident. I'm **now well** established in a consulting firm, and I have **no** worries about my future. Thank you, Global." *FA from Dubai*

## EXERCISE 2

| | |
|---|---|
| 2. a few | 11. a bunch of |
| 3. a great deal | 12. a couple of |
| 4. a little | 13. most of |
| 5. many | 14. a lot of |
| 6. any | 15. a great deal of |
| 7. a bit of | 16. a few of |
| 8. all | 17. a little |
| 9. A couple of | 18. a couple of |
| 10. every | |

## EXERCISE 3

| | |
|---|---|
| 2. No | 7. A few of |
| 3. Both | 8. many |
| 4. One | 9. much |
| 5. All | 10. a lot of |
| 6. A couple of | 11. any |

## EXERCISE 4

| | | |
|---|---|---|
| 2. All | 9. a number of | 16. a few |
| 3. many | 10. a little | 17. Most |
| 4. both | 11. Most | 18. several |
| 5. no | 12. a great many | 19. many |
| 6. each | 13. a lot of | 20. one |
| 7. Several | 14. many | 21. a couple of |
| 8. any | 15. some | 22. plenty of |

## EXERCISE 5

| | |
|---|---|
| 2. paycheck | 10. specialty |
| 3. time | 11. insurance |
| 4. expertise | 12. experience |
| 5. professional advice | 13. stock market |
| 6. vacation | 14. interests |
| 7. year | 15. money |
| 8. goals | 16. trust |
| 9. professionals | |

## EXERCISE 6

Many / ~~Much~~ / A lot of people in our town
1.
have been looking for a good Middle Eastern
restaurant. We have a few / ~~a little~~ / some Italian
2.
restaurants in the family style, a couple of /
3.
~~a great deal of~~ / ~~every~~ French bistros, several / a few /
4.
~~a little~~ Asian restaurants, and one / ~~some~~ / ~~every~~
5.
Mexican restaurant, but we haven't had ~~no~~ / any / ~~each~~
6.
good, authentic Middle Eastern restaurants—until now.
The new restaurant Sahara has excellent food
and service, along with some / ~~any~~ / ~~a few~~ exotic
7.

atmosphere: flowing red curtains, ~~plenty of~~ / lots of
8.
embroidered pillows on the floor, and ~~a great deal of~~ /
a great many / ~~every~~ colorful Moroccan lamps
9.
hanging from the ceiling. As soon as we arrived, we
were seated in a roomy booth. Almost immediately, a
waiter brought some / ~~a couple of~~ / ~~every~~ hot pita
10.
bread—nice and soft, not crisp—and some / ~~one~~ / ~~any~~
11.
olive oil to dip it in.
To begin, my companion and I chose two / ~~one~~ /
12.
~~both~~ different appetizers: She had ~~a little~~ / some / ~~one~~
13.
stuffed grape leaves, and I had a plate of creamy
hummus. Both / ~~Two~~ / ~~A couple~~ of them were
14.
delicious. Then, our main courses: the lamb kabob,
which consists of pieces of lamb and a few / ~~a little~~ /
15.
~~much~~ vegetables—onions, peppers, and mushrooms—
which was tender and tasty, and the chicken, which
had been cooked in a sauce made of ~~a little~~ / some /
16.
several mysterious spices, was out of this world. We
both had a side dish of yogurt with lots of / several /
17.
~~much~~ vegetables cut up in it. Of course, we wanted
dessert, and we chose the baklava, a delicate, flaky
pastry filled with some / ~~a little~~ / ~~plenty of~~ pistachio
18.
nuts and covered with a little / ~~a few~~ / ~~a couple of~~ honey.
19.
And, surprise! You will be pleased that the
restaurant is so affordable. You won't have to spend
much / ~~some~~ / a lot of money here. You'd better get
20.
to this restaurant soon. Before long, there will be a
long wait to get in.

## EXERCISE 7

                    much
It gives us ~~many~~ pleasure to write this letter
             some
to you. Our bank has ~~any~~ information which will
benefit you enormously. We are in possession of a
         deal of
great ~~many~~ money in an account with your name
on it!!! Yes, this is true. An unnamed person has
designated these funds for YOU!
In order to withdraw the money from the bank,
                a little / some
we need to request ~~a few~~ information from you:

1. What is your Social Security number? We need
*each / every*
this in order to access ~~all~~ account of yours.
2. What is your date of birth and where were you
*all / any*
born? We need this information to answer ~~every~~ questions about your identity.
3. Please send the name of your bank and your account number. We need this so we can
*any*
transfer the money easily without ~~no~~ problems
*each / every*
with international banking laws. Please write ~~all~~ number carefully.
4. What is the password for your bank account number? Please double-check this password,
*many*
and make sure it is up-to-date. A great ~~deal of~~ people have lost out on receiving their money because of incorrectly written passwords.
5. Please take these steps immediately. If the account is not settled by the last day of this
*any*
month, you will not be able to receive ~~some~~ money.

It has taken a while for us to find you. That's why you must respond quickly in order to meet the deadline for unclaimed funds. Do not take
*much / a lot of*                    *all*
~~many~~ time to respond or you will lose ~~each~~ of the money in your account!

Also, very important! Please keep this matter
*few*
confidential. Even if only a ~~little~~ people find out
*a lot of*
about this, it could make ~~many~~ trouble with the authorities.

## EXERCISE 8

*Answers will vary.*

### UNIT 9 (pages 73–79)

## EXERCISE 1

2. bright young
3. new spring
4. various international
5. exciting big
6. simple straight
7. smallest added
8. expensive silk
9. old Japanese
10. beautiful classic
11. elegant business
12. fabulous modern
13. brightly colored cotton
14. tropical South Sea
15. casual summer
16. liveliest new
17. long cotton
18. hot pink
19. turquoise and orange silk
20. well-known contemporary

## EXERCISE 2

2. flower gardens
3. vegetable gardens
4. work horses
5. show horses
6. house cats
7. family dogs
8. dog house
9. strawberry jam
10. blackberry tea
11. peach pie
12. kitchen table
13. childhood dreams
14. baby sister
15. summer night
16. childhood memories

## EXERCISE 3

2. hand surgery
3. experienced marathon runner
4. wonderful gourmet cook
5. absent-minded professor

## EXERCISE 4

2. 1 two-hundred-year-old dining room table
3. 8 velvet-covered dining room chairs
4. 2 century-old Tiffany lamps
5. 1 silver-plated samovar
6. 2 (one-) hundred-(and)-fifty-year-old rocking chairs
7. 1 hand-woven Persian carpet
8. 1 hand-written manuscript
9. 3 ivory-inlaid coffee tables
10. 4 hand-painted serving dishes
11. 2 hand-carved mahogany beds
12. 2 (one-) hundred-(and)-thirty-year-old, gold-inlaid vases

## EXERCISE 5

2. local coffee shop
3. student ethics council
4. international student activities
5. old, dilapidated houses / dilapidated old houses
6. attention deficit disorder
7. Four-Year Service Award
8. Five-State Volunteerism Award

## EXERCISE 6

I moved to Los Angeles ten years ago. I had expected to love "sunny" Los Angeles right away. However, my first months in the city were terrible. Here's what happened:
*fresh country*
Moving from the ~~country fresh~~ air to the awful, polluted stuff that city people breathe presents a shock to the body. Ten years ago, I had miraculously
*glamorous television*
obtained a well-paying job in the ~~television glamorous~~ world, and I moved with my wife and
*beautiful southwest*
two daughters from ~~southwest beautiful~~ Kansas,

with its ~~golden magnificent corn in the fields~~, *magnificent golden cornfields*

and ~~blue clear~~ skies, to Los Angeles, where there *clear blue*

appeared to us to be no skies at all, only ~~gray dirty~~ *dirty gray* smog.

Within a week, my wife and children and I all came down with a ~~respiratory mysterious~~ illness. *mysterious respiratory*

Coughing and sneezing, with eyes and noses dripping, we suffered for ten days. A ~~ten-days~~ stay *ten-day* inside a small four-room apartment felt like being

in a ~~cement, cold~~ jail cell. We were accustomed to *cold cement* being outdoors, in the open Kansas air. After only

two weeks at my ~~new prized~~ job, I got sick. And *prized new*

I was really sick! My 42-~~years~~-old, feverish body *year* ached as it had never ached before. ~~Iron enormous~~ *Enormous iron* hammers pounded in my head. My lungs felt like

~~lead huge~~ weights. I coughed constantly, and I never *huge lead*

had more than a two-~~hours~~ rest, even though I took *hour*

double the recommended dose of the ~~cough over-the-~~ *over-the-counter cough*

~~counter~~ medicine we had bought at the ~~drug corner~~ *corner drug* store. Finally, after ten days, we recovered physically,

although not psychologically, from our ~~Los Angeles~~ *rude Los Angeles* ~~rude~~ reception.

My first three weeks in the Los Angeles gave me the feeling that I was living in a foreign and hostile country—and it would be many months before I felt differently. The irony of all this is that I—the person

who had hated the ~~big terrible~~ city at first—now love *terrible big* Los Angeles. They have cleaned up the air here, and we see sunshine almost every day. I am really enjoying

my ~~active exciting~~ life in Los Angeles, and I hardly *exciting, active* miss Kansas at all.

## EXERCISE 7

*Answers will vary.*

## UNIT 10 (pages 80–87)

## EXERCISE 1

**A:** Is it really true <u>that a plant will grow better if you talk to it</u>?

**B:** Yes. Studies have shown <u>how much better plants grow when they are talked to</u>.

**A:** But plants don't have sound receptors or nervous systems, so can you tell us <u>why that is</u>?

**B:** Scientists know <u>that plants aren't responding to the specific words people say</u>. <u>What happens</u> is this: When you talk, you breathe out carbon dioxide and water vapor. <u>That plants need carbon dioxide and water in order to grow</u> is basic knowledge. They get a lot of these two vital nutrients from your breath. And soundwaves from your voice cause plant cells to vibrate. Experiments have demonstrated <u>that certain types and strengths of sound can affect plants</u>. These sounds can cause plants to grow better—or worse—than usual. For example, something amazing is <u>what plants have done after being exposed to classical music</u>: They grew thick, healthy leaves and developed good roots.

**A:** Only classical music? It makes a difference <u>if the plants hear classical music or other kinds of music</u>?

**B:** Well, it's interesting <u>that it does seem to matter</u>. Plants seem to care about <u>what kind of music they "hear."</u> Jazz has a beneficial effect too. And plants <u>exposed to country music</u> had normal growth. But plants <u>that were exposed to rock or rap music</u> did very poorly. Their root development was so terrible that the plants began to die.

**A:** No way! Do plants actually know <u>who they are listening to</u>—whether they are listening to Mozart or to Eminem?

**B:** Not exactly "know." They have an inclination, in a way, to like classical music. <u>What they do</u>, apparently, is sense the vibrations and respond differently to different types of rhythm.

**A:** Hmm. Well, here's <u>what I think</u>: <u>The fact that you talk to your plants</u> is good because it means <u>that you are paying attention to them</u>. <u>What you are doing</u> is giving them the water and food and pruning they need and not letting them die of neglect.

**B:** That's true. The issue of <u>whether plants live or die</u> depends on their receiving nutrients. But the answer to your original question—<u>whether or not plants actually do *better* when you talk to them</u>—is definitely "Yes." In health and longevity, plants <u>that you talk to</u> definitely outdo plants <u>that you don't talk to</u>.

## EXERCISE 2

2. that I have to forget about Lisa
3. that this is not going to be easy
4. that I can't forget about her
5. that I am not receptive to meeting people
6. that I get my life in order
7. that I should think about other things
8. that you have to be responsible on the job
9. that you have always been too casual about your work
10. That you adopt a better attitude
11. that you won't invest in any more iffy deals
12. that we are truthful with each other

## EXERCISE 3

2. (the summer Olympic Games of 2000) / (they) took place
3. (the symbol for ozone) / (it) is
4. (*numeracy*) / (it) means
5. (the largest organ of the body) / (it) is
6. (some fish) / (they) swim

## EXERCISE 4

2. whether (or not) / if the stores will be closed
3. whether (or not) / if the buses are running
4. whether (or not) / if there is enough food in the house
5. Whether (or not) / If the roads are safe
6. whether (or not) / if the electricity is going to go off
7. whether (or not) / if anyone wants to play Scrabble
8. whether (or not) / if he has to go to work
9. whether (or not) / if the doctors will be on call
10. whether (or not) / if the schools are going to be closed tomorrow too

## EXERCISE 5

2. what he said to (Marla) / (her)
3. That (Marla) / (she) is upset
4. where (Marla) / (she) is now
5. What (Marla) / (she) is going to do
6. whether (or not) (Marla) / (she) is going to get fired OR whether (Marla) / (she) is going to get fired (or not) OR if (Marla) (she) is going to get fired (or not)
7. whether (or not) (Marla) / (she) is going to be arrested OR whether (Marla) / (she) is going to be arrested (or not) OR if (Marla) / (she) is going to be arrested (or not)
8. what you are
9. What we are talking about

## EXERCISE 6

2. she was going to eat
3. she had liked the soup
4. what the stork was doing
5. I did this
6. what you think
7. what he deserved

## EXERCISE 7

Doctors have known for many centuries what *laughter can* ~~can laughter~~ do: Laughter can improve how ~~does~~ *a sick person feels* ~~a sick person feels~~; a sick person often *feels* much better when he or she laughs. However, growing evidence has revealed the fact *that* ~~what~~ laughter actually helps to *cure* the patient.

A famous and well-respected American editor, Norman Cousins, wrote about how *laughter helped* ~~did laughter help~~ cure him. It is a true story. This is what ~~did~~ *happened* ~~happened~~:

In 1964, he was experiencing severe joint pain and fever. It was just after *he had* ~~had he~~ returned from a strenuous trip abroad. The doctors diagnosed him with a serious illness that attacks the connective tissues of the body, and they hospitalized him.

While he was in the hospital, he began to research what *the effects of stress did* ~~did the effects of stress do~~ to the body. It became clear *that* ~~if~~ stress can be extremely damaging to the immune system. He read about the theory that *negative emotions are harmful to the body* ~~are harmful to the body negative emotions~~, so he wondered whether ~~that~~ the reverse was true: If negative emotions are harmful to the body, could positive emotions improve health?

What *he did* ~~did he do~~ next was dramatic. He checked out of the hospital and checked into a hotel suite in New York City. He supplanted his traditional medical treatment with an entirely different approach. He hired a nurse who read humorous stories to him and played funny movies for him. It was essential *that* ~~what~~ he laughed a lot and laughed hard every day. In addition, he took huge doses of vitamin C, a supplement he strongly believed in. He kept a very positive attitude.

That *the treatment turned out* ~~turned out the treatment~~ to be effective is well-known. It turned out to be so effective that in very little time Cousins didn't need any more painkillers or sleeping pills. He found *that* ~~what~~ the frequent and intense laughter relieved the pain and helped him sleep.

He returned to work and to an active life.

Because of who ~~was he~~ *he was* —a serious writer and editor—Cousins wrote about how ~~had the experimental treatment worked~~ *the experimental treatment had worked* in his book *Anatomy of an Illness*. In 1989, the medical profession acknowledged that his focused self-treatment was indeed ~~that~~ *what* had cured him. Cousins lived a healthy life for 16 more years after the illness. He died in 1990 at age seventy-five of a heart attack.

## EXERCISE 8

*Answers will vary.*

## UNIT 11 (pages 88–95)

## EXERCISE 1

The monthly meeting of the Board of Directors of the Towers Condominium was held on May 22. The meeting began at 6:40 P.M. when Ms. Janet Jones, president, said, "The meeting is called to order. Welcome, Board members, unit owners, and our manager."

### Reports of Officers and Committees

1. *East Side Homeowners Association.* Mr. Pantini <u>informed the Board that the County Commission had rejected the proposal for a new high-rise office building on our street</u>. The Commission was responding to the distressed residents, who don't want any more tall buildings in the area.
2. *The Towers Parking Committee.* Dr. Gardner <u>reported that a new system is going into effect on June 1</u>, and he <u>said that all the residents would be receiving new parking chips for their cars</u>. He <u>told everyone to place the new chips on the front windows of their cars</u> and <u>said that the cars would sound a "beep" when they pass the sensors at the gate</u>.

### Old Business

1. "Four companies have submitted estimates for the costs to repair the elevators," reported Harry Green, chair of the Elevator Repair Committee. He <u>stated that the Board would consider the proposals before the next meeting</u>.
2. "We are still short-handed in the front office," the manager reported. "We haven't had a secretary for two months," he added. He <u>asked if anybody knew of a good secretary</u>. Ms. Sloane <u>wondered whether the salary was too low</u>. She

<u>said that she is the CEO of a small accounting firm</u>, and she <u>knows that salaries have to be competitive</u>. She said <u>that the association should place a new ad on the Internet with a higher salary</u>.

### New Business

John Allen from InterRes, a satellite company, presented a short proposal for a new wireless system for our building. Mr. Allen said <u>that we could meet all our cable, telephone, and Internet needs by installing his system</u> and <u>said it would be much more economical than the systems we have</u>. He <u>asked the group who would be interested in the new system</u> and <u>asked where they could be contacted during the day</u>.

### Closing

Ms. Jones <u>asked whether there was any further business</u>, and the answer was negative. The meeting was adjourned at 8:05 P.M.

## EXERCISE 2

2. what your address is / was
3. when you were born
4. where you were born
5. if / whether I was your closest living relative
6. what your principal health complaint is / was
7. how long you have had this problem
8. if / whether you are / were in pain now
9. if / whether you have / had insurance
10. if I would ask you to sign this form

## EXERCISE 3

2. that if
3. would take
4. would tell him
5. (that) he would take the turtle / him
6. where the jewels were
7. that he didn't really know
8. that the turtle couldn't do that to him
9. that you shouldn't make a promise

## EXERCISE 4

2. (that) he had been / was elected last month to make great changes in the state
3. (that) he had been working hard to make those changes
4. (that) just the day before / the previous day he had signed a law to raise teachers' salaries
5. (that) in addition, the next / following day he would be signing / would sign a law to bring more benefits to the elderly

6. if / whether anyone had a question they would like to ask him
7. (that) she didn't have any children and (that) she was not elderly
8. why she had to pay for those services
9. if he could tell her why
10. that he understood how she felt
11. (that) well-educated children would grow up to be better citizens, which would benefit everyone
12. (that) one day . . . she was going to be elderly and then she too could enjoy the increased benefits for older people
13. (that) we had those / these problems and other serious problems in our state too, such as the economy, and he wouldn't sugar-coat the seriousness of those / these problems
14. (that) he would keep working hard with them to solve those problems.

## EXERCISE 5

2. 'd (had) better be ready
3. don't (do not) be
4. I want . . . starts
5. Remember . . . we get there
6. am going
7. I'm (am) going to dance . . . my
8. they play

## EXERCISE 6

*Polls Today* conducted its annual survey about the condition of the country today. The poll asked *what people thought* ~~did people think~~ about several issues and told them *to* ^ answer as honestly as possible. Here are some highlights from the survey:

### Question 1. In general, do you approve or disapprove of the way the president is doing his job?

When *Polls Today* asked if *they approved of the way the president was doing his job,* ~~"Do you approve of the way the president is doing his job?"~~ a little more than half (51%) said that they approved. However, a large percentage (48%) stated *that they did /do not* ~~not to~~ agree with the president on many issues, and 1 percent said that they didn't *have* ~~had~~ any opinion.

### Question 2. Is the government doing enough to protect the environment?

A large group (38%) stated *that* ~~what~~ the government was not doing enough to protect the environment. They wondered whether *the climate was* ~~was the climate~~ becoming too warm and whether *too many trees would be lost* ~~would be lost too many trees~~ within the next 10 years. An equal number claimed that the environment was probably in good enough condition and that they *did not* ~~not to~~ worry about it. The remaining 24 percent didn't say what ~~did~~ they ~~think~~ *thought* about this issue.

### Question 3. Do the citizens have access to good health care?

About one-third (32%) said that they had adequate health care for now and the future. About one-quarter (27%), though, wondered *what* ~~that~~ would happen to them if they became ill or disabled. Of this group, several expressed rancor and bitterness about the lack of health care available to them, compared with the universal health care that exists in several other countries. The remaining 41 percent said that they weren't sure.

### Question 4. Are taxes too high?

When asked *if / whether (or not)* ~~that~~ taxes were too high, 16 percent claimed that they were. This group is pushing hard to minimize both taxes and government services. Astonishingly, 38 percent stated that taxes were not high enough and that people would have to pay more for necessary services in the future. They said that they didn't want to pay more taxes, but the bottom line is that more money is necessary to maintain the services that exist now. The rest (46%) didn't *say* ~~said~~ what they thought.

### Question 5. Is the quality of life better or worse now than it was 10 years ago?

When asked how the quality of their lives was now, compared with what it had been 10 years ago, the population was again divided about 50–50. Forty-eight percent *told* ~~said~~ *Polls Today* that the quality of their lives had improved over the last 10 years, and 46 percent said that it had declined. A small percentage of this group believes that the government is putting a positive spin on reports about conditions in the country and is not telling the truth about how bad *things really are* ~~really are things~~. About 5 percent reported that they didn't have an opinion.

## EXERCISE 7

*Answers will vary.*

## UNIT 12 (pages 96–106)

### EXERCISE 1

This is the story of a very simple invention <u>that you can find in almost every office in the whole world today</u>. It is also the story of an inventor <u>whose creativity and persistence resulted in a very useful product</u>. What is the famous invention? It is Liquid Paper, the white liquid <u>that covers up the mistakes you make when writing or typing</u>. Bette Nesmith Graham—a secretary in Dallas, Texas, <u>who had begun using white paint to cover up the typing errors in her work</u>—invented it in the early 1950s.

At the time, Ms. Nesmith was a twenty-seven-year-old single mother. She was struggling to support herself and her young son by working as a secretary to the chairman of a big Dallas bank. When she began to work with her first electric typewriter, she found that the type marks <u>she typed onto the paper</u> didn't erase as cleanly as those from manual typewriters. So Ms. Nesmith, <u>who was also an artist</u>, quietly began painting out her mistakes with white paint <u>that she had prepared at home</u>. Soon she was supplying bottles of her homemade preparation, <u>which she called "Mistake Out,"</u> to other secretaries in the building.

When she lost her job with the company, Ms. Nesmith turned to working full time to develop the Mistake Out as a business, expanding from her house into a small trailer <u>she had bought for the backyard</u>. In hopes of marketing her product, she approached IBM, <u>which turned her down</u>. She stepped up her own marketing and within a decade became a successful entrepreneur. The product, <u>which came to be called "Liquid Paper,"</u> was manufactured in four countries and sold in nearly three dozen. In fiscal year 1979, <u>which ended about six months before she sold the company</u>, it had sales of $38 million. By the time Ms. Nesmith finally sold her business to Gillette in 1979, she had built her simple, practical idea into a $47.5 million business.

The story has a happy ending in more ways than one. Ms. Nesmith remarried and became Mrs. Graham. Her son, Michael, a musician <u>of whom she was understandably proud</u>, became very successful as one of the members of a music group called the *Monkees*, <u>which appeared on an NBC television show for several years in the mid-1960s</u>. Subsequently a country-rock musician, a songwriter, and a video producer, he then headed a production company in California, <u>where he also directed some charities</u>.

With some of her profits, Mrs. Graham established a foundation <u>whose purpose is to provide leading intellectuals with the time, space, and compatible colleagues that they need to ponder and articulate the most important social problems of our era</u>. Bette Nesmith Graham first developed a product <u>that there was clearly a need for</u>; then she used the substantial profits for charitable purposes, <u>which is a fine thing to do</u>.

The story of Liquid Paper and Bette Nesmith Graham is a story <u>everyone can appreciate</u>. It shows how an excellent product came to market because of the cleverness and perseverance of its inventor.

### EXERCISE 2

| | | |
|---|---|---|
| 2. whom | 7. who | 12. that |
| 3. who | 8. — | 13. that |
| 4. — | 9. which | 14. that |
| 5. where | 10. which | 15. whose |
| 6. which | 11. when | |

### EXERCISE 3

| | | |
|---|---|---|
| 2. which | 7. whose | 12. whose |
| 3. who | 8. who | 13. — |
| 4. whose | 9. when | 14. who |
| 5. — | 10. who | 15. that |
| 6. who | 11. who | 16. whose |

### EXERCISE 4

| | |
|---|---|
| 2. who | 14. where / that |
| 3. that / — / who / whom | 15. who |
| 4. who | 16. which |
| 5. that / — / which | 17. that / which |
| 6. that / which | 18. that / — / which |
| 7. that / — / which | 19. whose |
| 8. where | 20. who |
| 9. that / which | 21. when / that |
| 10. that / which | 22. that / — / which |
| 11. that / which | 23. that / which |
| 12. that / which | 24. that / which |
| 13. that / — / which | 25. that / — / which |

### EXERCISE 5

2. who feels energized around others
3. whose energies are activated by being alone
4. who / that pay attention to details in the world
5. who / that is more interested in relationships between people and things
6. that / which / — this test measures
7. who / that made decisions objectively
8. whose primary way to reach a conclusion was this
9. who / that took other people's feelings into consideration
10. that / which / — he or she has

11. where we prefer to work or live
(OR in which we prefer to work or live / which we prefer to work or live in / that we prefer to work or live in)

12. who / that prefer a planned and predictable environment

13. when / that / — / something happens
(OR at which something happens)

14. whose life must be planned in advance

15. where he or she should be placed to most enhance the company
(OR in which he or she should be placed to most enhance the company
OR that / which / — he or she should be placed in to most enhance the company)

16. where you would be the happiest and most productive

## EXERCISE 6

| | |
|---|---|
| **2.** a | **7.** a |
| **3.** b | **8.** a |
| **4.** b | **9.** b |
| **5.** a | **10.** b |
| **6.** b | **11.** b |

## EXERCISE 7

*that / which*
One of the ways ~~who~~ is used to describe people is to label them *extroverts* or *introverts*. However, there *that / which* are other methods ~~whose~~ people have used ~~them~~ to conveniently categorize members of the human race.

For example, for people whose size is a little outside the normal range, there is the division into *endomorphs*, who ~~they~~ tend to be fat, and *ectomorphs*, who are thin. The endomorph is stereotyped as a relaxed person without obsessions, in contrast to the *who* *who / that* ectomorph, ~~that~~ is stereotyped as a person ~~whom~~ is nervous and serious and who rarely smiles.

Another division defines people as Type A or Type B. Type A is the category which describes people *who / that* ~~they~~ are very serious, ambitious, and driven. Type A originally described people, usually middle-aged *who / that* males, ~~whom~~ were at risk of suffering a heart attack. Type B, on the other hand, labels a rather passive, *who / that* ambitionless person ~~which~~ others frequently take *who / that* advantage of and ~~which~~ is probably not a candidate for a heart attack.

Some people categorize human beings by their astrological signs. Astrology is the belief that stars and planets influence the Earth and human destinies. The date of a person's birth determines his or her astrological sign, which ~~it~~ is the name of one of the constellations of stars in the universe. This astrological sign that the person is born under determines their character and destiny. For example, *who / that* a person ~~whom~~ was born between April 22 and May 21 is called a Taurus and is supposed to possess certain characteristics, such as friendliness and tact. *whose* A person ~~that their~~ birthday is between June 22 and July 21 is a Cancer and is supposed to be stubborn but effective.

Another theory used to categorize people is the theory of left-brained vs. right-brained people. According to this theory in its simplest meaning, *who* right-brained people, ~~that~~ are intuitive and romantic, are the artists and creative people of the world. Left- *whose* brained people, ~~who their~~ thinking is very logical, often turn out to be mathematicians and scientists. *that / which* All of these theories—and many others ~~what~~ are too numerous to mention here—have provided attractive and sometimes amusing solutions to describe and understand people. Various theories for categorizing people, which ~~it~~ is always a difficult thing to do, will continue to come and go.

## EXERCISE 8

*Answers will vary.*

## UNIT 13 (pages 107–113)

### EXERCISE 1

Carolina Manning, daughter of Dr. and Mrs. John Manning of Hollywood, California, was married on Sunday to Matthias Wolfe, the son of Dr. Maria and Mr. Douglas Wolfe of Boston. Reverend Harry Carter performed the ceremony at the All-Faiths Religious Center in Hollywood.

Ms. Manning will continue to use her name professionally. She is well known as the originator of the children's television show *Hot Ice Cream*, of which she is both the writer and producer. She has a degree in film studies from the University of Southern California and she also received a master's degree in cinematography from New York University.

Her father, whose text on Shakespeare is required reading in many colleges, is a professor of English at Boston University. Her mother taught in the public school system for 30 years, the last 20 of which were at Grisham High School, where she was principal. She retired last June.

Mr. Wolfe is an independent producer. He previously produced movies for The Kallenbach Company, where he had worked for six years. He has a master's degree from the University of Southern California, <u>from which he graduated magna cum laude</u>, and subsequently taught film writing there. Mr. Wolfe's father is an editor at Koala Publications, a children's book publisher. His mother, Dr. Maria Lopez Wolfe, is a pediatrician, currently serving as chief of pediatrics at Children's Hospital. The bride and bridegroom met at the University of Southern California as students. They soon discovered that they had common interests such as art and film, and both belong to Art Outreach, a program dedicated to encouraging children in the arts. Mr. Wolfe occasionally publishes his letters of opinion, <u>some of which have drawn national attention</u>, in well-known newspapers.

## EXERCISE 2

2. most of which were
3. several of which were
4. a number of which came
5. all of which have entered
6. many of whose directors and producers deserve
7. two of which dealt
8. one of which was
9. the rest of which were
10. a few of which seemed
11. some of whom applauded
12. most of whom didn't like
13. an example of which is / of which an example is

## EXERCISE 3

2. looking for his missing son
3. trying to change his destructive lifestyle
4. brilliantly portrayed by Tom Cruise
5. adapted from the TV series
6. turned into a nightmare
7. zipping him from Amsterdam to Las Vegas
8. starring Leonardo DiCaprio and Kate Winslet
9. capable of a power that may destroy him
10. Francis Ford Coppola's Oscar-winning version

## EXERCISE 4

2. Cinema pubs offer independent sections of tables and comfortable swivel chairs, allowing you to feel like you are in your own living room.
3. Servers, most of whom are local college students, come to each table before the movie begins and take orders for food and beverages.
4. The ambience in the theater is similar to that in a cabaret, where there is an intimate feeling.

5. In accordance with the cozy atmosphere, the cinema pubs show small films, many of which are foreign.
6. Although you have come to the theater to see a movie, you will also find that the cinema pub is a gathering place where people like to socialize.
7. The idea of the cinema pub, already popular in the United Kingdom, is beginning to catch on in the United States.
8. Cinema pubs show recent films in a relaxed atmosphere, making them a welcome alternative to huge and impersonal movie multiplexes.
9. For a change of pace, see your next film at the cinema pub nearest to you.

## EXERCISE 5

After World War II, Europe was the center of important developments in filmmaking, ~~they~~ *which* strongly influenced motion pictures worldwide. In Italy, well-known movies, two of ~~them~~ *which* were Rossellini's *Open City*, made in 1945, and De Sica's *The Bicycle Thief*, made in 1948, started a trend toward realism in film. These directors, most of ~~them~~ *whom* preferred not to use artificial stories to spice up plots for entertainment, took their cameras into the streets. They wanted to make films ~~who~~ *that / which* showed the real difficulties of life in the years after the war.

In the next decades, Federico Fellini— ~~whose~~ *who* was an outstanding director— combined realistic plots with philosophical ideas. His films, the most famous of ~~them~~ *which* is *La strada*, are now classics. *La strada* is a movie that ̶ *which* seems to be about circus people in the streets but really is about the meaning of life.

In France, a group of young filmmakers, ~~calling~~ *called* the "New Wave," appeared during the 1950s. This group, ~~who their~~ *whose* focus was people, developed a new kind of film which stressed psychology instead of plot. It featured new camera and acting techniques, many of ~~that~~ *which* we can see in movies such as Truffaut's *400 Blows*.

In England, another group of filmmakers, ~~was~~ known as the "Angry Young Man" movement, developed a new kind of realism. In Sweden, Ingmar Bergman used simple stories and fables to look at complex philosophical and social topics, some of ~~whom~~ *which* are expertly explored in *The Seventh Seal*. The Spaniard Luis Bunuel, *whose* impressive film *Viridiana* made him famous, portrayed social injustices.

Postwar developments in filmmaking did not take place only in Western Europe. There was significant influence from Asian filmmakers, the first *of* which was Akira Kurosawa of Japan, who made *Rashomon* in 1950. Indian filmmakers, like Satyajit Ray, ~~who his~~ *whose* movie *Pather Panchali* showed us life on the subcontinent of Asia, became well known. Even in Russia, where filmmaking was under state control, it was possible to make movies like *The Cranes Are Flying*, showing the problems ~~whom~~ *that* individuals suffered.

In summary, after World War II, there were new types of movies on the scene telling different kinds of stories, ~~making~~ *made* by new filmmakers from around the world.

## EXERCISE 6

*Answers will vary.*

### UNIT 14 (pages 114–123)

## EXERCISE 1

**Storyville School Vandalized**
were stolen
was committed
was still being sought
could not be contacted

**Restaurant Burglarized After Hours**
was burglarized
had been altered
have been broken into
are being committed
is being made
will probably be arrested
have a better alarm system installed

**Hopeful Hijackers Arrested**
was not well developed
would never have been carried out
has not been established

**Cash Register Damaged, Waiter Is Fired**
was fired
(was) not arrested
have the incident documented
have the alleged offender barred
is estimated

## EXERCISE 2

2. will be caressed
3. lie
4. savor
5. will be thrilled
6. disappeared
7. were planned
8. were constructed
9. can be seen
10. numbered
11. collapsed
12. happened
13. have been fascinated
14. were grown
15. was cultivated
16. made
17. were domesticated
18. appeared
19. were often written
20. was done
21. was put
22. were ordered
23. made
24. were produced
25. were cut
26. were used
27. produced
28. was it destroyed
29. could have been caused by
30. was caused
31. think
32. remains

## EXERCISE 3

2. would actually be employed
3. is sustained
4. were sent
5. are maintained / have been maintained
6. must be controlled
7. cannot be grown
8. is obscured
9. has to be done
10. is produced
11. is recycled
12. are picked up
13. is done
14. has to be planned
15. are used
16. has been utilized
17. have been developed
18. am known
19. are made
20. can be found
21. have it collected
22. is filtered
23. is being built
24. will be completed

## EXERCISE 4

**A. Underlined Causatives:**
1. having their apartment sprayed
2. had some furniture sent
3. have it shortened
4. have future alterations done
5. have had it checked
6. have a car sent

**B. New Causatives:**
2. have your table looked at by an insurance adjuster
3. have the bill sent to him
4. can get the problem fixed
5. have your son picked up

## EXERCISE 5

2. get my car fixed
3. got towed
4. got charged
5. got stolen
6. got dumped
7. get hired
8. gets asked
9. get fired

## EXERCISE 6

2. **a.** it is made
   **b.** the meat is smoked
3. **a.** jicama is sold by street vendors
   **b.** that have been sprinkled
4. **a.** Avocados are considered
   **b.** they should be allowed
   **c.** A green salsa, guacamole, is made
   **d.** Avocados also are used
5. **a.** Meat is steamed
   **b.** the leaves must be softened
   **c.** the meat and other ingredients are wrapped
6. **a.** They can be eaten
   **b.** They are made
   **c.** Tortillas can now be found
7. **a.** Chilies are used
   **b.** Chili-seasoned foods have been consumed
8. **a.** Corn is used
   **b.** no part of the corn is wasted
   **c.** The ears, husks, silk, and kernels are used in different ways.
   **d.** Evidence has been found by archaeologists

## EXERCISE 7

I could tell you many things about radium and
radioactivity and how they were ~~discovering~~ *discovered*, but it would take a long time. Since we have only a short time, I'll give you a short account of my early work with radium. The conditions of the discovery were peculiar, and I am always ~~pleasing~~ *pleased* to remember them and to explain them.

In the year 1897, my husband, Professor Curie, and I ~~were worked~~ *were working / worked* in the laboratory of the School of Physics and Chemistry, where he held his lectures.

I was ~~engage~~ *engaged* in work on uranium rays, which had *been* discovered two years before by Professor Becquerel.

In my research, I found out that uranium and thorium compounds were active in proportion to the amount of uranium or thorium that they ~~got~~ contained; in other words, the more uranium or thorium ~~that contained~~ *that was contained / contained* in the compound, the greater the activity.

Then I thought that some unknown element must ~~be existed~~ *exist / have existed* among those minerals, one with a much greater radioactivity than uranium or thorium. And I thought that it should be found. I wanted to find and to separate that element, so I went to work on that with Professor Curie. We thought we would

have the project ~~doing~~ *done* in several weeks or months, but it was not so. It took many years of hard work to finish that task. There was not only one new element that we found—there were several. But the most important was radium.

Now, if we take a practical point of view, then the most important property of the rays is the way they influence the cells of the human organism. These effects may ~~use~~ *be used* for the cure of several diseases. Good results have ~~be~~ *been* obtained in many cases. What is considered particularly important is the treatment of cancer.

But we must not forget that when radium *was* discovered, no one knew that it would prove useful in hospitals. The work was one of pure science. And this is a proof that scientific work must ~~be not~~ *not be* considered from the point of view of its direct usefulness. It must be ~~doing~~ *done* for itself, for the beauty of science.

There is always a vast field which is left to experimentation, and I hope that we may have some beautiful progress in the coming years. It is my earnest desire that this scientific work should *be* carried on, hopefully by some of you, and that it will be ~~appreciating~~ *appreciated* by all of you, who understand the beauty of science.

## EXERCISE 8

*Answers will vary.*

## UNIT 15 (pages 124–129)

## EXERCISE 1

**Stative passives**

| | |
|---|---|
| is owned | is surrounded |
| is related | is composed of |
| is not connected | |

**Reporting passives**

| | |
|---|---|
| was known | is considered |
| is believed | are known |
| is thought | was said |
| was said | are assumed |

## EXERCISE 2

2. owned
3. claimed
4. were found
5. were said
6. was composed of
7. are also thought
8. are alleged
9. are located
10. said
11. are known

## EXERCISE 3

2. is believed
3. is said
4. is not known
5. is now assumed
6. was also thought
7. are now believed
8. is claimed
9. is known
10. was conjectured
11. is known
12. is thought
13. can be safely assumed

## EXERCISE 4

2. is believed
3. was previously thought
4. is understood
5. is well known
6. might be perceived
7. is widely confirmed
8. has been well established
9. are known
10. has been considered
11. can be assumed

## EXERCISE 5

    It *is* often said that a full moon causes many bad things to happen. More crimes, disasters, and accidents are ~~alleging~~ *alleged* to occur during the times when the moon is full, so many people take extra care during these times. People have been known to plan their lives around the phases of the moon; for example, *it* is believed by some that certain phases of the moon are ~~relate~~ *related* to the best times for certain activities, such as getting married, making important financial decisions, or praying at a shrine.

    These beliefs about a full moon, however, are not true, according to many scientists. Numerous studies have been conducted, and no relationship between a full moon and higher rates of anything has been proven. A full moon is not ~~connect~~ *connected* in any way to increases in the rates of murders, traffic accidents, crisis calls to police or fire stations, births of babies, major disasters, assassinations, aggression by professional hockey players, psychiatric admissions, emergency room admissions, sleepwalking, or any other events that are often ~~believe~~ *believed* to be affected by the moon.

    If the appearance of a full moon is really not ~~relating~~ *related* to these kinds of occurrences, why are these moon myths ~~assuming~~ *assumed* to be true by so many people? Sociologists say that the basis of many moon myths *is* found in old folk tales. For example, it has *been* claimed

since ancient times that more births occur during a full moon and more crimes are committed during a full moon, even though reliable statistics have never confirmed these ideas. Beliefs like these are advanced by the effect of today's media; movies and books often depict strange happenings during a full moon. It makes a strikingly good story when events are seen as being controlled by the moon.

    There are also some misconceptions that a full moon has a powerful effect on the human body. For instance, some people claim that, because both the Earth and the human body ~~have~~ *are* composed of 80 percent water, the moon influences the body just as it does the Earth's tides. But this is not entirely true. Eighty percent of the *surface* of the Earth is water. The moon influences only *unbounded* bodies of water, such as oceans and seas. Unbounded bodies of water are those that have no boundaries; they ~~don't~~ *aren't / are not* surrounded by anything. But the water in the human body is bounded by the limits of the skin surrounding the entire body.

    Even though the powers of the moon have been discredited by some scientific research, the moon is still ~~considering~~ *considered* a strong symbol of romance and mystery all over the world.

## EXERCISE 6

*Answers will vary.*

## UNIT 16 (pages 130–139)

## EXERCISE 1

    Thank you for <u>writing</u> to Zenith University. You have asked what qualities are necessary for <u>gaining</u> admittance to the freshman class.

    Zenith University seeks to attract academically talented students who will have the greatest possibility of <u>succeeding</u> and <u>thriving</u> here, and who will also participate in <u>contributing</u> to the growth of the university community. The most important factors are:

- <u>Completing</u> high school with a grade point average (GPA) of 3.5 or higher
- <u>Achieving</u> a score of 1875 or higher on the standardized Scholastic Aptitude Test (SAT)
- <u>Being recommended</u> by high school teachers and counselors
- <u>Demonstrating</u> evidence of <u>being involved</u> in the world

In addition, the Board considers the overall level of achievement, enrollment in honors courses, individual academic strengths, and class rank. For example, you must be in the top quarter of your high school class, and the higher your rank, the greater your chance of <u>becoming</u> part of our student body. Of course, <u>receiving</u> good recommendations from teachers and counselors also tells us that you will be able to succeed in your academic work here.

    <u>Taking</u> interest in the world is shown by your <u>having participated</u> in extracurricular activities in high school, such as <u>playing</u> sports, <u>writing</u> for the school newspaper, and <u>taking</u> part in student government. Involvement is also evidenced by your <u>showing</u> concern for your community, in the context of activities like <u>volunteering</u> in hospitals and <u>being</u> active in political campaigns. <u>Displaying</u> an interest in other cultures coincides with an active curiosity, and the university looks favorably upon candidates who have spent time <u>studying</u> or <u>traveling</u> abroad.

    Along with your application, you will send a personal essay. <u>Writing</u> this essay carefully is important, because it demonstrates your skills in <u>thinking</u> and in <u>expressing</u> yourself. The Board of Admissions carefully reviews every application for undergraduate admission in <u>deciding</u> whom to admit.

    We wish you good luck in your application process.

## EXERCISE 2

**2.** h    **3.** g    **4.** a    **5.** c    **6.** d    **7.** b    **8.** e

## EXERCISE 3

**2.** carving
**3.** Playing
**4.** Knitting
**5.** Traveling
**6.** telling
**7.** taking
**8.** Collecting
**9.** keeping
**10.** riding
**11.** reading

## EXERCISE 4

**2.** not having been
**3.** having stopped by
**4.** having seen
**5.** having met
**6.** having telephoned
**7.** having become
**8.** not having stopped

## EXERCISE 5

**2.** having been employed / being employed
**3.** being hung up on
**4.** being interrupted
**5.** being bothered
**6.** being left alone
**7.** being bombarded
**8.** being trapped
**9.** not being disturbed
**10.** being solicited
**11.** Being required
**12.** being / having been interrupted
**13.** being concerned
**14.** being / having been annoyed
**15.** being distracted
**16.** being upset

## EXERCISE 6

**2.** Her finding / having found
**3.** Mary's working / having worked
**4.** George's coming / having come
**5.** Henry's constant upgrading
**6.** Nicole's falling down
**7.** her constant complaining
**8.** Jim's leaving
**9.** his meandering

## EXERCISE 7

    On February 28, 2004, Keizo Miura celebrated his birthday by ~~ski~~ *skiing* down a 2-mile run at a Rocky Mountain ski resort. A man's skiing 2 miles down a mountain run is not usually worthy of being noticed, but in this case it was—this birthday was his 100th birthday.

    Miura celebrated his 100th year by ~~descend~~ *descending* the mountain together with more than 120 friends and family members from Japan, all regular and robust skiers. After the descent, Miura said, "There is no better way to celebrate my 100th birthday than being able to wholeheartedly enjoy ~~ski~~ *skiing* with my family and friends."

    ~~Him~~ *His* succeeding in this descent was just one more of his many accomplishments. The year before, for his 99th birthday, Miura skied down Mont Blanc in the French Alps together with his eldest son, Yuchiro, and his grandson Yuta. Yuchiro is a champion skier too, no doubt because of having been ~~inspiring~~ *inspired* by his father. Another of Miura's activities is mountain ~~climb~~ *climbing*. At age seventy-seven, he succeeded in ~~climb~~ *climbing* Mount Kilimanjaro, the tallest mountain in Africa.

    Miura was a skiing teacher and a photographer of mountain landscapes. He was known for his fitness and his ~~participate~~ *participating / participation* in outdoor sports at an advanced age. Miura might not have embraced the sport without ~~have~~ *having* worked at the Aomori Forestry Bureau as a young man; it was there that his strong interest in skiing developed. After ~~retire~~ *retiring* at age fifty-one, he continued ~~put~~ *putting / to put* his energies into the sport, not only by ~~ski~~ *skiing* frequently, but also by ~~to work~~ *working* on the technical committee for the Ski Association of Japan.

To what did Miura credit his having stayed in shape for all those years? One thing was eating well. He ate nutritious food, such as unpolished rice, fish, seaweed, and soybeans. Another thing was exercising regularly. Every morning he went through a routine of ~~move~~ *moving* his neck left and right 100 times, ~~open~~ *opening* his mouth wide, and ~~stick~~ *sticking* out his tongue. He said that this prevented the area around his mouth from ~~be~~ ~~wrinkling~~ *being wrinkled*. He also did squats and other exercises for ~~to strengthen~~ *strengthening* the body, and he walked 3–4 kilometers each day.

Miura benefited enormously from ~~having been~~ ~~eaten~~ *having eaten* healthfully and having ~~exercising~~ *exercised* religiously for a half-century. "I still feel good," he said, almost at the end of his life. "It's about diet, it's about exercise . . . It's about making the most out of a long life." He said, "~~Ski~~ *Skiing* isn't really the reason for my long life. The reason for my long life is my passion for ~~ski~~ *skiing*."

Keizo Miura's long life ended just a few weeks before his 102nd birthday.

## EXERCISE 8

*Answers will vary.*

**UNIT 17** (pages 140–148)

## EXERCISE 1

Human beings need <u>to be loved and cared for</u>. When warm feelings exist between people, it is natural <u>to give</u> and <u>to accept</u> love. In fact, a common proverb is: "It is better <u>to give</u> than <u>to receive</u>."

Children who do well in school seem <u>to be receiving</u> strong and consistent love and support from their families. On the other hand, many antisocial adolescents appear <u>not to have been given</u> much tender, loving care during their childhood. In fact, their childhoods can be described as wretched. In their desire <u>to be included</u> in a group, some teenagers are easily seduced into gangs. Often they are disappointed <u>not to receive</u> from other gang members the love that they had been yearning for.

After spending years in a gang, it is common for these young people <u>to become hardened</u>; their hardened attitude is "a tough nut <u>to crack</u>," according to police officers and social workers. It becomes

extremely difficult for them <u>to re-enter</u> society. Unfortunately, most are expected <u>to continue</u> through their lives in this sad and hopeless scenario. However, some who are fortunate enough <u>to have been reached and touched</u> by enlightened and caring social workers do reform and become productive members of society. With guidance and help, it is possible, even for those exhibiting antisocial behaviors, <u>to be rehabilitated</u>.

The purpose of this paper is <u>to identify</u> agencies and facilities in this state which have done significant work in rehabilitating troubled youngsters and <u>to outline</u> their programs of treatment. In the final section of the paper, I attempt <u>to evaluate</u> these programs.

## EXERCISE 2

2. to celebrate
3. to spend
4. to sing
5. to enjoy
6. to see
7. to be included / to have been included
8. to know
9. to be given
10. to have been remembered / to be remembered
11. to joke
12. to tell
13. to be teased

## EXERCISE 3

2. (d) I would go to the Caribbean (in order) to sail, swim, dive, and snorkel.
3. (f) I would go to Switzerland or Colorado (in order) to ski.
4. (e) I would go to Egypt (in order) to visit the pyramids.
5. (i) I would go to Japan (in order) to see Mount Fuji.
6. (a) I would go to Kenya (in order) to photograph large wild animals.
7. (b) I would go to Paris (in order) to shop for original designer clothes.
8. (j) I would go to Italy (in order) to walk around the ruins of ancient Rome.
9. (c) I would go to Brazil (in order) to dance the samba and bossa nova.
10. (g) I would go to Disneyland (in order) to meet Mickey Mouse and Donald Duck.

## EXERCISE 4

2. to leave
3. to think
4. to have
5. to change
6. to design
7. to be
8. to complete
9. to start
10. to finish
11. to focus
12. to go
13. to make
14. to avoid
15. to have been
16. to have possessed

## EXERCISE 5

2. to love
3. to be
4. to be picked up
5. (to be) given
6. to ride
7. to be invited
8. to visit
9. to make
10. to talk
11. to tell
12. (to) imagine
13. (to) try
14. to go
15. to be attacked
16. to walk
17. to go
18. to drive
19. to let / to have let
20. to have been
21. To lose / To have lost
22. to have had

## EXERCISE 6

2. to learn
3. to work
4. to do
5. to flunk
6. to get
7. To be
8. to show up
9. to take
10. to leave
11. to allow
12. to give
13. to have gotten
14. to have been given
15. to be taken
16. to invest
17. to have been tricked
18. to tell
19. to forget
20. to pursue
21. to be
22. to talk
23. to be told
24. To get
25. to behave
26. to go out

## EXERCISE 7

"To be or not ^to be"—this is a famous quotation from Shakespeare's *Hamlet*. The quotation is relevant to me because for the past two years, I have been thinking about what I am and what I want ~~being~~ ^to be.

In spite of having quite an average upbringing, I was different from my friends because I preferred ~~to not~~ ^not to watch TV, but to read. Not that I didn't participate in childhood games and high school sports—I was involved like most young people, and my parents encouraged ^me to take part in several activities. But I also chose to ~~reading~~ ^read for a few hours each day, or more likely, each night. Sometimes I didn't even stop ~~going~~ ^to go to sleep. As a child, I read the usual children's books, but I soon attempted to read newspaper articles and magazines about science, and a few years later, about philosophy. Since I had learned to read without difficulty at age three, it was easy enough for me ~~stepping~~ ^to step up to a higher level.

Because of my interests in science and philosophy, I have always tended to balance the one area with the other in my mind. The result

of spending so much time reading and trying to integrate everything I was absorbing was that I became quite a reflective person. I didn't appear ~~being~~ ^to be an intellectual kid with its connotation of "geek." (I have always been a computer geek, though. I have almost never written in longhand.)

I seemed ~~acted~~ ^to act like everybody else. And, in truth, I was like everyone else except that I also had a more introspective side than most kids.

This description of myself is meant to show that I have been thinking about myself and what I wish ~~becoming~~ ^to become. The truth is that I do not know yet; it is too soon know. This is why I hope to attend Zenith University— ^to get a broad exposure to all the humanities and sciences and to ~~finding~~ ^find the field where I will be able ^to maximize my abilities and find fulfillment. At the moment, I think I would like ^to be an archaeologist and do research about the beliefs and religious practices of ancient peoples. But I will seek to expose myself to many disciplines at Zenith and to benefit from learning about all of them.

In Zenith's motto, the words "To learn is to grow" are meant for me. That is what I expect ^to do and will endeavor to ~~doing~~ ^do at Zenith University.

## EXERCISE 8

*Answers will vary.*

## UNIT 18 (pages 149–155)

## EXERCISE 1

1. Never **N**
   Clearly **S**
2. only **F**
3. essentially **S**
4. not only **N**
   Certainly **S**
5. Nearly **F**
   hopefully **S**

1. Actually **S**
   almost **F**
2. just **F**
3. Mainly **S**
4. significantly **S**
   Even **F**
5. basically **S**
   Surely **S**

## EXERCISE 2

2. almost
3. you are
4. I am
5. hardly
6. almost
7. scarcely
8. ever
9. rarely
10. Not only
11. never
12. Never
13. never
14. Obviously
15. just
16. rarely
17. even
18. just
19. No way
20. Little
21. ever
22. even
23. Only

## EXERCISE 3

2. But really he used up the state's money.
3. He put only his friends in the best jobs.
4. He even paid for his friends' so-called business trips.
5. He did merely the minimal work.
6. He simply appeared in his office, dispensed favors, and went out to play golf.
7. He just didn't care about the people of this state.
8. This state will be saved only if you elect Don Deare.

## EXERCISE 4

2. Seldom does he take a vacation.
3. Rarely is he able to spend much time with them, however.
4. Never does he neglect his family.
5. No way would he accept a bribe.
6. Only then does he take action.
7. Little do people realize how many hours he has volunteered at the shelter for the homeless.
8. Never does he think of himself first.
9. Not only has he served the people very well as a civic volunteer, but he will do even more for them as a senator.

## EXERCISE 5

**Situation 2:** here he is
**Situation 3:** Here You Come Again
**Situation 4:** here I come
**Situation 5:** there lies the problem
**Situation 6:** There goes the president

## EXERCISE 6

Have you seen the TV ads for different medications? A national physicians' group wants to prohibit the advertising of medicines on TV. Not only ~~the~~ *do* the ads make people interested in those medicines, but they compel many of those people to ask their doctors to prescribe them. Consumers want a "quick fix" for their health problems, and may not fully understand the risks involved.

The physicians say this kind of advice from patients to their doctors is not a good idea. A doctor does not like to refuse patients' requests, but the medicine the patient asks for could be the wrong one. The doctor ~~wants just~~ *just wants* the patient to improve and he or she knows which one is best. Requesting an advertised drug challenges the medical doctor's judgment.

Here ~~a story is~~ *is a story* from a doctor. A patient came to the doctor, wanting a medication he had seen on TV. The medicine was a strong pain reliever, and the patient wanted it to relieve his headaches. He ~~begged~~ *even begged* ~~even~~ the doctor for the medicine. ~~Only he wanted~~ *He only wanted / He wanted only* the attractive pink pill he had seen on TV. But the doctor wanted to find out what was causing the headaches, not to find a temporary cure ~~just~~ *only*. The doctor persuaded the patient to have a general physical examination. He took many blood tests and ~~did even~~ *even did* an electrocardiogram to examine the patient's heart. The doctor found that the patient was allergic to many environmental products and to ~~all almost~~ *almost all* kinds of fish. Those allergies were causing the headaches. It's a good thing that the doctor didn't ~~write just~~ *just write* a prescription for the patient's headache relief. By persevering, ~~not only the doctor found~~ *the doctor not only found* the correct diagnosis, but he was able to cure the patient.

On the other hand, a pharmacists' organization disagrees about TV advertising. ~~The~~ *Basically, the* pharmacists think that advertising ~~basically~~ medications is a good thing. They say that advertising the medicines on TV sheds some light on what is available. They say that more knowledge about medicines ~~only is~~ *is only* good; it can't be bad.

The pharmacists say that the ads educate consumers about diseases and the options for treatment. They encourage TV viewers to visit their doctors and ask about the advertised medicine.

Some people believe that TV advertising should be uncensored and that companies should be able to advertise whatever product they want. Since it is not compulsory to buy the advertised product, consumers can make their own choices. ~~It~~ *Obviously, it* is good to have ~~obviously~~ information, but when it comes to advertising medicines on TV, the issue remains controversial.

## EXERCISE 7

*Answers will vary.*

## EXERCISE 1

**A:** Dr. Scope, just what *does* make a happy family?

**B:** There is a cliché that all happy families have
*contrast*
some things in common. <u>While this may be trite</u>,
it is also true.

**A:** Really? What are these things?

**B:** Well, in happy families, <u>even though family</u>
*contrast*
<u>members may argue</u>, they have a basic concern
*reason*
for each other. <u>Since every person needs to</u>
<u>know that somebody really cares for and about</u>
<u>him or her</u>, this caring is perhaps the most
prevalent factor.

**A:** Is caring enough to keep young people on the
road to productive lives and certainly away
from nonsocial behavior?

**B:** No. Of course it's not so simple, but . . . a person
who feels connected to others is more likely to
act in socially acceptable ways, <u>whereas a</u>
*contrast*
<u>person who does not feel connected often acts</u>
<u>in antisocial ways</u>.

**A:** So, is being connected the principal factor?

**B:** It is very important.

**A:** Tell us what else is important.

**B:** <u>When family members support each other's</u>
*time*
<u>goals</u>, the family feels united.

**A:** Give us an example.

**B:** Well, <u>if a parent is hoping to be promoted at</u>
*condition*
<u>work</u>, everybody is supportive and shows
interest. <u>If a youngster is trying to make the</u>
*condition*
<u>basketball team</u>, the other family members
show encouragement and warmth.

**A:** What happens in times of trouble?

**B:** <u>When one family member is having trouble</u>, the
*time*
others should exhibit concern and try to help.
Suppose, for example, that a family member has
been fired from a job. This person may suddenly
feel totally worthless in society, <u>although, of</u>
*contrast*
<u>course, this is not true</u>. In face, precisely
*reason*
<u>because this person doesn't have a job</u>, he or she
needs to feel valued as a human being.

**A:** So, is that the key word, *valued*?

**B:** I think it is. People need to feel valued,
appreciated. They also need to feel secure

among the family members. They need to know
that their families will always be there for them
*condition*
<u>even if they are irritable, depressed, ill,</u>
<u>unemployed—or whatever</u>.

**A:** Does the economic status of the family matter?

**B:** Of course, economic stability is favorable. But
*place*
happy families exist <u>wherever you look</u>, in all
economic strata. And unhappy families as well.

**A:** Well, thank you very much doctor. We certainly
feel a little more enlightened than we did before.

## EXERCISE 2

2. whenever
3. Even if
4. because
5. By the time
6. As soon as
7. After
8. Even though
9. Only if
10. wherever

## EXERCISE 3

2. as soon as the warmer weather arrives
3. Wherever a busy person travels
4. anywhere you shop
5. When you want
6. Even though he may already have
7. If your loved one loves
8. even if it's raining outside

## EXERCISE 4

2. As soon as
3. Until
4. Wherever
5. If
6. even though
7. Unless
8. while

## EXERCISE 5

2. When we turn to certain sports channels
on TV, we see athletes at various venues,
jumping, diving, somersaulting over dangerous
landscapes, and otherwise contorting
themselves. OR
We see athletes at various venues jumping,
diving, somersaulting over dangerous
landscapes, and otherwise contorting themselves
when we turn to certain sports channels on TV.

3. Because these athletes push themselves to
dangerous and extreme levels, this category of
sports is called "extreme sports." OR
This category of sports is called "extreme sports"
because these athletes push themselves to
extreme and dangerous levels.

4. Although extreme sports are dangerous, they are becoming more and more popular among young people all over the world. OR
Although they are becoming more and more popular among young people all over the world, extreme sports are dangerous.

5. As these sports are extreme and dangerous, it is inevitable that something will go awry at one time or another. OR
It is inevitable that something will go awry at one time or another as these sports are extreme and dangerous.

6. Even though extreme sports are not seen at the Olympic Games yet, there are twice-yearly competitive games showing extreme sports on some sports channels. OR
There are twice-yearly competitive games showing extreme sports on some sports channels, even though extreme sports are not seen at the Olympic Games yet.

7. Since "X" represents the word *extreme*, these games are called "The X-Games." OR
These games are called "The X-Games," since "X" represents the word *extreme*.

8. Since they first appeared on television in 1995, they have been increasingly popular. OR
They have been increasingly popular since they first appeared on television in 1995.

9. Wherever there are young people who want to compete in "real adventure," there will be more and more participants in extreme sports. OR
There will be more and more participants in extreme sports wherever there are young people who want to compete in "real adventure."

## EXERCISE 6

**RAY:** Hello, football fans! What a fantastic game this is! We're coming to you from Starz Stadium now, ~~by the time~~ *while* the two best football teams in the league are on their half-time break. The score stands at 0–0. The Panthers and the Leopards have each been undefeated ~~after~~ *since* this season began. They've won wherever they've played, at home or away. This game will decide the league championship. Arnold, what do you think? When the game ~~will be~~ *is* over, which team is going to have the higher score?

**ARNOLD:** That's impossible to say, Ray. Both teams are in great shape. They're just about equal. We don't know who will win. ~~Unless~~ *If* the Panthers win, it will be because of their terrific offense. They've been perfecting

their offense ever since the new coach arrived. On the other hand, if the Leopards win, ~~will it~~ *it will* be because of their superb defense, which is just about perfect this year.

**RAY:** I think that the Panthers have the edge with their offense. Unless they ~~will~~ make a big mistake, that offense is going to win the game for them.

**ARNOLD:** You may be right, Ray, but don't forget— the Leopards have won all their games ~~although~~ *because* their defense has been so great. ~~Only~~ *Even* if the Panthers' offense is fantastic, they won't be able to score because the Leopards' super defense will stop them.

**RAY:** Could be. At the beginning of the game, it looked like the Panthers were going to score. But then, right after Lowell—the Panthers' top scorer—got possession of the ball, Brown—the Leopards' strongest player—blocked his shot and stopped the point.

**ARNOLD:** I think we agree. ~~Since~~ *Although / Though* the Panthers have a terrific offense, they can't score easily against the Leopards' defense.

**RAY:** Right. I think the Panthers could score. But only if the Leopards make an unlikely error in defense ~~the Panthers will~~ *will the Panthers* score.

**ARNOLD:** Right! This sure is one exciting game!

**RAY:** You bet! ~~Whereas~~ *Because* the teams are equally good, the game is going to be really close until the last second of play. We won't know the winner until the game ~~will be~~ *is* over.

## EXERCISE 7

*Answers will vary.*

## UNIT 20 (pages 164–171)

## EXERCISE 1

While in the car
When in a boat
Riding in a boat
On seeing another boat
Having docked
Being able to swim
While in the water
Having learned these rules
When riding bicycles
Suffering from severe sunburn

Before going out in the sun
not wanting to wear a hat
When buying sunglasses for children

## EXERCISE 2

2. After having rained
3. While driving
4. hitting
5. crashing
6. Stunned
7. Being dazed
8. Being
9. Before realizing
10. having crashed
11. After acknowledging
12. waiting
13. Having arrived
14. Not having been
15. Since notifying

## EXERCISE 3

2. Hoping to lower their cholesterol levels, people minimize their intake of animal fats.
3. Knowing that fiber in the diet is excellent for digestion, people are consuming more fresh fruit, vegetables, and whole wheat products.
4. Knowing that they weigh too much, heavy people diet to lose weight.
5. Not wanting to become decrepit, many senior citizens exercise regularly to avoid this.
6. Having been told / Told that vitamin C, vitamin E, and beta-carotene greatly reduce cancer risk, people began buying these nutrients in large quantities.
7. Having known for a long time that too much salt and sugar is unhealthful, people buy a lot of salt-free and sugar-free products.
8. Having learned / Upon learning that using good sunglasses will protect their corneas, many people have bought good sunglasses.
9. Believing that eating fish will raise their intelligence level, some people eat a lot of it.
10. Realizing that they can contribute to their own good health, people eat much more knowledgeably than they used to.

## EXERCISE 4

| | | |
|---|---|---|
| 2. c | 6. a | 10. a |
| 3. b | 7. b | 11. c |
| 4. b | 8. b | 12. a |
| 5. c | 9. c | 13. b |

## EXERCISE 5

Shakira Isabel Mebarak Ripoli, ~~having~~ _known_ professionally as Shakira, is a singer, songwriter, dancer, and philanthropist. Born and ~~raising~~ _raised_ in Barranquilla, Colombia, Shakira began performing in school, ~~being shown~~ _showing_ her vocal ability with rock and roll, Latin, and Middle Eastern music at an early age.

She wrote her first poem at age four, and she recorded her first album at age thirteen. After ~~have had~~ _having / having had_ a commercial failure with that album and with another, Shakira decided to produce her music herself. In 1995, upon ~~released~~ _having released / releasing_ Pies descalzos (translation in English: _Barefoot_), she became famous all over Latin America and in Spain. Since then, Shakira's music has been very well received, and she has been enormously successful.

There is another side to Shakira, besides that of being a performance star. She has a lot of compassion for poor people, especially children, who cannot obtain an education. As a young girl, Shakira had seen the suffering of street children ~~slept~~ _sleeping_ in parks every night, and she made a promise to herself to help them someday. Having ~~achieving~~ _achieved_ career success, she used much of the money she had earned to improve the lives of children. She created a foundation ~~having provided~~ _providing_ education and meals for poor children in her country. She said, "~~Because growing~~ _Growing_ up in Colombia, I saw that education can be a child's way out of poverty and a way to fulfill his or her potential."

The name of the foundation, ~~taking~~ _taken_ from her first successful album, is _Pies descalzos_. The first school was built in a small Colombian city. After that, Shakira's foundation built many more schools ~~served~~ _serving_ disadvantaged children and their families through education, counseling, nutrition, and income-generating projects. ~~Inspiring~~ _Inspired_ by the success of the Pies Descalzos Foundation in Colombia, Shakira founded the U.S.-based Barefoot Foundation in 2008. ~~Having supported~~ _Supporting_ worldwide education today, it encourages governments to increase spending on educational programs.

~~Recognizing~~ _Recognized_ for her education advocacy, she is the Goodwill Ambassador for UNICEF, a United Nations agency, and she is also the Honorary Chair of the Global Campaign for Education, an organization ~~having held~~ _holding_ governments responsible for their commitment to securing education for all.

Shakira's life shows that a person can have success and fame while ~~work~~ _working_ to make the world a better place. With Shakira's compassion, a blow has been struck against poverty.

## EXERCISE 6

*Answers will vary.*

**UNIT 21** (pages 172–179)

## EXERCISE 1

Good evening, ladies and gentlemen. We are here to bring you the latest news from Hollywood.

<u>First of all</u>, a major new studio has been created. The three biggest motion picture producers have just joined forces to form the core of a new studio. <u>As a result</u>, Big Three Productions, as it is going to be named, will be the largest studio ever in Hollywood. <u>Moreover</u>, it has more money behind it than any studio in Hollywood has ever had. <u>In addition</u>, seven megastars have joined the group as junior partners; <u>therefore</u>, they will have a financial interest in the success of the company. Big Three Productions is expected to produce excellent financial results from the start.

There are, <u>however</u>, several lawsuits pending against the three partners, <u>because of</u> the complicated business dealings they had with their previous studios. <u>For instance</u>, the ex-wife of one of the partners has brought a lawsuit against him; she claims that he and their previous studio owe her $7 million for her starring role in *Turner Towers*. She left the movie set <u>because</u> she couldn't get along with the director; <u>nevertheless</u>, she says that she vividly recollects being fired by the director, <u>so</u> she was prevented from making a living.

<u>Next</u>, we have reports that movie queen Rosalinda Rock has finally found happiness. She and actor Fox Craft were married secretly last month in a small town in Nevada. There had been reports that Fox was involved with an Italian starlet, <u>but</u> these reports have turned out to be false. Rosalinda and Fox are on their honeymoon now; <u>afterwards</u>, they'll be in residence at their home in Sun Valley, <u>or</u> they'll be at their beach house in Santa Monica. Fox gave Rosalinda a diamond-and-emerald necklace as a wedding present; he had already given her a 10-carat diamond ring several weeks earlier. Rosalinda says she wants to stay home, at one of her homes, to have children while enjoying domestic life. She's going off to Tahiti right after the honeymoon, <u>nonetheless</u>, for several months on location.

<u>Finally</u>, nobody can predict who this year's winners of the Academy Awards are going to be. <u>First</u>, the pictures this year seem better than ever before. <u>For example</u>, the adventure story *Running in Space* has stunned everyone with its special effects, <u>and</u> it has impressed the critics with its incredible plot. It's a definite contender for the best picture award. <u>Likewise</u>, *I Remember When*—a beautiful film that taps into everyone's nostalgia—moved even the

most macho of men to tears. <u>On the other hand</u>, the award could go to any one of several fine comedies, <u>or</u> the brilliant horror movie *Drackenstein* might be the first of its genre to win.

The suspense over the Academy Awards is tremendous, <u>and</u> everybody is eagerly awaiting the big night. <u>Meanwhile</u>, join us again every night at 9:00 to learn more of what's really going on Around the Stars.

## EXERCISE 2

| | |
|---|---|
| **2.** i | **6.** h |
| **3.** a | **7.** c |
| **4.** g | **8.** d |
| **5.** b | **9.** e |

## EXERCISE 3

2. (however / ~~besides~~ / instead)
3. (First / ~~Next~~ / ~~Finally~~)
4. (~~Yet~~ / ~~Therefore~~ / Otherwise)
5. (Furthermore / ~~In contrast~~ / In addition)
6. (for instance / for example / ~~nevertheless~~)
7. (And / ~~But~~ / ~~Plus~~)
8. (~~moreover~~ / ~~however~~ / so)
9. (Therefore / ~~Otherwise~~ / ~~Nor~~)
10. (~~However~~ / For instance / ~~Nevertheless~~)
11. (Plus / Besides / ~~Instead~~)
12. (~~finally~~ / but / ~~so~~)
13. (~~Thus~~ / Furthermore / ~~Nor~~)
14. (and / ~~though~~ / ~~therefore~~)
15. (In the meantime / ~~Therefore~~ / ~~So~~)

## EXERCISE 4

**2.** b   **3.** b   **4.** c   **5.** c   **6.** a   **7.** c   **8.** c

## EXERCISE 5

| | |
|---|---|
| **2.** however | **6.** besides |
| **3.** though | **7.** Plus |
| **4.** meanwhile | **8.** In spite of |
| **5.** Otherwise | |

## EXERCISE 6

I'm the center on my basketball team. I like to play basketball for a lot of reasons:

*First*
~~Next~~, I like the teamwork. It really feels good to be part of a group whose members depend on each

*For example / For instance*
other. ~~In contrast~~, when I throw the ball to one of my teammates, I know that he will almost certainly

*and*
catch it. We have practiced hundreds of times ~~but~~ have perfected our skills pretty well. Thus, a win is due not only to a teammate's scoring, but in part to my passing, and in part to each member of the team.

Second, I like the competition. I like the feeling

*and*

of playing to win, ~~nor~~ the adrenaline rush when you

*consequently / as a result / so*

know that you have to fight hard; ~~otherwise~~, your heart beats faster, you breathe more rapidly, and you sweat a lot.

Third, I like the physical exercise. I think pushing myself to my physical limit is good for my body. It regulates the glucose level, among other things. I am not afraid of overdoing the exercise, nor do I have fears of being hurt during a game.

Finally, I like the glory. I love it when the crowd roars to encourage us, and I love it when I hear the

*In addition / Besides / Plus / Likewise*

cheerleaders shouting my name. ~~However~~, it sure makes a guy feel important to be recognized around town as a big hero.

Are there any drawbacks? Yes. It's terrific to play

*however / though / but*

basketball, ~~because~~ there are some negative aspects.

*however / nevertheless / still / on the other hand*

Being part of a team is great; ~~furthermore~~, you have to practice all the time and you don't have much of a private life. Playing in competition is exciting,

*however / but*

~~moreover~~ you don't get much chance to relax. Getting all that physical exercise feels wonderful;

*however / nevertheless / still / on the other hand*

~~therefore~~, you might get seriously hurt. (A guy I know was temporarily paralyzed because the left lobe of his brain had been injured.) In fact, there's a negative aspect to each of the things I like about

*but*

basketball, ~~and~~ these drawbacks are relatively unimportant.

In conclusion, I totally enjoy being a basketball

*because*

player ~~although~~ I love the teamwork, the competition, the physical exercise, and the glory.

## EXERCISE 7

*Answers will vary.*

## UNIT 22 (pages 180–189)

## EXERCISE 1

Dictionaries define *chocoholic* as a person who has an obsession for chocolate. The world is full of chocoholics. <u>Yet, if an unusual sequence of events had not occurred, these people would probably never have tasted chocolate.</u>

Chocolate was unknown outside of the Americas until the early 1500s. That's when it was discovered that the Aztec Indians there drank a delicious, dark, foamy beverage called *chocolatl*, made from the beans of the native cacao plant. These cacao beans were so highly valued in the area that they were used by the natives as money in the marketplaces; a pumpkin could be bought for 4 cacao beans, for example, and a rabbit could be bought for 10. The Aztecs evidently had chocoholics as well as chocolate. Their king, Montezuma, normally drank 50 pitchers of *chocolatl* a day; it is said that if <u>he didn't, he felt a very strong physical need for it.</u>

When the Europeans first tasted chocolate, it was too bitter for their tastes, so they added sugar to it. <u>If they hadn't added sugar, they wouldn't have been able to consume it.</u> With the added sugar, they liked the drink very much and brought it back to Spain. Chocolate first appeared in Europe as a thick, sugared, chilled beverage. Soon chocolate houses, like coffee houses, sprang up; however, only the rich people could enjoy the drink because of its high cost. <u>The common people could have enjoyed chocolate much sooner if it hadn't been so expensive.</u> It remained largely a privilege of the rich until the invention of the steam engine. which made mass production possible in the late 1700s. <u>If the steam engine had not been invented, mass production of chocolate would not have been possible at the time.</u>

Doctors of the era reported that chocolate was an effective medicine which gave people energy. When people wanted to feel stronger quickly, they could take some chocolate. Chocolate contains theobromine, a substance similar to caffeine; it is actually the theobromine which causes people to feel energized after drinking chocolate. <u>If chocolate didn't contain theobromine, it wouldn't have the stimulating effect that it has.</u>

Chocolate was primarily a beverage until the 1800s, when a Swiss chocolatier discovered that chocolate combined well with milk solids. <u>If that chocolate maker had not made the discovery, chocolate would not have evolved into the solid milk chocolate that we know.</u> Of course, <u>someone else would probably have invented the solid milk chocolate if the chocolatier hadn't already invented it.</u> Since solid chocolate was invented, we have had chocolate candy, chocolate cakes, chocolate cookies, and chocolate ice cream, and many people all over the world enjoy chocolate.

While too much chocolate is not good for you, recent medical reports have brought good news to chocoholics. Dark chocolate is healthful! Dark chocolate contains a large number of antioxidants, which help destroy bad things in the body. A small bar of it every day can help keep your heart and cardiovascular system in good condition. Says one chocoholic who has chocolate every day, "Quite frankly, <u>if I had a day without chocolate, it would be like a day without sunshine.</u>"

## EXERCISE 2

2. (Chocolate) was brought back to Europe by explorers
   (It) is popular today
3. (Air-conditioning) was developed in the 20th century
   (Places like Florida) have become popular locations to live
4. (Sweltering tropical areas) have air-conditioning
   (People) can live there comfortably
5. (Dinosaurs) don't roam the Earth
   (Humans) are living today
6. (Butterflies) have wings
   (They) can flutter over flowers
7. (It's) raining
   (We) can't hail a taxi
8. (I) don't have a large bureau
   (There) isn't room (in it) for all my socks, T-shirts, and underwear
9. (Sam) loves Sue
   (He) gave her that nice engagement ring as a token of his love and commitment
10. (I) don't know how to speak Russian well
    (I) mutilate the language

## EXERCISE 3

| | | | |
|---|---|---|---|
| 2. d | 6. g | 9. f | 12. e |
| 3. b | 7. m | 10. j | 13. h |
| 4. i | 8. c | 11. a | 14. l |
| 5. n | | | |

## EXERCISE 4

2. If Saudi Arabia were not an oil-rich country
3. Canada would not import oranges
4. If Thailand didn't have a tropical climate / If Thailand had a colder climate
5. Brazil wouldn't have become a large producer of coffee
6. it wouldn't have 11 time zones
7. If the Chinese government hadn't made huge efforts to save the panda

## EXERCISE 5

A. 2. I met the right man, I would (I'd) have a different feeling about it
   3. I didn't have a lot of friends, I would (I'd) be lonely
   4. I didn't like my job, I would (I'd) be unhappy
   5. (that) people would leave me alone
   6. I could meet the perfect man tomorrow
   7. (that) I had it all / I could have it all

B. 1. they start
   2. I often don't say it / often, I don't say it
   3. nobody will understand you
   4. I don't speak
   5. Mr. Right doesn't come along
   6. Mr. Right comes along

## EXERCISE 6

2. wouldn't have eaten / wouldn't have had to eat
3. wouldn't have been
4. never would / would never have suffered
5. had met
6. had never met
7. hadn't / wouldn't have happened
8. hadn't made
9. would've passed

## EXERCISE 7

Robert and Cynthia are good friends and are both lawyers at the Marks and Hobbs law firm. They both hope to be selected as partners at the end of the year. If a person ~~will be~~ *is* selected to be a partner, he or she will become a part-owner of the law firm and therefore, would ~~had~~ *have* a secure future there. Robert and Cynthia's supervisor, Henry Marks, has told Robert that he is likely to get a partnership at the end of the year but that Cynthia isn't. *Should Robert tell Cynthia this?*

**What should Robert do?**
*He should tell her. (And he might tell her.)* If Cynthia ~~had~~ *does* not become a partner, she will have no future in the firm. Robert and Cynthia are good friends, and they should be honest with each other. If Cynthia ~~will find~~ *finds* out the truth now, she can get another job. Furthermore, if Robert ~~would~~ *does* not tell her, he will have to lie to Cynthia for the rest of the year. In addition, Robert should think, "If the situation ~~is~~ *were* reversed, would I want to know the truth?" The answer is "Yes."
*He shouldn't tell her, and in fact, he has decided not to tell her. He thinks:* If he ~~has told~~ *told* her, it would destroy the confidence that his boss has in him. In fact, if Robert ~~would~~ broke the confidence, he himself might not be promoted; Henry would ~~lost~~ *lose* confidence in him.

**What happened?**

Robert told Cynthia, who confronted Henry. Henry, of course, was angry at Robert for breaking a trust, and he told Robert that he was no longer a candidate for the promotion.

**What does everyone think now?**

*Robert*: What a mistake! I wish I ~~don't tell~~ *hadn't told* Cynthia! She could have worked happily for the remainder of the year if I ~~haven't~~ *hadn't* told her. My intuition told me that I shouldn't tell her in order to spare her feelings; however, my wish to be honest with her was more important to me. But it ended badly for both of us. If I hadn't told her, I ~~will~~ *would* be in line for a promotion now. Now neither of us will be promoted.

*Cynthia*: I appreciate Robert's friendship, but I'm really sorry he has lost his own opportunity. If I ~~am~~ *were* Robert and the situation ~~be~~ *were* reversed—would I have told him? Maybe not.

*Henry*: I never should have told Robert anything. If I had kept the information to myself, none of this would ~~had~~ *have* happened. Now I have lost the trust and confidence of two good colleagues. I wish I ~~have~~ *had* their confidence again, but that's not possible. If only it ~~is~~ *were* easy to be the boss of this law firm!

## EXERCISE 8

*Answers will vary.*

### UNIT 23 (pages 190–199)

## EXERCISE 1

Without the simple little tool   IMP
that we have (circled)
Were there no can openers   INV
Were there no can openers   INV
But for canned tuna   IMP
A better way to open cans had to be found; if not   IMP
it had to be used correctly. If not   IMP
Had the U.S. military not discovered this primitive can opener   INV
there be (circled)
Without canned goods   IMP
can openers were invented; otherwise   IMP
should there be an emergency   INV
that every family have (circled)

## EXERCISE 2

2. would not be
3. will have
4. can arrange
5. be put
6. be given
7. be thrown
8. that the room be neat
9. be organized
10. Without
11. would never have gotten
12. that my husband get rid of
13. Had I not seen
14. would never have believed
15. that we put up

## EXERCISE 3

2. not fought; would not have been known
3. might not have won
4. would not have grown
5. not succeeded; would have succeeded
6. would not have developed
7. would have already become

## EXERCISE 4

2. we would have to use our fingers to eat
3. not been discovered, we wouldn't have electric lights, movies, television, or computers
4. existed 100 years ago, people would have traveled extensively then
5. not available throughout the world, fashion, music, and basic values would not be very similar in many places
6. not been developed, businesses wouldn't be able to obtain the data they need to function in today's world
7. the general public wouldn't have easy access to extensive information
8. have a cellular phone, he or she would not be able to communicate from remote places

## EXERCISE 5

2. Julius Caesar not conquered several areas of the world, people in those areas would not speak "Romance" languages
3. the Spanish and Portuguese settled North America, people there would not speak English, but Spanish or Portuguese OR
the English not settled North America, people there wouldn't speak English
4. blue jeans not been invented in 1849, everyone all over the world wouldn't be wearing blue jeans today
5. penicillin not been discovered in 1928, hundreds of millions of lives would have been lost OR
penicillin not been discovered in 1928, hundreds of millions of lives would not have been saved
6. Dolly the sheep not been cloned in 1997, certain amazing scientific possibilities and troubling ethical questions would not have been raised

7. there gravity in a spaceship, objects wouldn't float in the air there
8. the polar ice caps melt, certain coastal areas might be flooded

## EXERCISE 6

2. that drivers stay on the left side of the road
3. that people remove their shoes before going inside a house
4. that people keep their shoes on
5. that people not eat pork products
6. that a sick person be treated with modern medicine
7. that a sick person use herbal remedies
8. that a waiter be summoned by whistling
9. that a waiter not be summoned by whistling
10. that a traveler learn about customs in various places

## EXERCISE 7

I have often fantasized about the perfect world. It would be perfect not only for my family and me, but for everyone.

First of all, ~~we were~~ *were we / if we were* living in a perfect world, there would be food for everyone. No one would be starving or without regular sources of food. Second, in this perfect world, everything would ~~been~~ *be* clean and free of pollution. With clean air and toxin-free water, humans, animals, and plants would ~~stayed~~ *stay* healthy. Third, all diseases would be conquered; we ~~will~~ *would* be free of cancer, AIDS, and heart disease. Without those diseases, people could ~~lived~~ *live* longer and be free from terrible suffering. ~~Scientists had~~ *If scientists had / Had scientists* already discovered a cure for these diseases, we could now be anticipating a much longer lifespan. Fourth, were the world in perfect condition, there ~~will~~ *would* be no crime. Societal and psychological factors would not breed the violence that they do. And last, there would be no wars. All countries and all peoples would live together, harmoniously, as one.

While these goals may appear unrealistic, it would be wise not to abandon them. Had diplomats abandoned the idea of one world, we ~~don't~~ *wouldn't* have the United Nations today, or other organizations to help global populations. Had scientists given up their search for cures, we ~~will~~ *would* not have found the means to conquer polio, tuberculosis, some types of pneumonia, and many bacteria-caused diseases. Had civic-minded individuals been less tenacious, we ~~did~~ *would* not have cleaned up the cities and water and air as much as we have. Had ~~not we~~ *we not* learned and taught better methods of agriculture and food distribution, many more people would be starving today.

What if there ~~are~~ *were* a universal law like this: All the *haves*—those people who *have* a decent life and more than enough material things—must make concrete contributions to a perfect world? Local governments would require that citizens ~~gave~~ *give* a specified amount of time or money each year to a recognized community project. What if it were required by law that young people ~~studying~~ *study* the histories of all major cultures? Knowing about other cultures would ~~have~~ expand people's minds and help them to understand each other better. Would such compulsory programs work? They might. They would, hopefully, help the citizens of the world to think of others who live in different situations. It is absolutely essential that hope ~~are~~ *be* expressed not only in words, but also in actions; otherwise, the world ~~would~~ *will* not be a better place tomorrow than it is today.

## EXERCISE 8

*Answers will vary.*